The Globalization of Merchant Banking before 1850

London merchant bankers emerged during the 1820s in the wake of financial turmoil caused by the wars of American Independence, the Napoleonic campaigns and the Anglo-American war of 1812. Although the majority of merchant bankers remained cautious in their affairs, Huth & Co. established an impressive global network of trade and lending, dealing with over 6,000 correspondents in more than 70 countries. Based on archival research, this comparative study provides a new chronology of early nineteenth-century commercial and financial expansion.

Huth & Co. was a true market-maker and acted as a key intermediary of commodities and capital flows in the international economy. This is an important example of a firm shaping globalization well before the transport and communication revolution of the last quarter of the nineteenth century. But rather than a case study, this is a comparative study concerned with the commercial and financial activities of the leading merchant bankers of the period.

This book will be of great interest to business and economic historians interested in the nature of the early decades of globalization.

Manuel Llorca-Jaña is Associate Professor of Economic and Business History at Universidad de Santiago, Chile.

Financial history
Series Editors: Farley Grubb and Anne L. Murphy

Slave Agriculture and Financial Markets in Antebellum America
The Bank of the United States in Mississippi, 1831–1852
Richard Holcombe Kilbourne, Jr.

The Political Economy of Sentiment
Paper credit and the Scottish Enlightenment in Early Republic Boston, 1780–1820
Jose R. Torre

Baring Brothers and the Birth of Modern Finance
Peter E. Austin

Gambling on the American Dream
Atlantic City and the casino era
James R. Karmel

Government Debts and Financial Markets in Europe
Edited by Fausto Piola Caselli

Virginia and the Panic of 1819
The first great depression and the Commonwealth
Clyde A. Haulman

Towards Modern Public Finance
The American war with Mexico, 1846–1848
James W. Cummings

The Revenue Imperative
The Union's financial policies during the American Civil War
Jane S. Flaherty

Guilty Money
The city of London in Victorian and Edwardian culture, 1815–1914
Ranald C. Michie

Financial Markets and the Banking Sector
Roles and responsibilities in a global world
Edited by Elisabeth Paulet

Argentina's Parallel Currency
The economy of the poor
Georgina M. Gomez

The Rise and Fall of the American System
Nationalism and the development of the American economy, 1790–1837
Songho Ha

Convergence and Divergence of National Financial Systems
Evidence from the Gold Standards, 1871–1971
Edited by Patrice Baubeau and Anders Ogren

Benjamin Franklin and the Invention of Microfinance
Bruce H. Yenawine

The Development of International Insurance
Edited by Robin Pearson

Federal Banking in Brazil
Policies and competitive advantages
Kurt E. von Mettenheim

The Development of the Art Market in England
Money as muse, 1730–1900
Thomas M. Bayer and John R. Page

Camille Gutt and Postwar International Finance
Jean F. Crombois

Taxation and Debt in the Early Modern City
Edited by José Ignacio Andrés Ucendo and Michael Limberger

Money in the Pre-Industrial World
Bullion, debasements and coin substitutes
Edited by John H. Munro

Reforming the World Monetary System
Fritz Machlup and the Bellagio Group
Carol M. Connell

Debt and Slavery in the Mediterranean and Atlantic Worlds
Edited by Gwyn Campbell and Alessandro Stanziani

Bonded Labour and Debt in the Indian Ocean World
Edited by Gwyn Campbell and Alessandro Stanziani

The Globalization of Merchant Banking before 1850
The case of Huth & Co.
Manuel Llorca-Jaña

Monetary Statecraft in Brazil
Kurt von Mettenheim

The Globalization of Merchant Banking before 1850
The case of Huth & Co.

Manuel Llorca-Jaña

LONDON AND NEW YORK

First published 2016
by Routledge
2 Park Square, Milton Park, Abingdon, Oxon OX14 4RN

and by Routledge
711 Third Avenue, New York, NY 10017

Routledge is an imprint of the Taylor & Francis Group, an informa business

© 2016 Manuel Llorca-Jaña

The right of Manuel Llorca-Jaña to be identified as author of this work has been asserted by him in accordance with Sections 77 and 78 of the Copyright, Designs and Patent Act 1988.

All rights reserved. No part of this book may be reprinted or reproduced or utilised in any form or by any electronic, mechanical, or other means, now known or hereafter invented, including photocopying and recording, or in any information storage or retrieval system, without permission in writing from the publishers.

Trademark notice: Product or corporate names may be trademarks or registered trademarks, and are used only for identification and explanation without intent to infringe.

British Library Cataloguing in Publication Data
A catalogue record for this book is available from the British Library

Library of Congress Cataloging in Publication Data
A catalog record for this book has been requested

ISBN: 978-1-848-93607-2 (hbk)
ISBN: 978-1-781-44880-9 (ebk)

Typeset in Times New Roman.
by Saxon Graphics Ltd, Derby

To my wife Ana María and our son Román, many thanks for all the support, as always.

In loving memory of Philip L. Cottrell (1944–2013) and my mother (1951–2014).

Contents

List of figures xi
List of tables xiii
Acknowledgements xv

Introduction 1

1 **Early life and activities of Frederick Huth, founder of the company, *c*.1777–1822** 11

2 **Expansion of the firm during the 1820s–1830s and the South American branches** 29

3 **Huth & Co.'s Spanish and German connections during the 1820s–1840s** 55

4 **The Liverpool branch, agents in Britain and the US connection** 79

5 **A global enterprise of trade and lending** 101

6 **Risk-management credit strategies** 117

7 **Conclusions** 136

Bibliography 145
Index 155

Figures

2.1	UK re-exports of quicksilver to Chile, Peru and Bolivia, 1827–1859	45
2.2	UK imports of quicksilver from Spain, 1827–1859	46
4.1	UK exports to the US, 1820s–1860s. Declared value of the produce of the UK, annual averages	90
4.2	Huth & Co.'s acceptances on American account (£), 1835–1850 (London and Liverpool branches)	94
6.1	Value (£) of bills accepted by Huth & Co. between October 1845 and September 1846	123
7.1	Huth & Co.'s capital, thousand of £ each year, 1809–1850	139

Tables

1.1	Location of Frederick Huth's correspondents *c.*1812–1813	15
1.2	Share of the main products within the UK's exports of British and Irish produce to Spain, 1814–1818	16
1.3	The UK's imports of raw wool. Share of main origins, 1812, 1813 and 1815	17
1.4	Location of Huth & Co.'s correspondents in 1822	20
3.1	Geographical distribution of Huth & Co.'s correspondents (*C*) in Spain: a sample for 1812–1851	56
3.2	Geographical distribution of Huth & Co.'s correspondents in Germany: a sample for the main cities, *c.*1812–1848	73
4.1	Huth & Co.'s correspondents in Britain. A sample for selected cities, *c.*1812–1848	81
4.2	Location of Huth & Co.'s correspondents. A sample for 1833–1835	83
5.1	Location of Huth & Co.'s correspondents. A sample for 1846–1848	105
7.1	Location of Huth & Co.'s correspondents. A sample for *c.*1812–1850	138

Acknowledgements

My interest in Huth & Co. goes back to 2005, when I started my PhD research on British textile exports to South America during the first half of the nineteenth century.[1] Huth was one of the main conduits of British textile exports to Latin America during this period, so it made sense to consult the available collections on this merchant. What I did not know when I first visited UCL Special Collections was that Huth's export of textiles to Latin America was just one of the many activities performed by the firm. I was immediately struck by the huge wealth of primary information available for the business, and in particular by the geographical diversification of the company's activities. When I told Philip L. Cottrell, then my PhD advisor, about it, his immediate answer was: 'now you have a second big project waiting for you.' And indeed, Phil thought that, given the prominence of Huth & Co. within the London merchant-banking community before 1850, I was very lucky that no one else had had the time (or inclination) to prepare a monograph on this firm. So, my thanks go first and foremost to Philip Leonard for identifying a new avenue of research. He is sadly missed by his relatives, friends, other colleagues and certainly by me too.[2]

I would like to thank Huw Bowen and Bernard Attard, from my days at Leicester, Anne Murphy for encouraging me to submit this book, Katharine Wilson for polishing the whole monograph, Xabier Lamikiz (as usual) for carefully reading and commenting on several chapters (often directing me to relevant literature and enhancing my prose style, as well as preventing me from many embarrassing pitfalls), as well as to many colleagues, relatives and friends who have always supported me. Amongst them I would like to mention in particular Mark Latham, Rory Miller, Pat Hudson, Herbert Klein, Marcello Carmagnani, Xavier Tafunell, Tristan Platt, Geoff Jones, Bernardo Bátiz-Lazo (of great help in particular with Chapter 6), Juan Navarrete (of great help with the proof-reading), Francisco Betancourt, Adrian Pearce, Chris Evans, Cristián Copaja, Diego Barría, Lilibette Correa, Bernarda Ramírez, Cristián Ducoing, Erica Salvaj, Pedro Verdugo, Claudio Robles and my colleagues at Universidad de Santiago. Last but not least, and indeed most important of all, my wife and my son have always been a permanent support throughout my entire academic career. I am also grateful to my sister, my brother, Pipe Abraham and my family more generally.

Finally, it is important to mention that this book was funded by Universidad de Santiago de Chile (Facultad de Administración y Economía), the Chilean Fondecyt (project 11100022), Universitat Pompeu Fabra (Department of Economics and Business) and 'Convenio N°4 del Proyecto Basal por Desempeño, Hacia una cultura de indicadores en la educación superior, USA1298, Usach'. My thanks go also to UCL Special Collections, The National Archives (Kew), Guildhall Library, The Rothschild Archives and all other archives that allowed me to access their collections.

Notes

1 It was subsequently published as: Manuel Llorca-Jaña, *The British Textile Trade in South America in the Nineteenth Century*, Cambridge University Press (New York, 2012).
2 An obituary by his son can be read at http://www.theguardian.com/theguardian/2014/jan/06/philip-cottrell-obituary, and two others by David Williams at http://www2.le.ac.uk/departments/history/people/pcottrell/obituary and by Youssef Cassis at the *Financial History Review*, Volume 21–1, 2014, pp 1–3.

Introduction

This book discusses the nature and extent of the global networks of trade and lending established by the London merchant bankers Huth & Co. during the first half of the nineteenth century. Trade in this context means trade in commodities but also in securities. Although the book is focussed on a case study of Huth & Co., it is also a comparative monograph concerned with the commercial and financial activities of the leading merchant bankers of the period. That is, whenever possible or convenient for the reader, Huth & Co.'s experience is compared to that of contemporary competitors. The main reason of focussing on the company, this being a work on commercial networks, is that, as stated by Marzagalli, 'the most obvious way of studying networks is to analyze the activities carried out by a single firm and its correspondents'.[1]

Merchant bankers were a heterogeneous group that emerged mainly in London during the 1820s and 1830s. Yet, despite their heterogeneity, they performed some key common activities. These encompassed trading goods on own/joint account, or obtaining consignments of products for themselves, their agents or friends; trading in securities (on own account or on commission), including floating them on the European markets; bullion dealing; accepting (granting of advances) or financing of international trade and even financing the trade of securities; provision of marine and fire insurance (as underwriters or brokers); exchange (negotiating foreign exchange rates or getting acceptance of bills of exchange on behalf of other merchants resident in other markets); provision of shipping services (owning of vessels or shipping brokerage); provision of strategic information for clients and friends; and active participation in the issuing of public debt.

That is, merchant bankers performed sophisticated transactions, despite the apparent simplicity of international business before the first wave of globalization. They were major actors in nineteenth-century international business, moving their own goods, helping others to trade, reducing the risks associated with international trade, facilitating the movement of capital across borders and financing many trade and capital movement operations. In other words, they were important intermediaries in international trade and international finances, linking sellers and buyers of goods and securities, thus greatly reducing transaction costs across borders.[2] To accomplish these tasks they had to be effective at building information and trust networks in an era of poor communications and weak enforcement of commercial contracts across borders. They had to nurture and expand their connections, thus increasing their social capital (i.e. connections among individuals).

Merchant bankers also shared other common and important characteristics. First, international trade (rather than finance) was the background of most merchant bankers during the first half of the nineteenth century.[3] That is, they were all traders before becoming financiers, even though most of them concentrated on finances subsequently. Second, they were not organized as modern firms with limited liability but instead were all partnerships, and more generally they remained family firms during the whole period covered by this monograph.[4] Indeed, in the merchant-banking sector, family-based possession and direct control continued unchallenged until as late as the first half of the twentieth century.[5] That is, they were an intrinsic part of the so-called 'family capitalism' associated with the early phases of modern industrialisation in Europe,[6] and which remained strong in Britain in particular.

Yet despite the important role played by London merchant bankers in the first half of the nineteenth century, they have received comparatively little attention within the economic, managerial, financial and business historiography, particularly when compared to the industrial sector. Indeed, according to Lisle-Williams, 'economists seem to regard the merchant banks as curiosities', while for theorists of managerial control 'they are dinosaurs in the mammalian age'.[7] This relative neglect is important because multinational trading companies (including merchant bankers) 'present intriguing theoretical challenges to explain differences in the strategies chosen by firms',[8] when comparisons are made between major players of the period. Indeed, there were many different (albeit reasonable) ways of operating from London before 1850 and, therefore, key decisions had to be taken.

For example, merchant bankers of the 1820s–1840s had to decide about: whether to go global or to concentrate on one or a few markets only; whether to focus on a few products (either trading or financing) or to become involved in as many goods as possible; whether to trade on commission and/or their own account;[9] whether to carry on trading only, or to combine trading with the financing of trade, or just concentrate on financing trade and other financial activities, thus abandoning purely mercantile activities. If they were financing international trade, they would need to consider whether to finance the trade of primary products only (and how many) or to finance trade in manufactures as well. They would also need to think about whether to execute all (or most) or just a few of the most common duties performed by merchant bankers of the time, and finally about whether to deal with a few selected correspondents (namely, contacts) or with as many businessmen as possible. These were all crucial decisions with no obvious answers, and they shaped the *modus operandi* and structural organization of merchant banks. Each of these decisions is analyzed in the chapters of this book, with special attention given to the case of Huth. A full comparative balance is given in Chapter 5.

But who were Huth & Co., my main focus of study? Why focus on them? Huth & Co. was a successful London-based merchant banker (although its founder was

German-born with close links to Spain) that operated in London from 1809 to 1936, when the company was eventually dissolved. In 1936 the banking business was acquired by British Overseas Bank Ltd., and the fur business by C. M. Lampson & Co. Ltd.[10] Yet this monograph is concerned only with the early years of the enterprise, *c*.1809–1850. The reasons for this are manifold. First, the extant information available on this firm for this period is rich and challenging enough to merit a full monograph, and has previously been neglected by other authors working on this area. Second, this is by far the best-documented period for this enterprise. Finally, to cover the subsequent period (*c*.1850–1936) would be in itself a major research project beyond the scope and ambitions of this book, and for which little information has survived, rendering such a task nearly impossible.

More importantly, by concentrating on Huth & Co. and the first half of the nineteenth century, this book sheds new light on the unique and impressive global network of trade and lending created by a particular merchant banker before 1850. Its network embraced over 6,000 correspondents in more than 70 countries (using modern geographical borders), in over 600 cities and on all continents. But the diversification of the company was not only geographical. Far from it, in fact: it also involved an important product diversification of both manufactures and primary products. Indeed, Huth & Co. was regularly dealing with an impressive range of different items, including commodities traded extensively around the world but also 'exotic' goods as well as securities. Finally, the company advanced funds to many of the merchants involved in these trades. Therefore, the risk management strategies used by the company to protect against the risks arising from lending to so many people involved in so many different products in so many locations during a period of profound information asymmetries are also explored.

I should stress that I am not aware of any other London-based merchant banker trading to this extent and with such a geographical reach before 1850, and who in turn financed many of these international flows of goods and securities. We are therefore analyzing a unique enterprise during this early nineteenth century period of globalization. And indeed, as shown in Chapter 5, most London merchant bankers of the 1820s–1840s remained cautious and did not diversify the remit of their operations geographically or in the products they traded during this period, nor did they engage with a wide range of clients.

Most of the leading merchant bankers in London at this time made their fortunes in the financial sector and/or by trading commodities in lesser numbers and across fewer locations,[11] with a select group of clients, while smaller merchants specialized in a handful of countries and/or fewer products. Yet Huth & Co. took a completely different path, establishing the impressive global network of trade and lending noted above. This uniqueness is in line with Jones and Friedman's assertion that 'entrepreneurs and firms, not governments or markets, have driven and shaped globalization',[12] otherwise one would expect other competitors to have adopted a similar strategy. Furthermore, it is remarkable that this network of contacts was established at the end of the so-called 'Age of Commerce' (*c*.1650–1850), well before the transport and communication revolutions that began (or at least were disseminated and popularised) during the second half of the nineteenth century. That is, during a period when access to information was relatively limited.

But the interest on Huth & Co. goes beyond the above-described two-fold diversification and the unique globalization strategy the firm pursued. In 1836 and 1850, the firm's capital reached the staggering sums of £123,000 and nearly £500,000, respectively.[13] To put these numbers in context, 'towards the middle of the nineteenth century, £100,000 was considered a large capital sum for a British merchant'.[14] Huth & Co. had reached five times this threshold by 1850. Indeed, it was part of a select group of just some 15 merchant bankers operating in London during the first half of the nineteenth century.[15] Amongst the most prominent ones were Baring Brothers, Rothschild & Sons, Brown Shipley, Fruhling & Goschen, J. S. Morgan & Co., Kleinworts, Schroders, Morrison & Co. and Hambro & Co.

The small number of firms operating in this sector was due to three important barriers to entry: merchant bankers needed large capital sums, vast and wide-reaching commercial intelligence and a sound international reputation. More importantly, within this elite group of first-class operators in existence during the period of this study, by 1850 Huth & Co. ranked immediately below the two leading merchant bankers of the British market at that time: Baring Brothers and Rothschild & Sons.[16] This makes Huth & Co. an interesting case of study on its own, in particular considering the extremely humble origins of its owner, Frederick Huth, which make the firm an exception in yet another context. Indeed, according to Rubinstein (who was unaware of Frederick Huth's history), in his celebrated study of the very wealthy in Britain since the Industrial Revolution, 'it is not possible to speak of a single wealth-holding banker who was, strictly speaking, a "self-made man"'.[17]

Regarding the specific epoch chosen (dictated in part by the availability of sources), it is worth explaining in further detail the environment in which Huth & Co. operated. To start with, this was a period characterized by an important British hegemony in world manufacturing and, therefore, in world exports of manufactures (textiles in particular). Britain was also the largest cross-border exporter of capital (perhaps the only important one before 1850), and dominant too in the services supporting the movements of both goods and capitals. In addition, and in part due to this British supremacy, this period provided 'spectacular new opportunities for trade companies' in Britain,[18] including merchant bankers. But this situation had not arisen solely due to increasing British industrial production and capital accumulation. Indeed, the period studied in this book was preceded by a forty-year spell of conflict affecting Britain, including the American Wars of Independence (*c.*1775–1782), the Napoleonic Wars (*c.*1799–1815) and the Anglo-American War of 1812. During these major international military conflicts many British merchants either retired, having lost patience with so many long-term disruptions to trade or, even worse, were bankrupted for the same reason, thus leaving plenty of room for newcomers to prosper. Particularly affected were the British houses trading mainly with Europe: it is estimated that 90 per cent of all London's continental Europe houses failed during the Napoleonic Wars,[19] to the great benefit of Huth and other potential market entrants, given their natural interests in countries such as Spain and Germany, about which they had an expert knowledge. To this situation must be added the end of regulated trade systems (i.e. the monopoly trading rights of the British chartered trading companies),[20] the collapse of the Spanish American empire during the 1810s–1820s[21] and the opening up of Brazil to international trade from 1808,[22] all of which gave greater stimulus to multinational traders based in Britain (or willing to move there), and in particular offered new opportunities to expand worldwide from London, the capital of industrialising Britain.[23]

This long period of warfare and trade expansion also brought 'to an exceptional degree, the mixing of merchants of different nationalities' in the English capital.[24] Many refugees from continental Europe came to London looking for a new base for their businesses. Amongst the foreign merchants who came to London during this epoch were Frederick Huth, who arrived in 1809 following Napoleon's invasion of Spain where he was working, and also Johann Heinrich Schroder, the founder of J. H. Schroder & Co. of London, who had arrived in England seven years prior in 1802, also in the midst of the so-called Napoleonic Wars.[25] The cosmopolitan atmosphere generated by the European merchants was a new phenomenon at the beginning of the nineteenth century, and it certainly shaped merchant bankers' future activities since they all began their careers as merchants at this time. Indeed, there was a notorious preponderance of foreigners within the London merchant-banking community of the first half of the nineteenth century.[26]

Yet despite the attractiveness of this period, as well as of these family-owned enterprises, the bulk of the research published to date on British multinational trading companies (including merchant bankers) focuses on the second half of the nineteenth century and the twentieth century.[27] In fact although there is a sizeable and respected body of literature on merchant banking, there is no work which fully assesses the nature and scope of the global networks established by members of this select group of merchants before 1850, let alone a comprehensive work on Huth & Co. In this vein, Lisle-Williams rightly notes that 'merchant banks have played a significant but little recognised part in the development of British capitalism'.[28] We cannot but agree. Even Chapman, the undisputed authority on European merchant banking, has recognised that despite his enormous contribution there are still major gaps in our knowledge of the sector: 'the history of the mercantile side is still unexplored territory.'[29]

This historiographic debt is evident in particular for several merchant bankers of the period. Indeed, despite Huth's unique global trading and financing networks, as well as its prominence within the British merchant-banking sector, no other author has dealt with Huth's global activities during the first half of the century (or any other period). There is only one important academic work on Huth & Co., but it deals solely with the connections made in the United States (which was not by any means the most important part of Huth's business as we shall see),[30] thus providing a very narrow view of the company's activities. This study has also (wrongly) led many colleagues to believe that Huth & Co.'s concerns were mainly in the US. Additionally, the firm has also been mistakenly labelled as a 'central European specialist'.[31] Finally, there is also a fine biography of Frederick Huth,[32] which, although useful for family historians, deals principally with family affairs rather than international business.

This is not to say that there are no other works on Huth & Co.'s activities before 1850. I note that in the most important general works on merchant banking so far published,[33] there is some mention of Huth's activities, but such references are mainly in passing and usually based on secondary sources.[34] Finally, bearing in mind that Huth opened branches in Chile and Peru (the only branches the company opened outside Britain before 1850), some authors have explored this particular connection, but without relation to the rest of the world economy and while ignoring the richest primary sources.[35] Overall, this book is the first comprehensive monograph on Huth's global networks. Furthermore, most previous scholars with an interest in Huth have completely neglected the richest extant collection on Huth for 1810–1850, in particular those working on Chile, Peru or Spain.[36]

The richest collection for Huth & Co., and therefore the main primary source of information for this book, is the Huth papers available at University College London (UCL) Special Collections (now at Kew).[37] This collection contains 183 volumes of out-letters for $c.$1812–1855 and about 70 folders of incoming correspondence for $c.$1814–1850. It also contains accounts books (including bills payable, bills receivable, journals, cash books, and insurance ledgers). Despite this wealth of data, few scholars have used this collection before. Freedman drew on it, but only to study Huth's connections with the US $c.$1835–1850, and he himself admitted that his work did not 'purport to offer a full inquiry into the worldwide interests of the house'.[38] Other academics who used these papers before (for published works) include: McGrane, but also in connection with the US only, and selected volumes only;[39] Reber, albeit sparingly, for a work on British merchant houses in Buenos Aires;[40] Curry-Machado and Cervantes-Rodriguez, who used only one volume of correspondence in connexion with Cuba;[41] and Jones, who produced a short (though very useful) biography on Frederick Huth, based mainly on information gleaned from secondary sources.[42] Scholars who have studied Huth's activities in Chile or Peru have used instead the Huth papers at the Guildhall Library (as I did for this book), but those papers are of comparatively minor interest, in particular for the 1810s–1840s.

So why have the Huth papers at UCL not been used more widely? That is a very difficult question to answer, especially given that the main difficulty of research in merchant banking is that the 'historical records of most firms have disappeared'.[43] In other words, you would expect more colleagues to have been attracted to this ocean of information. Nonetheless, it could be the case that these papers have received relatively scant attention because in many volumes the handwriting is difficult to decipher, while other volumes are in a very poor condition. Another difficulty could be that the letters are in Spanish, English, French and German. Likewise, in order to cover the whole period under study, a vast amount of information must be explored and consequently the time to be spent on the archive would be considerable. Finally, although at least 15 major merchant banks were founded in London before 1850, it is true that it was only *after* this date that they became a more distinctive social group and more powerful than during the period covered by this monograph, at least in terms of economic muscle, wealth and political influence. As a result, economic and business historians have understandably concentrated on this latter period.

Regarding other sources of information, and bearing in mind that Huth had so many correspondents all over the world, it is unsurprising that there are many collections of other merchants which contain useful material on Huth. Therefore, papers in the following repositories in Britain were consulted: The Rothschild Archive, which contains rich evidence of Huth's profitable partnership with Rothschild to market quicksilver in the Americas; Baring Brothers' papers at ING, containing valuable reports on Huth & Co. and merchants linked to the firm; the Plymouth and West Devon Record Office, containing Huth's correspondence with an agent (James Olver) in Plymouth very early on; the Lancashire Record Office, containing exchanges with a supplier of manufactures; Glasgow University Archives, containing letters to and from some of Huth's agents in Scotland; Nottingham University Library, containing the records of William Brandt, which were extremely useful regarding factual information about Huth's partners; and the University of Leeds, home to the John Anderton papers, one of Huth's main textile suppliers. Outside of the United Kingdom, the following collections were also consulted: Smith College, Northampton (US), in particular the Hiram Putnam Papers, which contain material on Chilean copper exports supported by Huth; New South Wales State Library (Australia), which holds information on Australia's wool cargoes to London; and the National Archives of Chile, which are a rich source of data on Huth's activities in Chile and Peru. Useful searches were also run in *The Times* digital archives and in the House of Commons Parliamentary Papers, also online. Finally, the main secondary literature on merchant banking was consulted.

After this introduction, this book contains another six chapters. Chapter 1 deals with the early life of Frederick Huth, in particular his early training in Basque merchant houses in Hamburg and Corunna, *c*.1791–1805. It also addresses the beginnings of Huth's career as a lone merchant, first in Corunna (1805–1809) and subsequently in London from 1809 to 1815, ending with the incorporation of a first partner into the company and the early years of operations under this new arrangement, *c*.1815–1822. Chapter 2 covers the period from 1822 until the late 1830s, concentrating on the opening of branches in Peru and Chile in the early 1820s and the operations of the company from these quarters, but also on Huth's interests in other Latin American quarters. Chapter 3 deals in detail with Huth's activities in Spain, which together with the dealings in Germany constituted by far the most important parts of the company's business. Due to this, a small section of this chapter deals exclusively with Germany.

Chapter 4 discusses the opening of Huth & Co.'s Liverpool branch in the late 1830, the only one the firm opened in the UK. The chapter also covers the US connection and the relations between Huth and key agents appointed to the British textile districts, ending with the company's policy of incorporating partners. Chapter 5 is a comparative analysis of key decisions to be taken by merchant bankers during my period of study, albeit centred on Huth & Co., in order to draw

8 *Introduction*

useful comparisons between this company and its main competitors. These decisions relate to geographical and product coverage, whether to trade and finance trade or just finance trade, client numbers, the nature of products whose trade was financed (i.e. manufactures and/or raw materials), and the range of other activities performed by merchant bankers. Finally, before a concluding chapter, Chapter 6 deals with the risk management credit strategies pursued by Huth & Co. to protect itself from the risks arising to lending to so many people in so many places and in so many different products.

Notes

1. S. Marzagalli, 'Establishing Transatlantic Trade Networks in Time of War: Bordeaux and the United States, 1793–1815', *Business History Review*, 79 (2005), p. 838.
2. We must bear in mind that, given the state of communications, these were times when the main obstacles to trade were lack of information and lack of trust, and in turn these obstacles accounted for most transaction costs. M. Casson, 'The Economic Analysis of Multinational Trading Companies', in G. Jones (ed.), *The Multinational Traders* (London: Routledge, 1998), p. 23; G. Jones, 'Multinational Trading Companies in History and Theory', in G. Jones (ed.), *The Multinational Traders* (London: Routledge, 1998), p. 16.
3. R. Roberts, *Schroders: Merchants and Bankers* (London: Macmillan, 1992), p. 22.
4. G. Jones, *Merchants to Multinationals: British Trading Companies in the Nineteenth and Twentieth Centuries* (Oxford: Oxford University Press, 2000), p. 21.
5. There was, indeed, 'an extraordinary tenure of family capitalism in the merchant banking sector'. For instance, the mighty N. M. Rothschild & Sons abandoned the partnership form as late as in 1970, when they become a limited liability, private company. M. Lisle-Williams, 'Beyond the Market: The Survival of Family Capitalism in the English Merchant Banks', *British Journal of Sociology*, 35 (1984), pp. 241, 244, 262.
6. On this, see G. Jones and M. B. Rose, 'Family Capitalism', *Business History*, 35 (1993).
7. Lisle-Williams, 'Beyond the Market', pp. 246–247.
8. Jones, 'Multinational Trading Companies', p. 4.
9. For a theoretical discussion of this topic, see M. Llorca-Jaña 'The Organization of British Textile Exports to the River Plate and Chile: Merchant Houses in Operation, c.1810–1859', *Business History*, 53 (2011), pp. 829–831.
10. It was then led by the great-grandsons of Frederick Huth. The company had been in relative decline since the late 1860s, but in particular during the First World War, and was in danger of failure by 1921, when it had to be supported by the Bank of England. C. Jones, 'Huth, Frederick Andrew (1777–1864)', *Oxford Dictionary of National Biography* (Oxford: Oxford University Press, 2004), p. 4; M. Lisle-Williams, 'Coordinators and Controllers of Capital: the Social and Economic Significance of the British Merchant Banks', *Social Science Information*, 23 (1984), p. 257.
11. Before 1850, other merchant bankers, such as Baring Brothers or Schroder, concentrated on trade with the US, while Rothschild & Sons concentrated on trade with Europe. Likewise, Kleinwort specialized in Russia, the US and the West Indies. S. D. Chapman, *The Rise of Merchant Banking* (London: George Allen & Unwin, 1984), p. 22; Jones, *Merchants to Multinationals*, pp. 23–24; Roberts, *Schroders*; R. W. Hidy, *The House of Baring in American Trade and Finance* (Cambridge: Harvard University Press, 1949); N. Ferguson, *The House of Rothschild. Volume 1* (London: Penguin, 1999).

12 W. A. Friedman and G. Jones, 'Business History: Time for Debate', *Business History Review*, 85 (2011), pp. 3 and 5–6.
13 For 1836, HPJ-228. For 1850, see A. Murray, *Home from the Hill* (London: Hamish Hamilton, 1970), pp. 141 and 182.
14 Chapman, *The Rise*, p. 40.
15 M. Lisle-Williams, 'Merchant Banking Dynasties in the English Class Structure', *British Journal of Sociology*, 35 (1984), p. 339.
16 Jones, 'Huth, Frederick Andrew', p. 2.
17 W. D. Rubinstein, *Men of Property: The Very Wealthy in Britain Since the Industrial Revolution* (Surrey: Croom Helm, 1981), p. 96.
18 Jones, *Merchants to Multinationals*, pp. 18–21; S. D. Chapman, 'The International Houses: The Continental Contribution to British Commerce, 1800–1860', *Journal of European Economic History*, 6 (1977), p. 7.
19 S. D. Chapman, 'Financial Restraints on the Growth of Firms in the Cotton Industry, 1790–1850', *Economic History Review*, 33 (1979), pp. 217–218; S. D. Chapman, *Merchant Enterprise in Britain. From the Industrial Revolution to World War I* (Cambridge: Cambridge University Press, 1992), pp. 47–48, 68–70; Chapman, *The Rise*, p. 10.
20 Thanks to this development, India (1813) and China (1834) were opened up to British merchants. M. Greenberg, *British Trade and the Opening of China, 1800–42* (Cambridge: Cambridge University Press, 1969). This is not to say that the region was unknown to private traders hitherto, they could now operate more freely than before, and many new entrants followed. Private business networks became more influential as regulated trading companies declined in importance. R. Pearson and D. Richardson, 'Social Capital, Institutional Innovation and Atlantic Trade before 1800', *Business History*, 50 (2008), p. 766.
21 The independence wars in Spanish America encompassed, roughly speaking, the period between 1808 and 1824. The literature for this crucial episode of Latin American history is huge, but J. Lynch, *The Spanish American Revolutions, 1808–1826* (London: W. W. Norton & Company, 1986) remains an important work to start with the political side of the story. On the economic side, see V. Bulmer-Thomas, *The Economic History of Latin America Since Independence* (Cambridge: Cambridge University Press, 2003), chapter 1; and L. Bértola and J. G. Williamson, 'Globalization in Latin America before 1940', in V. Bulmer-Thomas, J. Coatsworth, and R. Cortés-Conde (eds), *Cambridge Economic History of Latin America* (Cambridge: Cambridge University Press, 2006), amongst many other works. After independence many British mercantile establishments opened offices in the new Latin American republics. Indeed, during *c*.1810–1859 over 260 British merchant houses operated in the River Plate or Chile alone, but many more opened offices in the rest of Latin America. M. Llorca-Jaña, *The British Textile Trade in South America in the Nineteenth Century* (New York: Cambridge University Press, 2012).
22 On this topic, see in particular E. De Fiore and O. De Fiore, *The British Presence in Brazil, 1808–1914* (Sao Paulo: Editora Paubrasil, 1987); L. H. Guenther, *British Merchants in Nineteenth-Century Brazil: Business, Culture, and Identity in Bahia, 1808-1850* (Oxford: Oxford University Press, 2004); A. K. Manchester, *British Pre-Eminence in Brazil: its Rise and Decline* (New York: Octagon Books, 1964); M. Llorca-Jaña, 'British Merchants in New Markets: the Case of Wylie and Hancock in Brazil and the River Plate, *c*.1808–1820', *Journal of Imperial and Commonwealth History*, 44 (2014). To give an idea of the British presence in the area during this early period, by 1810 there were probably over 200 British mercantile establishments operating in Brazil.
23 Jones, *Merchants to Multinationals*, p. 21; D. Kynaston, *The City of London. Volume 1: a World on its Own 1815–1890* (London: Chatto & Windus, 1995), pp. 25–27; C.

10 *Introduction*

       Jones, *International Business in the Nineteenth Century* (Brighton: Wheatsheaf, 1987), p. 2; Chapman, 'Financial Restraints', p. 217.
24 Jones, *International Business*, p. 2; Chapman, 'The International Houses'. For the activities of Spanish merchants in London during this period, see in particular X. Lamikiz, *Trade and Trust in the Eighteenth-Century Atlantic World* (London: Boydell & Breaver Press, 2010), pp. 45–50, 146–150.
25 Roberts, *Schroders*, p. 30.
26 Lisle-Williams, 'Beyond the Market', p. 248.
27 Amongst the most celebrated works we have Chapman, *The Rise*; Chapman, *Merchant Enterprise in Britain*; Roberts, *Schroders*; J. Wake, *Kleinwort Benson: the History of Two Families in Banking* (Oxford: Oxford University Press, 1997); Hidy, *The House of Baring*; Ferguson, *The House of Rothschild*; Jones, *Merchants to Multinationals*.
28 Lisle-Williams, 'Coordinators and Controllers', p. 95; Lisle-Williams, 'Beyond the Market', pp. 241–243.
29 Chapman, *Merchant Enterprise in Britain*, p. 3.
30 J. R. Freedman, *A London merchant banker Anglo-American trade and finance, 1835–1850*. PhD Thesis (London: University of London, 1968).
31 Lisle-Williams, 'Coordinators and Controllers', p. 257.
32 Murray, *Home from the Hill*. There are also two biographical works touching on Daniel Meinertzhagen, one of Huth's partners. G. Meinertzhagen, *A Bremen Family* (London: Longmans, 1912); and R. Meinertzhagen, *Diary of a Black Sheep* (London: Oliver and Boyd, 1964).
33 Chapman, *Merchant Enterprise in Britain*, and Chapman, *The Rise*; Jones, *International Business*; Jones, *Merchants to Multinationals*.
34 Wake, *Kleinwort Benson*; Roberts, *Schroders*.
35 E. Cavieres, *Comercio Chileno y Comerciantes Ingleses* (Santiago de Chile: Editorial Universitaria, 1999); J. Mayo, *British Merchants and Chilean Development* (Boulder: Westview Press, 1987).
36 Cavieres, *Comercio Chileno*; Mayo, *British Merchants*.
37 The vast majority of UCL collections are currently housed temporarily at The National Archives in Kew, Richmond, and are available to users in a dedicated reading room.
38 Freedman, *A London Merchant Banker*, p. ii.
39 R. C. McGrane, *Foreign Bondholders and American States Debt* (New York: MacMillan, 1935).
40 V. B. Reber, *British Mercantile Houses in Buenos Aires* (Cambridge: Harvard University Press, 1979).
41 J. Curry-Machado, 'Running from Albion: Migration to Cuba from the British Isles in the 19th Century', *International Journal of Cuban Studies*, 2 (2009), p. 6; M. Cervantes-Rodriguez, *International Migration in Cuba: Accumulation, Imperial Designs, and Transnational Social Fields* (Pennsylvania: The Pennsylvania State University Press, 2010), p. 90.
42 Jones, 'Huth, Frederick Andrew', p. 2.
43 Jones, *Merchants to Multinationals*, p. 14.

1 Early life and activities of Frederick Huth, founder of the company, c.1777–1822

Early training in Hamburg and Corunna, 1791–1809

Nowadays Huth & Co. is recognized as a leading London merchant banker of the nineteenth century. Yet Huth's commercial origins must be traced to Germany[1] and northern Spain. Frederick Huth, the founder of Huth & Co., was born in Stade, Hanover (nowadays part of Germany) in 1777.[2] Although he died a very wealthy man in 1864 (aged 87), his origins were humble. Frederick was the son of a soldier who settled with his family in 1781 at Harsefeld (south-west of Hamburg), where Frederick attended local schools. His future did not look particularly promising. By then, Frederick's father was working as a tailor, earning barely enough to support his growing family. But things were to change for the better. Aged 14, Frederick was fortunate enough to be admitted as apprentice to a Basque[3] merchant house in Hamburg (called Brentano Urbieta & Co.).[4] Huth was given a little room in Urbieta's premises, and apart from learning on the job, twice weekly he attended the local and prestigious *Handelsakademie* (business school) to receive a formal education in commerce.

The location of this Spanish house was not unusual at that time, since many Basque merchants established themselves in European Atlantic ports during the 1780s–1790s, including places like Bayonne, Bordeaux, Amsterdam, Ostend, London and Hamburg.[5] With its good connections to other leading seafaring cities, such as London and Amsterdam, Hamburg was an important entrepôt of colonial produce, in particular that garnered from outposts of the British and Spanish empires.[6] Hamburg has thus justifiably been described as 'a wonderful city for a future merchant, for it was a city on the move'.[7] For example, from Hamburg, Urbieta's dealings included imports of Spanish produce from Malaga and Cadiz, including re-exports of Havana's sugar, Venezuela's coffee, Central America's cochineal and indigo, and Buenos Aires' hides.[8] In turn, merchants in Hamburg were well connected to several of the most important European consumer centres of the time.[9] But Hamburg was also one of the prime exit doors of German manufactures (linens in particular, but also ironware), which were re-exported to France, England, the Netherlands, Spain, her colonies, and many other places. Indeed, most of the 'production from the famous manufacturing regions in Germany's interior was destined for foreign and overseas markets'.[10]

Furthermore, when in 1795 Amsterdam was taken by the French, Hamburg made further commercial gains. Many of the merchants who had been working in Le Havre, Amsterdam and Antwerp emigrated to Hamburg, bringing with them vast trade networks as well as their capital,[11] thus increasing the cosmopolitan character of this city. In short, Frederick Huth could not have asked for a better European port in which to start his commercial education, and in particular to gain a good understanding of the international trading networks operating from Europe at that time, including the keys to succeed in multilateralizations of trade involving other (distant) regions. Incidentally, Joseph Hambro, the founder of Hambro & Son of London (a competitor of Huth & Co.), also served his apprenticeship in Hamburg, and according to the biographers of this company, 'there could be no better place for a future merchant to serve his apprenticeship'.[12]

Indeed, it was in Hamburg that Frederick Huth swiftly learned the most basic tricks of international trading. Frederick did so well that, in 1795, aged just 18, he was promoted to senior clerk by Juan Antonio Urbieta, the head of Brentano Urbieta & Co. By then Huth's period of apprenticeship had ended. The following year Urbieta took him on his annual linen-buying tour of Silesia.[13] Linen accounted for a high proportion of the goods sent to Spain by Brentano Urbieta & Co. (many of which were subsequently re-exported to the Americas),[14] this being one of the few products they purchased directly from producers, including those in remote locations.[15] It is worth stressing here that Huth's knowledge of this product will prove influential in his future dealings from London. In any case, only two years later, Huth's performance continued to be so outstanding that in 1797 Juan Antonio decided that Frederick would be of better use in Corunna, where Brentano Urbieta & Co. had a branch house that was contributing significantly to the firm's overall revenues.[16]

Several changes in Spanish law underlie this decision. The most important of these enabled foreign Protestants (such as Frederick Huth) both to live and to work in Spain. Previous to that, in 1764 the Spanish crown created its first postal service connecting Spain with Spanish America (*correos marítimos*, or maritime mail, in a monthly basis), with Corunna (rather than Cadiz) being chosen as the port from which the packet boats would depart. There was no better place in Spain to access timely information regarding Spanish America.[17] A year later, in 1765, Corunna and other nine ports were allowed to trade with the Spanish Caribbean, a concession which was further enhanced in 1778 when Corunna (and twelve other Spanish ports) was allowed to trade directly with the entirety of Spanish America, the combined effect of which increased Galician foreign trade beyond all previous limits. This development will be of future importance because it was in Galicia that Huth became familiar with direct trades with Spanish America. Indeed, from Corunna Huth was sent to South America several times acting as the Urbietas' supercargo between the late 1790s and early 1800s. During these trips Huth landed in places such as Rio de Janeiro, Callao, Valparaiso and Buenos Aires. Corroborating the excursions of Brentano, Bovara (another partner)[18] and Urbieta in that region, according to data collected by Barbier, in 1802 two vessels chartered by this Basque house arrived at the River Plate, and another three between 1804 and 1808. In this later period, the firm also chartered another three ships for Callao,[19] and it was as part of these trips that Huth gained valuable firsthand knowledge of these markets, which must surely have showed him the potential of the region, in particular after independence. In fact these travels may have led to Huth's decision in 1822 to open branches in Peru (and in Chile two years later), as discussed below.

More importantly, Huth's appointment in Galicia is crucial to understanding his later and strong connections with Spain after he moved to London in 1809. Having spent nigh on twelve years in Spain, Frederick Huth not only had a first-mover advantage over potential competitors but had also longstanding friends who could be trusted – and who trusted him – at a time when one of the main obstacles to international trade was the lack of trust, and trust was intimately linked with another crucial element of cross-border business: reputation.[20] Frederick's reputation began to grow as a result of his early training in Hamburg, and it was surely enhanced in Spain amongst those who knew him well. And indeed, apart from Britain and Germany, it was in Spain that Huth & Co. of London concentrated most correspondents for the entirety of the period 1809–1850. In turn, the links with Spain were instrumental to the firm's strategy of business diversification.

The Corunna house was led by Cypriano Urbieta, a brother of Juan Antonio, who soon started to rely heavily on Huth. Apparently Cypriano had other (more) important interests than commerce,[21] and therefore Frederick was free to shine, winning an enhanced reputation with the Urbietas in the process, so much so that after his final trip as supercargo to South America, Frederick was made chief clerk (and junior partner) of the Corunna house, thus completing a meteoric ascendancy within the firm. Despite this new responsibility, and the consequent salary increase, two years later in 1805 he decided that – thanks to the invaluable commercial experience and formal training he had gained in Hamburg, Corunna and South America – it was time to open his own business.[22] Furthermore, by then he had married a young Spanish lady called Manuela Felipa Mayfren (1785–1856), which also prompted him to set up on his own. Although an orphan, it was thought that Manuela was actually the daughter of a senior courtier to the king of Spain,[23] a connection that would prove very useful for Huth & Co.'s future business operations from London.

Huth's activities as a sole merchant in Corunna between 1805 and 1809 are poorly documented, but this is not surprising given the small scale of his activities at this time. We can, however, presume that during these years he traded principally with Hamburg, other German provinces, France, Russia and South America, thus replicating some of Urbieta's businesses at both Hamburg and Corunna, and surely making the most of the contacts he had previously cultivated while working for the Basque house. Yet Huth's independent business in Galicia proved to be short-lived. Napoleon's invasion of Spain in 1808 forced him, his wife and their two children[24] (and many other residents) to leave Corunna a few months later and the Huths arrived in London in 1809,[25] with no more than £700 in funds and a few letters of introduction given by his friend and merchant Juan Francisco Barrié,[26] a senior member of the Real Consulado de Comercio of Corunna. Although of French origin, Barrié had taken Spanish nationality in 1803.[27] They became very close friends during Huth's time in Galicia,[28] and indeed it is believed that Barrié assisted Huth when he opened his own business there in 1805.[29] But Huth also had some valuable London contacts he had previously cultivated while working for Brentano Urbieta & Co. Indeed, amongst those who also helped Huth in his early days in London was Fermín[30] de Tastet (1793–1863), head of Tastet & Co., 'a well known Spanish house' of London,[31] and a contact provided directly by the Urbietas when Huth moved to England.[32] Firmín, like so many London-based merchants, was very active in the re-export of many products from London to several Atlantic ports.[33] Indeed, in the mid-1800s de Tastet and the Urbietas entered into several joint-account operations involving multilateral trades between London, Corunna and the River Plate, in some of which Huth even acted as supercargo. In turn, Firmín had a brother (Juan Antonio de Tastet), a respected merchant resident in Cádiz, who also had a dense network of contacts in other quarters of Europe, South America and the US.[34] Thus, the Tastet brothers' networks could be, and indeed were, rapidly used by Huth from London to engage in commission business.

The Tastets proved instrumental in Huth's swift assimilation into England in 1809, providing him with useful contacts in many quarters. Furthermore, when in 1815 Huth decided to take a first partner on board, the chosen one was none other than John Frederick Gruning, at that time working for Tastet in London.[35] Given that Gruning remained Huth's principal partner until his death, Tastet's (and Spain's) long-term influence on Huth should be read as critical. That said, another early influential friend in London was Marcial Francisco del Adalid, a merchant originally from Corunna, and once also principal commissioner of the Banco Nacional de San Carlos, who by this time was also a refugee resident in the English capital.[36] Finally, Manuel de Florez-Mendez, also originally from Corunna, but resident in London until 1814, proved helpful to Huth during his early years in England, providing key contacts in Spain before the end of the Napoleonic Wars. All in all, it is clear that without the Spanish connection, the establishment of Huth in London and its subsequent expansion worldwide would have been extremely difficult, if not impossible.

At 32 years old, Frederick was not a young man, and his English was limited. He did not come from a rich family, which in itself makes him unusual among merchant bankers.[37] But he spoke German, French and Spanish, and, above all, he was persistent, and had gained the reputation of being an honest man. He had also either lived or visited more places than most of the merchants of his generation. His wife had good political connections in Spain. Starting a new career in London would not be easy, but he nonetheless had some assets many competitors would want to posses.

The early years as a standalone merchant in London, 1809–1815

After settling in London with his Spanish wife and children, Huth resumed business as a general commission merchant, probably in the same way that he had done in Corunna between 1805 and 1809, but operating from a location with far greater potential (albeit stronger competition). We know very little about the first three years of operations. The first regular business correspondence available is for 1812, although we do have some patchy written communication for 1810–1812, plus a few pieces of additional information such as current accounts. From 1812 onwards, though, the information at hand is of excellent quality and quantity. Table 1.1 summarizes the location of Huth's full list of correspondents for 1812–1813, and certainly gives us a clear sense of his early activities in the English capital.

As can be inferred from this table, trade with Spain was the main core of the business at this early stage: over half of all correspondents were based there. The English connection was obviously very strong too,[38] in particular in London and southern England, but Huth did not have many connections elsewhere in Britain, with noticeable omissions in the textile-focused quarters of northern England and Scotland (although Huth already traded with textiles) that would become so influential later on. Huth clearly relied heavily on his Spanish contacts, particularly those in Corunna. He had just one correspondent in Germany (unsurprisingly Brentano, Urbieta & Co. of Hamburg),[39] and a handful of others elsewhere in Europe, but this should not surprise us given the negative impact of the Napoleonic Wars on British and continental Europe's foreign trade and international communications.

Table 1.1 Location of Frederick Huth's correspondents c.1812–1813

Location	Number of Correspondents	Share	Location	Number of Correspondents	Share
Spain	58	*51.3%*	*England*	37	*32.7%*
Corunna	28	24.8%	London	11	9.7%
Santander	5	4.4%	Portsmouth	5	4.4%
Santiago de Compostela	5	4.4%	Plymouth	4	3.5%
Bilbao	4	3.5%	Bristol	3	2.7%
Cadiz	3	2.7%	Falmouth	3	2.7%
Gijon	2	1.8%	Birmingham	2	1.8%
San Sebastian	2	1.8%	Others in England	9	8.0%
Rivadeo	2	1.8%			
Others in Spain	7	6.2%	*Rest of Europe*	7	*6.2%*
			Bordeaux	1	0.9%
Americas	8	*7.1%*	Hamburg	1	0.9%
Buenos Aires	6	5.3%	Others in Europe	5	4.4%
Havana	1	0.9%			
Montevideo	1	0.9%	*No Available*	2	*1.8%*
			TOTAL	113	100%

Source: HPSL-154.

16 *Early life and activities of Frederick Huth*

Table 1.2 Share of the main products within the UK's exports of British and Irish produce to Spain (calculated from declared values series), 1814–1818

Year	British and Irish produce								
	Cottons	Woollens	Linens	Silks	Hardwares & Cutlery	Iron & Steel	Tin	Corn, Grain & Flour	Other products
1814	42%	26%	6%	4%	3%	2%	1%	3%	13%
1815	18%	25%	7%	8%	8%	4%	1%	10%	20%
1816	20%	20%	14%	8%	5%	4%	3%	10%	16%
1817	8%	35%	22%	14%	6%	4%	4%	1%	8%
1818	5%	32%	19%	13%	7%	5%	2%	0%	17%

Source: BPP, several volumes.

A more detailed analysis of Frederick Huth's business correspondence for these foundational years shows that his principal contacts in Spain around this time included: Lopez Doriga (Santander); Marcial Francisco de Adalid (Corunna); Pedro Llano (Corunna);[40] Antonio Francisco Casas (Rivadeo); Aguirre Hermanos (Santander); Garcia & Co. (Santiago de Compostela); Pedro Ventura Marzal (Corunna); Antonio Gonzalez (Luarca); Jose Altuna Cruz (San Sebastian); Miguel Francisco Demblans (Bilbao); and Carlos Frige (Bilbao). Essentially, Huth consigned to Spain a wide range of British products, such as cottons, woollens, silks, cutlery, pottery and wheat (understandably most of the main products exported by Britain to Spain at that time, as seen in Table 1.2), and also re-exported non-British products such as tallow, hides, cinnamon, pepper, tobacco, Indian cottons, cod, rum and sugar.[41]

Around this time, Huth's strongest trade from Britain was not in British manufactures but in foreign (mainly colonial) produce. For instance, Huth was an enthusiastic participant of London's public auctions of East Indies species, having over 45 interested clients in Spain wanting to receive black pepper, pimento or cinnamon.[42] For all of these transactions Huth charged a small commission on invoices and sales of no more than 2.5 per cent for exports to Spain, certainly a modest fee given all the savings customers would make by not having to search for information, agree prices and look for trusted buyers or sellers themselves.

In exchange for exports to Spain, Huth received consignments of wool and many other products such as ham, wine and cochineal via the Spanish Central American colonies. For most of these operations Huth also arranged marine insurance on behalf of a wide range of Spanish merchants, not only for shipments between Britain and Spain, but also for consignments from places such as Havana or Veracruz to Corunna or Cadiz.[43] Should we need to rank the relevance of Huth's operations, however, it has to be said that Spanish wool occupied the bulk of Huth's energies during this early period.[44] Wool ranked as one of Spain's principal exports and in turn Spain was one of the leading suppliers of this product for Britain (Table 1.3). Huth's Spanish correspondents for this product sent the wool to London or Bristol. (If sent to the latter, Hill & Sons and Greaves & Son received and sold the wool on Huth's behalf.[45]) In turn, Huth's Spanish connections would draw against Huth after shipping the bales.

Table 1.3 The UK's imports of raw wool. Share of main origins, 1812, 1813 and 1815 (from volumes imported)

Origin	1812	1813	1815
Portugal	38%	66%	16%
Spain	54%	24%	43%
Germany	1%	0%	22%
Others	7%	10%	19%

Source: BPP, several volumes.

During this early period, Frederick Huth operated mainly under consignments, that is, receiving Spanish and Spanish colonial produce on consignment and encouraging British suppliers to consign their merchandise to his contacts in Spain. Thus, he typically acted as an intermediary between sellers and buyers. But why could Spanish buyers not engage directly with British sellers, or British buyers with Spanish sellers? The main reason for this was that there were high transaction costs involved in these international trade operations. Moreover other obstacles to international commerce before 1850 included lack of direct contact, trust, product specifications and agreement on prices, not to mention the language barrier.[46] Thus, the major transaction cost components of these obstacles lay in finding out key information, sampling products, setting prices, monitoring quantity and quality, and ensuring punctual and reliable delivery. We must bear in mind that during this period 'the circle of people who had access to information from beyond their immediate locality was very small'.[47]

Spain and England aside, the River Plate connection was also important for Huth during the early years of operation in London. These were contacts surely cultivated by Frederick himself during his voyages there as supercargo of Urbieta & Co., and further promoted by well-connected Galician merchants known to him. At this time Buenos Aires provided hides, tallow and silver for the European markets.[48] Huth regarded the River Plate produce so highly that he even considered chartering a whole vessel for the River Plate in ballast, just sending gold to Buenos Aires because it was more expensive there than in Europe, and exchanging the gold directly for hides and tallow.[49] Local merchants such as Llano Brothers (Juan de Llano and his brother were relatives of Llano of Corunna),[50] Jaime Alsina (a connection facilitated by Mariano Serra of Corunna)[51] and Jose and Antonio Galup were amongst Huth's first contacts there.[52] Others were Manuel Giroud and Geronimo Merino Villanueva (another connection brokered by Mariano Serra). By this time Frederick Huth was already an expert in South American produce, and he exploited this advantage. In exchange, Huth sent to the River Plate a wide range of British and non-British products, including cottons, mustard, glasses, woollens, hardware and Spanish wine.

So this was the situation until 1815: a lone London merchant with a limited geographical reach and product portfolio. Things were about to change, however, and quickly. After the Napoleonic Wars, the German connection started to become more important (as was to be expected during peacetime), as did that with other European countries such as France, Portugal, the Netherlands and Russia.

Intra-European trades started to boom during this conflict-free period. By 1815 Huth had 28 correspondents in Germany (having had just one three years earlier), where many merchant houses provided textiles and other manufactures such as glass for Huth's friends in Spain and those further afield in Cuba and the River Plate region. Houses such as Justus Ruperti (Hamburg), J. C. Godeffroy (Hamburg), L. A. Huffel (Hamburg), J. F. Scheinert & Co. (Hamburg), Chapeaurouge & Co. (Hamburg), Groning & Co. (Hamburg),[53] and J. G. Schutte & Co. (Bremen) sent manufactures to the likes of Lopez Doriga (Corunna), Antonio Prado (Rivadeo), Rochelt Brothers (Bilbao) and other houses thanks to Huth's intermediation. If German manufactures were sent to Huth's friends, thanks to Huth's networking, then a commission was paid to the London merchant. This was a trade Huth had learnt very well while working for Urbieta & Co. Likewise, Huth promoted re-exports of Cuban produce from London and Spain to Hamburg and other European quarters: for example, Llano of Corunna sent sugar to Thornton in Hamburg during these early years,[54] as did many others.

Frederick Huth becomes Huth & Co: The early years of the first Huth & Co. partnership, 1816–1822

The nature of the business above described for c.1809–1815 was simple, chiefly involving bilateral trades and a few products across a few locations. In other words, it was characterized by a high geographical and product concentration. It was also greatly affected by the Napoleonic Wars, as noted above, but the enterprise prospered. Indeed, by the early 1810s Huth even had the capital to buy his first ship, the *Manuela*, in order to promote trade with Spain. And furthermore, in 1814, Frederick intended to buy a second vessel, this time of 164 tons, also intended for intra-European trades.[55] That said, in the absence of any evidence of the firm's profits during this period, we should not exaggerate Huth's success at this stage; Frederick's own capital was surely less than £20,000.[56]

Nonetheless, the end of the Napoleonic Wars was clearly an inflection point in the development of the firm. Huth's intra-European trades expanded substantially: by the end of 1815 Huth's correspondents had increased to some 200, nearly doubling those recorded just two years earlier. The correspondents were still primarily concentrated in Spain (43 per cent of them were resident there), but now Germany had also become very important (accounting for 15 per cent of all correspondents). Huth was also now trading in a wider range of products than in the early 1810s, and not only on commission, as he explained to an old friend: 'my business is now extended to all branches of trade, not only on commission but also on own account or in joint-account with other merchants.'[57] Own account operations required a larger amount of capital too, which we should take as another indicator that the firm's funds were on the rise and that there were no liquidity problems.

With peace returning to Europe, the future looked even more prosperous, so much so that in late 1815 Frederick Huth thought that it was the right time to bring his first partner into the business. It is unclear how and why, but another German

Early life and activities of Frederick Huth 19

(originally from Bremen, now working in London) was the chosen man. His name was John Frederick Gruning.[58] We know little about him, unfortunately, although it is believed that he was one of the Grönings of Bremen.[59] But Gruning was not related to Huth, and given that family was viewed as 'the main supplier of trustworthy associates and agents'[60] at this time, this must have seemed like a risky choice. Most merchant bankers of the period were drawn from the higher social echelons,[61] so that more often than not they resorted to relatives (e.g. brothers, brothers-in-law or sons) when incorporating partners into their firms.

Having more humble beginnings, Huth was an exception to this rule.[62] One explanation for his unconventional choice of partner could be the fact that Gruning had worked before for Huth's good friend, Fermín de Tastet, who as noted above had had dealings with the Urbietas.[63] In other words, it was likely that Gruning's character could be vouched for. Furthermore, despite his being an outsider to the firm, Gruning was German, and even though Huth's trade with Germany was increasing, he did not yet have an in-country branch. But perhaps more important than his references, anthropologists tend to believe that 'ethnicity has a great influence on how we judge other people's trustworthiness',[64] so that in this case Gruning's own background played an important role in his selection.

Thus, after formalizing Gruning's incorporation into the firm, from 1816 the trading house was styled Huth & Co. and remained so until its dissolution in 1936. Time proved that Frederick Huth had made the right decision, and that those who had recommended Gruning to Huth had done well: the partnership was dissolved only after the inevitable happened, when one of them (Gruning) died. More importantly, relations between both partners remained very good for the entirety of their association.

It is unclear how much capital Gruning brought into the firm in 1815,[65] but the first mission entrusted to him by Huth was to further promote the European side of the business by visiting various cities in Spain as well as Amsterdam, Paris and Bordeaux, which Gruning did during most of 1816.[66] Likewise, Gruning's incorporation further enhanced the importance of Germany for the house, in particular the Bremen connection. In 1815 Frederick Huth had only one correspondent in Bremen; by 1822 and 1827–1828, Huth & Co. had 20 and 28, respectively. Business associations with the Bremen house of G. Loning and the Hamburg houses of Justus Ruperti and J. C. Godeffroy proved useful and long-lasting. Huth's correspondent numbers in Germany boomed – from 28 in 1815 to 161 in 1822 and 228 in 1827–1828 – and the country became so important to the firm that it warranted the compilation of a separate correspondence volume besides the Spanish and English series.[67] Indeed, by 1827–1828 Huth had more correspondents in Germany than in Spain. To what extent this was mainly due to Gruning's incorporation it is difficult to tell, but it certainly helped.

Beyond Gruning's immediate impact on the firm, another significant fact to highlight regarding Huth & Co.'s geographical diversification was the increasing importance of France, Austria, Bohemia, Norway,[68] the Netherlands and Poland during the second half of the 1810s and early 1820s (Table 1.4). Likewise, if compared to the situation in 1812–1813 (indicated in Table 1.1), many new

Table 1.4 Location of Huth & Co.'s correspondents in 1822

Country	Number of Correspondents	Share	Country	Number of Correspondents	Share
North America	*20*	*3.0%*	*Britain*	*110*	*16.5%*
USA	8	1.2%	England	100	15.0%
Mexico	12	1.8%	Scotland	10	1.5%
Caribbean	*20*	*3.0%*	*Europe*	*434*	*65.3%*
Cuba	8	1.2%	Austria	3	0.5%
Curazao	3	0.5%	Belgium	1	0.2%
Haiti	2	0.3%	Czech Republic	1	0.2%
Jamaica	2	0.3%	Denmark	1	0.2%
Puerto Rico	2	0.3%	France	34	5.1%
St Thomas	3	0.5%	Germany	162	24.4%
			Gibraltar	2	0.3%
South America	*67*	*10.1%*	Ireland	1	0.2%
Argentina	11	1.7%	Italy	5	0.8%
Brazil	6	0.9%	Latvia	6	0.9%
Chile	2	0.3%	Malta	2	0.3%
Ecuador	9	1.4%	Netherlands	17	2.6%
Uruguay	1	0.2%	Norway	6	0.9%
Peru	38	5.7%	Poland	10	1.5%
			Portugal	4	0.6%
Asia	*3*	*0.5%*	Russia	1	0.2%
India	2	0.3%	Spain	178	26.8%
Philippines	1	0.2%			
			No available	*8*	*1.2%*
Africa	*3*	*0.5%*			
South Africa	3	0.5%	*Total*	*665*	*100%*

Source: HPSL-159.

countries in the Americas were also incorporated into the company's trade networks. These included Mexico, the US, Peru, Chile, Ecuador, Brazil, Haiti, Jamaica, Puerto Rico and St Thomas, amongst others.

Mexico (in particular Veracruz and Mexico City) and Peru became increasingly important as Huth & Co. entered the silver market. Cuba also gained strategic value for the firm: Huth & Co. was becoming an expert trader in the international sugar market. During the 1810s, the company made its first connections in Havana with the likes of Vidal & Sirven and Layseca & Co., the latter becoming Huth & Co.'s business agent in Cuba after regular dealings led to a trusting relationship.[69] The Cuban connection provided vast consignments of sugar, but also of rum and tobacco, not only for London but also for Germany, Spain, France and the Netherlands. Havana was also used as a destination for Buenos Aires' jerked beef (used to feed slaves employed in sugar-cane plantations), which Huth's correspondents in the River Plate (e.g. Zimmerman, Frazier & Co.) sent to Cuba in payment for Huth's consignments to Buenos Aires.

By the early 1820s, it was clear that the remit and volume of Huth & Co.'s business had expanded drastically. In 1812 and 1815 Frederick Huth had correspondents in 'only' 13 and 19 countries, respectively, and these were mainly concentrated within Europe. In 1822 Huth & Co. sustained correspondence with merchants in 37 countries in the Americas, Europe, Asia and Africa. But this is not to say that the Spanish or the German connection lost momentum. On the contrary, the volume of trade with all quarters was expanding. By 1822 Huth & Co. was corresponding with over 175 people in Spain and over 160 in Germany. This took the level of businesses with Spain (as it did with Germany) to a different level.

Indeed, I am not aware of any other London merchant banker having so many connections in Spain at this early stage. Most prominent merchant bankers of the period concentrated on Anglo-American trades or on one or two other markets,[70] among which Spain was not always a preferred option. Such was the case, for example, for Baring Brothers,[71] Brown Shipley & Co.,[72] Swire & Co.,[73] Cropper & Benson[74] and Rathbone Brothers & Co., all of which remained highly focussed on the US. Likewise, other comparable London multinational traders specialized in European markets, but these were further afield than Spain, as was the case for Brandt Sons & Co.[75] and Ralli Brothers.[76] This issue is discussed in depth in Chapter 5.

Keeping our focus on the Iberian peninsula, as part of this process of consolidating and enhancing Huth & Co.'s position in Spain, it is worth noting that its involvement in the Spanish wool market remained strong. Product diversification was also ongoing, however. Apart from wool, another Spanish product which became very important for the firm's dealings was wine, in particular the fortified Jerez variety (better known in the UK as sherry), which was at that time one of the main Spanish exports, especially to Great Britain.[77] The company's main contact in Spain for this product was Haurie & Nephews of Xerez, an important local dealer in this commodity. Thus, Huth & Co. in London received vast quantities of Jerez which were redistributed elsewhere within Britain. But Haurie was also instructed to send the wine directly to places such as Liverpool, Dublin, Bristol, where Huth & Co. had confidential agents – such as Castellain in Liverpool[78] – who took care of redistributing the wine elsewhere. Other suppliers of wine, this time from Cadiz, were Charles F. A. Uhthoff.

Finally, beyond Germany and Spain, Huth & Co.'s connections within Britain had also increased considerably. If in 1812 Frederick Huth had only 37 correspondents in England, by 1822 this number had increased to 100. Likewise, Scotland had been incorporated as a valuable connection as a result of the company becoming very active in the textiles trade, in particular in cottons, worsteds and woollens. These started to be exported to a wide range of correspondents all over the world. Huth & Co. had also begun trading in earthenware and iron products and thus the major industrial cities of Birmingham and Sheffield became important suppliers of manufactures for Huth's connections, as did Wales. Frederick Huth committed to Britain on a personal level too, first by joining the Church of England in 1815[79] and then obtaining British citizenship in 1819.[80] He would never leave Britain.

Regarding the structure adopted by the firm within Britain and the partnerships arrangement, it is worth noting that, despite the growth of the business, by this stage Huth & Co. still had only one office (in London) and two partners (Frederick Huth and John F. Gruning). Given the growing volume of trade, however, a new partner joined the team during the mid-1820s. This time Frederick Huth followed the more traditional and secure approach, and Charles Frederick Huth (1806–1895), Frederick's eldest son, joined Huth & Co. as a third partner.[81] Frederick was thus, in part, trying to replicate a merchant banking system overwhelmingly controlled by dynasts and their appointees' sons.

Additionally, in order to support trade with so many locations, during this 'foundational period' Huth & Co. used the services of many people in key British ports. These agents were businessmen who performed commercial activities on behalf of other businessmen based elsewhere (they were sometimes also called business partners[82]). And so in London, Liverpool, and other key strategic places, Huth & Co. hired the services of specialized brokers to facilitate the sales of the products they were trading or helping others to trade.[83] These relationships were cultivated slowly, initially via regular correspondence, and then a probation period when trust was built up sufficiently. If things went well, the business relationship was formalized, although it is clear from Huth's correspondence that there was a great diversity in the terms under which Huth's agents worked for Huth & Co. (both for inland and overseas agents).

For example, in Falmouth Fox & Co.[84] acted as Huth & Co.'s agents, charging a commission for several services, including handling correspondence, shipping intelligence, but most importantly, market intelligence on many products. The idea was to assess which British port (or other location) was more convenient for the sale of Huth & Co.'s imported cargoes.[85] Similar services were provided in other ports by Hill & Sons or G. Edwards & Co. in Bristol.[86] As time passed, these business partners started to provide not only commercial but also political intelligence. In all, Huth & Co.'s network was, therefore, asymmetric, in the sense that nothing but Huth's London headquarters was at its very centre. In turn, the London headquarters was strongly supported by specialized clerks. In 1822, for instance, Huth & Co. employed the services of senior clerks such as George Child, J. B. Cabanyes, James Tate, Mr. Misler, C. L. Vidal, Mr. Hellman, J. D. Launburg and Mr Hodgkinson. Judging from the surnames alone, most of them were surely employed in particular to support the British, Spanish and German connection.[87]

Overall, by the early 1820s Huth & Co. was a sound merchant house on the London market, with capital of £30,000.[88] The company was strong in specific import markets, namely raw wool (from Spain and Germany), sugar and tobacco (from the Caribbean), hides (from Brazil and the River Plate),[89] tallow (from Russia and the River Plate), coffee and cocoa (from the Caribbean and northern South America), timber (from Norway), grains (whenever they were in short supply in Britain, brought from many quarters) and, increasingly, silver (from Mexico and Peru). Huth & Co. was also becoming an important exporter of British manufactures, which were sent to continental Europe, the Americas and Asia. Huth also remained important in the re-export side of British trade, sending colonial produce to Europe and the Americas.

By this time, however, in contrast to 1812, the company had become more active in trades that never even touched British ports. It was, for example, the essential link between many merchants in Spain, Germany and France and their counterparts in the Americas. The same European merchants who had formerly received sugar cargoes from Huth & Co. in London were now also getting them directly from places such as Havana and Rio de Janeiro. The company also started increasingly to fund trade operations, some of which passed through Britain and some of which did not, thus becoming a de facto merchant banker, although still on a limited scale by the early 1820s.[90] For example, Layseca in Havana was a regular sugar consigner for Huth & Co. in London, but started to consign sugar to Galicia upon the company's request and intermediation, with Huth & Co. making advances for both sorts of operations. The structure of the firm began to change too, not by incorporating new partners or agents, but rather by opening the first branches of the company, which takes us to the next chapter.

Notes

1. During our period of study, Germany as such did not exist yet. By this stage what would become Germany in the future was perhaps best described as a league of sovereign states.
2. Jones, 'Huth, Frederick Andrew', pp. 1–3.
3. We can confirm that Urbieta was from the Basque country, although I was not able to confirm that this was also the case for Brentano. If Brentano was not Basque, then perhaps 'Spanish firm' is a more accurate term for this house.
4. This happened thanks to the intervention of Pastor Brandt of Harsefeld, who recommended young Frederick Huth to Doktor Pratje, an influential figure of the Lutheran Church in Bremen. Murray, *Home from the Hill*, p. 20.
5. A. Angulo-Morales, 'Bilbao, Madrid, Londres. Ganaderos, Comerciantes y Cambistas Vascos en los Mercados Financieros y Laneros del Atlántico', in J. A. Ocampo (ed.), *Empresas y Empresarios del Norte de España a Fines del Antiguo Régimen* (Madrid: Marcial Pons, 2011), pp. 198–200; A. Aragón and A. Angulo-Morales, 'The Spanish Basque Country in Global Trade Networks in the Eighteenth Century', *International Journal of Maritime History,* 25 (2013), p. 171. It is worth mentioning that there were movements in the opposite direction. For example, merchants from Germany established offices in the principal ports of France, Spain (in particular Cadiz) and Britain. K. Weber, 'The Atlantic Coast of German Trade: German Rural Industry and Trade in the Atlantic, 1680–1840', *Itinerario*, 26 (2002), p. 104.
6. The territories of the German Empire, at this stage, lacked the colonial dimension of Germany's western neighbours. Weber, 'The Atlantic Coast', p. 100; B. Bramsen and K. Wain, *The Hambros, 1779–1979* (London: Michael Joseph, 1979), pp. 148–150. It was only during the 1870s that Germany started to acquire colonies.
7. Bramsen & Wain, *The Hambros*, p. 148.
8. During the last quarter of the eighteenth century there was an important commercial exchange between Germany and Spanish America via Spain, and directly between Germany and Spanish America during wartime, all thanks to the neutral trade allowed by the Spanish crown during warfare to avoid isolating Spanish colonies during military conflicts. H. Asdrúbal, 'Hamburgo y el Río de la Plata: Vinculaciones Económicas a Fines de la Epoca Colonial, *Jahrbuch für Geschichte Lateinamerikas*, 21 (1984), p. 190.
9. Weber, 'The Atlantic Coast'.
10. Weber, 'The Atlantic Coast', pp. 100–102.
11. Jones, *International Business*, pp. 36–37; Roberts, *Schroders*, pp. 14–15; Wake, *Kleinwort Benson*, p. 10.

24 *Early life and activities of Frederick Huth*

12 Joseph Hambro served his apprenticeship just a few years later than Frederick Huth did, between 1797 and 1800, in the Hamburg house of Furst, Haller & Co. Bramsen and Wain, *The Hambros*, pp. 148 and 150.
13 Jones, 'Huth, Frederick Andrew', p. 1.
14 See for example, B. Stein and S. Stein, *Edge of Crisis: War and Trade in the Spanish Atlantic, 1789–1808* (Baltimore: Johns Hopkins University Press, 2009), p. 254. According to Weber, 'more than three quarters of Silesian linen was destined for the Atlantic nations of Western Europe or for the Americas'. This was possible thanks to a navigable waterway connecting Silesia directly with Hamburg and the Atlantic. Weber, 'The Atlantic Coast', pp. 101 and 103.
15 Murray, *Home from the Hill*, p. 26; Jones, *International Business*, p. 37. It is worth noting that Andrew Murray, the author of Frederick Huth's biography, was Frederick's great-great grandson.
16 Hamburg developed close links with Corunna in particular during the 1790s. Jones, *International Business*, p. 37.
17 Lamikiz, *Trade and Trust*, p. 98. The exact route was Corunna–Havana. From Havana the mail was redistributed elsewhere in Spanish America. Likewise, another mail service was inaugurated in 1767, when between four to six ships per year departed from Corunna to Buenos Aires carrying mail intended for some regions of South America. Lamikiz, *Trade and Trust*, p. 99.
18 Also referred to as Vobara in both primary and secondary sources.
19 J. A. Barbier, 'Comercio Neutral in Bolivarian America', in R. Liehr (ed), *América Latina en la Epoca de Simón Bolívar* (Berlin: Colloquium Verlag, 1989). See also Asdrúbal, 'Hamburgo y el Río de la Plata', pp. 194, 199, 202; Weber, 'The Atlantic Coast', p. 109. From 1797, during times of war, the Spanish crown authorized her American colonies to trade with neutral nations. A. Pearce, *British Trade with Spanish America, 1763-1808* (Liverpool: Liverpool University Press, 2007). As part of this agreement, Brentano Urbieta & Co. traded directly between Hamburg and the River Plate, as many other firms based in Germany did.
20 Lamikiz, *Trade and Trust*, introduction; Casson, 'The Economic Analysis', p. 23.
21 The biographer of Frederick Huth described Cypriano Urbieta rather crudely, as a 'paler edition of his brother' Juan Antonio. Murray, *Home from the Hill*, p. 46.
22 Murray, *Home from the Hill*, pp. 70–73; and Jones, 'Huth, Frederick Andrew', p. 2.
23 Freedman, *A London Merchant Banker*, pp. 12–13; Jones, 'Huth, Frederick Andrew', p. 1; Murray, *Home from the Hill*, p. 72.
24 They were Charles Frederick (born in 1806) and Ferdinand (born in 1808). While living in London, Frederick and Manuela had another nine children.
25 Incidentally, this was the same year that Rothschild & Sons was founded as a bank in London. R. Liedtke, 'Modern Communication: the Information Network of N. M. Rothschild & Sons in the Nineteenth-Century Europe', in Feldman, G. D. and Hertner, P. (eds), *Finance and Modernization, a Transnational and Transcontinental Perspective for the Nineteenth and Twentieth Centuries* (Surrey: Ashgate, 2008), p. 155.
26 Murray, *Home from the Hill*, pp. 90 and 106. Barrié was not only a merchant, but also a hat-maker. Indeed, he was the only hat-maker in Galicia at that time, employing around 180 hands in total. J. A. Barbier, 'Peninsular Finance and Colonial Trade: the Dilemma of Charles IV's Spain', *Journal of Latin American Studies*, 12 (1980), p. 36; J. L. Labrada, *Descripción económica del Reino de Galicia* (Ferrol: Editorial Galaxia, 1804), p. 46; D.Vedia y Goosens, *Historia y Descripción de la Ciudad de Coruña* (Ferrol: D. Puga, 1845), p. 222.
27 F. Dopico, 'Felicidad Pública y Libre Mercado. El Surgimiento de Valores Liberales en la Ilustración Gallega', *Revista Galega de Economía*, 16 (2007), pp. 1–19. According to Alvarez, Barrié was also an important slave trader. L. A. Alvarez,

Comercio Colonial y Crisis del Antiguo Régimen en Galicia, 1778-1818 (Santiago de Compostela: Xunta de Galicia, 1986), p. 184.

28   Barrié also moved to London, but returned to Corunna around 1815. In gratitude, Huth was quick to assist his old friend once Barrié resumed business in Galicia. For instance, Huth started to consign Barrié some products such as wheat, and tobacco. Huth also convinced their Paris friends Foxes & Sons to consign their wheat to Barrié in Corunna. See letters in HPSL-156.

29   Freedman, *A London Merchant Banker*, pp. 11–12.

30   Also seen in primary sources as Firmin.

31   Chapman, 'The International Houses', p. 12. Fermín de Tastet was a Basque, born in San Sebastian, and son of a very wealthy merchant of that city (Antonio Tastet). I am very grateful to Xabier Lamikiz for information on this house.

32   SP 46/147/47, Harrys versus Tastet. Statement by Huth, 1819. On the activities of Spanish merchants in London during this period, see Lamikiz, *Trade and Trust*, pp. 45-50, 146-150. Born in Bilbao but nationalized English, Fermín de Tastet was also the agent in London of the Royal Company of the Philippines. Aragón & Angulo-Morales, 'The Spanish Basque Country', p. 170; A. Aragón, 'La Guerra de la Convención, la Separación de Guipúzcoa y los Comerciantes Vasco-Franceses y Bearneses', *Pedralbes* 31 (2011), p. 207.

33   For example, in 1808 Tastet is mentioned as importing several large cargoes of Jesuits' bark from South America into England 'with the view of forwarding them to different continental Europe ports in the usual course of his trade'. J. L. Campbell, *The Lives of the Lord Chancellors and keepers of the Great Seal of England* (London: John Murray, 1847). Likewise, Tastet & Co. of London is also mentioned in contemporary accounts as trading a wide range of products between the US, the Caribbean and Europe. See for example, House of Commons Parliamentary Papers, *Journals of the House of Commons*, From January the 21st, 1808, in the Forty-eighth Year of the Reign of King George the Third, to January the 16th, 1809, in the Forty-ninth Year of the Reign of King George the Third, (1808), p. 560.

34   Aragón & Angulo-Morales, 'The Spanish Basque Country', p. 155.

35   HC 16/1, Undated, *c.*1830s, report No. 47.

36   Even after Marcial Francisco del Adalid (subsequently styled as Adalid e Hijos) returned to Corunna around 1812, his company remained important correspondents of Huth for the entirety of the period covered by this monograph. See HPSL, all volumes.

37   According to W. D. Rubinstein, *Men of Property: The Very Wealthy in Britain Since the Industrial Revolution* (Surrey: Croom Helm, 1981), p. 96, 'almost none of the immigrant bankers were literally penniless when they moved to London, but were mainly the sons of established bankers abroad'. This was certainly not Huth's case – far from it.

38   The number of London correspondents is surely underestimated in Table 1.1 since many dealings with London's neighbours did not involve formal correspondence, for instance for marine insurance broking or banking activities. Indeed, Huth's journals (HPJ) and the insurance ledgers of the company show a great deal of activity within London which is not captured in Table 1.1 and other similar tables for subsequent periods shown in this monograph.

39   It speaks volumes for Frederick Huth that he remained on good terms with his former employers for the rest of their lives. It is confirmed, for example, that Huth did not 'poach' Urbietas' clients when he set up his own business in Corunna and later in London.

40   For several years Pedro de Llano was perhaps the most important of all Huth's correspondents, at least judging from the profuse number of letters they exchanged. Indeed, Llano was one of the main consignors of wool for Huth. See for example, HPSL-154, Frederick Huth to Hill & Sons (Bristol). London, 8 April 1812 and 29 September 1812.

41 HPIL/S/SP/1. José Altuna to Frederick Huth (London). San Sebastian, 30 May 1814; HPSL-154. Frederick Huth to J. N. Ezcurdia (Corunna). London, 3 June 1812.
42 HPIL/R/38. Account Current, 1817.
43 Even Brentano Bovara & Urbieta of Hamburg would ask Huth to obtain marine insurance in London for shipments between Lima and Spanish ports. HPSL-157.
44 This is clear from Huth's business correspondence, but further confirmed in a Baring Brothers' report (HC 16/1), where Huth is plainly described as a wool merchant.
45 HPSL-154. Frederick Huth to Hill & Sons (Bristol). London, 8 April and 29 September 1812; Frederick Huth to J. N. Ezcurdia (Corunna). London, 3 June 1812; Frederick Huth to Lopez Doriga (Santander) and Pedro Llano (Corunna). London, all letters for 1812 and 1813. Although Huth's main dealings with Hill & Sons were in relation to wool, Hill & Sons performed many other services, such as receiving Spanish dollars in Bristol belonging to Huth, and forwarding them to the Bank of England to be credited into Huth's account there. Something similar happened with other agents in key southern England ports. For example, Huth's agents in Portsmouth would also receive Portuguese gold coins for Huth and forward them to London. HPSL-154. Huth & Co. to Day & Phillips (Portsmouth). London, 15 May 1812.
46 Jones, 'Multinational Trading Companies', p. 17; Casson, 'The Economic Analysis', p. 23; Chapman, *Merchant Enterprise in Britain*, p. 25.
47 Liedtke, 'Modern Communication', p. 155.
48 Hides in particular were very important for the River Plate's economy. A recent work has shown that, if statistics for Buenos Aires and Montevideo are combined, hides exported from the River Plate to the world amounted to about 1 million units during 1817–1841. M. I. Moraes and N. Stalla, 'Antes y Después de 1810: Escenarios en la Historia de las Exportaciones Rioplatenses de Cueros desde 1760 hasta 1860', *Documentos de Trabajo* 11, Sociedad Española de Historia Agraria (2011), p. 13.
49 HPSL-157. Frederick Huth to Pedro de Llano (Bordeaux). London, 14 November 1815.
50 For some examples, see HPSL-154. Frederick Huth to Juan de Llano y Hermano (Buenos Aires). London, 7 July 1812 and 15 March 1813. Llano of Buenos Aires had also sent a brother to Montevideo to enhance their businesses in the River Plate. HPSL-155.
51 HPSL-154. Frederick Huth to Jaime Alsina (Buenos Aires). London, 7 July 1812.
52 HPSL-154. Frederick Huth to Juan de Llano y Hermano (Buenos Aires). London, 7 July 1812 and 15 March 1813.
53 Groning & Co. was also instrumental in brokering insurance between London and Hamburg. HPSL-154. Frederick Huth to Groning & Co. (Hamburg). London, 7 October 1814.
54 HPSL-156. Frederick Huth to Pedro Llano (Corunna). London, 6 January 1815.
55 It was piloted by Josef Bonifacio Arrarte. HPSL-154. Frederick Huth to Day & Phillips (Portsmouth). London, 15 May 1812. HPSL-155. Frederick Huth to Ramon Lopez-Doriga (Santander). London, 18 May 1814.
56 The first evidence I managed to gather on Frederick Huth's own capital is for 1822, and it shows that his capital invested in the firm (by then Huth & Co.) was £22,272.
57 HPSL-156. Frederick Huth to Juan Francisco Barrié (Corunna). London, 6 January 1815.
58 HPSL-157. Frederick Huth to John F. Gruning (Madrid). London, 26 September 1815; HPSL-157. Huth & Co. to Pedro de Llano (Bordeaux). London, 16 February 1816.
59 Freedman, *A London Merchant Banker*, p. 12.
60 X. Lamikiz, 'Social Capital, Networks and Trust in Early Modern Long-Distance Trade: A Critical Appraisal', in M. Herrero and K. Kapps (eds), *Connectors of Commercial Maritime Systems: Merchants and Trade Networks between the Atlantic and the Mediterranean, 1550–1800* (London: Pickering & Chatto, 2016), p. 13. See

also Y. Ben-Porath, 'The F-connection: Families, Friends, and Firms and the Organization of Exchange', *Population and Development Review*, 6 (1980).
61 Lisle-Williams, 'Beyond the Market', p. 244; Rubinstein, *Men of Property*, pp. 96–97.
62 It was only during the 1820s–1830s, when Frederick Huth's sons came of age, that some of them were incorporated as either partners in London or Liverpool, or sent to Chile, Mexico, Spain and Austria as agents of the company.
63 Both Tastet and the Urbietas had dealings in connection with Corunna well before 1806, and both houses got involved in chartering vessels on joint-account for Spanish America before independence. See for example, J. Ortiz de la Tabla, *Comercio Exterior de Veracruz, 1778–1821* (Sevilla: Escuela de Estudios Hispano-Americanos, 1978), pp. 319-320.
64 Liedtke, 'Modern Communication', p. 158.
65 In 1822 John Frederick Gruning's capital within Huth & Co. was £7,200 (or 24 per cent of the total capital of the firm), so that we can presume that in 1815 this figure was much lower. HPJ-224, Balance for 1822.
66 HPSL-157. Huth & Co. to Pedro de Llano (Bordeaux). London, 16 February 1816.
67 Freedman, *A London Merchant Banker*, p. 13.
68 In Norway, Andreas Gruning & Co. was of tremendous importance, sending Huth wool, timber, while also receiving a wide range of manufactures and primary products. See transactions recorded in HPJ-224, any month.
69 See, for example, HPSL-155. Huth & Co. to Vidal & Sirven (Havana). London, 11 December 1813, and letters in HPSL-159. Huth & Co. to Layseca & Co. (Havana). London, 30 July 1822. Francisco Layseca was a contact provided by Brentano, Urbieta & Co., with whom Layseca had regular dealings from earlier on.
70 Chapman, *The Rise*, p. 38.
71 Austin, *Baring Brothers*, pp. 65–67; Chapman, *The Rise*, pp. 26–27. It was only during the 1870s that the Barings focussed their attention on other quarters beyond the US and the Far East.
72 Perkins, *Financing Anglo-American Trade*, pp. 17, 112–113; Chapman, *Merchant Enterprise in Britain*, p. 152.
73 It was only during the second half of the century that their business expanded geographically. Jones, *Merchants to Multinationals*, p. 37; Jones, *International Business*, pp. 145–146.
74 The core of their business was Anglo-American trade and finance. Wake, *Kleinwort Benson*, pp. 39–40, 42–45.
75 Chapman, *The Rise*, p. 122.
76 Jones, *Merchants to Multinationals*, pp. 24–25; Roberts, *Schroders*, p. 53; Kynaston, *The City of London*, p. 56.
77 L. Prados de la Escosura, 'Comercio Exterior y Cambio Económico en España, 1792–1849', in J. Fontana (ed.), *La Economía Española al Final del Antiguo Regimen, Volumen III, Comercio y Colonias* (Madrid: Alianza Editorial, 1982), pp. 208–210.
78 HPEL-17. Huth & Co. to Haurie & Nephews (Xerez). London, 2 and 5 January 1837.
79 Jones, 'Huth, Frederick Andrew', p. 2.
80 *Journal of the House of Lords*, George III, year 59, 18 June 1819, p. 706. Apparently during this time it was very common for foreign merchants resident in London to be nationalized British, as the Copenhagen born Carl Joachim Hambro did, for instance. Bramsen & Wain, *The Hambros*, p. 228.
81 Charles Frederick became very active within the business and outside the firm. For instance, he was one of the first directors of the Marine Insurance Company and one of the first directors of the Imperial Anglo-Brazilian Canal. 'The Marine Insurance Company', *The Times*, 14 June 1836; 'Imperial Anglo-Brazilian Canal', *The Times*, 12 September 1835. Later on he became Director of the Bank of England, and even married a daughter (Frances Caroline Marshall) of a Lord Mayor of London (Sir Chapman Marshall).

28 *Early life and activities of Frederick Huth*

82 Liedtke, 'Modern Communication', p. 155.
83 Referred to as 'sundry brokers' or 'sundry tradesmen'. Between 1817 and 1823, Huth & Co. employed the services of at least 60 sundry brokers. HPJ-224. They specialized in one or several products. For instance, Palmer & King dealt with wool, coffee, pimento, rice and sugar, but Thompson, Forman & Sons dealt in iron products only.
84 See for example, HPIL/R/34. G. C. & R. W. Fox & Co. to Huth & Co. (London). Falmouth, 8 September 1821.
85 HPIL/R/33. Fox to Huth & Co. (London). Falmouth, 8 September 1821; HPEL-3. Huth & Co. to Fox (Falmouth). London, 14 and 30 January 1829.
86 Edwards took over Hill & Sons. HPSL-183. Huth & Co. to Edwards (Bristol). London, 3 and 20 September 1822.
87 Payments to these clerks varied between £10 to £30 per month, that is, some £120–£360 per annum. HPJ-224.
88 Of this capital, three-quarters belonged to Frederick Huth and the remaining 25% to John Frederick Gruning. HPJ-224, 1822.
89 By this stage, the British house of Dickson & Montgomery was very active in getting hides cargoes for Huth & Co. and their friends. See for example, HPSL-159, Huth & Co. to Dickson Montgomery & Co. (Buenos Aires). London, 21 and 27 June 1822.
90 To give an idea of the firm's scope, in 1822 Huth & Co. accepted 491 bills of exchange, against over 5,000 bills accepted every year during the late 1840s. See HPBP, volumes for 1822 and 1845–1846.

2 Expansion of the firm during the 1820s–1830s and the South American branches

As outlined in the previous chapter, by the early 1820s Huth & Co. was an established merchant house on the London market, having built an important reputation after a few years operating in England. The firm was also expanding its network of international contacts quickly, and would grow them further in the forthcoming years. The transition from being an international business to a truly global one was well under way. It was as part of this globalizing process that the company decided to appoint confidential[1] agents worldwide, including in countries as diverse as the United States, Mexico, Cuba, River Plate Provinces, Spain, France, Germany, the Netherlands, China and India – to name but a few. This process is discussed in depth in Chapter 5.

More importantly for the purposes of this chapter, and supporting this internationalization of the company's interests, Huth & Co. also decided to open branch houses in the south-west Pacific in two recently independent republics[2] – Chile and Peru – that had formerly been part of the Spanish American Empire. These were the only branches the firm opened outside Britain for the entirety of the period covered by this book (they were styled Huth, Gruning & Co. for most of that time). Why the company chose these locations in particular is certainly an intriguing question, given the strong links it had in so many places. But it is also interesting from the point of view of the receptor countries because Huth & Co. was the only merchant banker of the period to establish operations in these countries.

However, it may be argued that the merchant house of Antony Gibbs & Sons (also of London) is an exception here. It too established branches in Chile and Peru at this time, but prior to the 1840s, Gibbs & Sons would have been better described as pure merchants rather than merchant bankers on account of their limited capital. Indeed, this firm prospered only after 1842, when it became involved in the profitable guano trade.[3]

But why should we care in particular about Huth & Co.'s activities in Chile and Peru? We know that it was the only London merchant banker to open branches in the South Pacific before the 1840s, and that Huth, Gruning & Co. had the wealthiest parent house among all British merchant houses operating in these countries before 1850. This chapter sheds new light on the vast global networks brought to Chile and Peru by these British merchants during the 1810s–1850s, and how these international networks provided these peripheral countries with new trading opportunities beyond Britain during early nineteenth-century globalization. Firms like Huth & Co. were instrumental players in smoothing the process of these countries' insertion into the international economy after they gained independence from Spain.

Despite this pivotal role played by these London merchant bankers, the extant literature on Anglo-Chilean or Anglo-Peruvian economic relations for the period 1810s–1850s has focused to date on admittedly important topics such as the development of bilateral trades, British (still limited) investments in the region, the general impact of British merchants on local economic development (including the mining and financial sector), the nature of British influence on the Chilean or Peruvian economy (i.e. positive or detrimental, including theories of imperialism and economic dependency), the role played by British merchants in Chilean and Peruvian local trade and production, the loans extended by Britain to Chile and Peru in the early 1820s, and the role of Valparaiso and Callao as emporia in the south Pacific.[4] Yet this valuable historiography does not cultivate a global historical approach, which in the case of Huth & Co. is of great consequence given the pan-continental nature of the firm. Indeed, the economic history of Anglo-Chilean and Anglo-Peruvian economic relations for the period c.1810–1850 (trade relations in particular), has been mainly told in isolation from the rest of the world economy, and the cosmopolitan and truly international character of Huth & Co. before 1850 has not been taken into account. For example, when Cavieres describes the activities of Huth, Gruning & Co. in Valparaiso, his main conclusion is that this branch of Huth & Co. of London was solely concerned with importing British manufactures, exporting Chilean produce to Britain and to a lesser extent with importing French manufactures as well.[5] This type of analysis, however, misses the positive impact of the firm's global networks on Chilean (and Peruvian) foreign trade with locations far beyond Britain or France. Finally, from the point of view of Huth & Co. of London, it also omits the new business opportunities available to the firm thanks to its South American branches.

Establishing operations in Peru and Chile, 1822–1824

In 1822 Huth & Co.'s capital had increased to almost £30,000 (from £700 in 1809), unquestionably a remarkable achievement. Frederick Huth had been in London for 13 years by this time, and his partnership with Gruning had worked well for more than five of them. Frederick was now a British citizen and Huth & Co.'s connections in Britain had also increased markedly, since he now had over 100 correspondents nationally, and was adding presence in the English industrial heartland. Similarly in Scotland, Glasgow and Edinburgh had been incorporated as valuable connections, reflecting Huth & Co.'s increasing expertise in the textiles trade.

In all, Huth & Co.'s business had solid foundations on the British market, and the time was deemed to be right for international expansion. The chosen location was South America, which is not entirely surprising given the ongoing collapse of the Spanish American Empire and the new world of opportunities emerging there for foreign merchants. British merchants soon began to arrive in great numbers in the region,[6] and in 1822 Latin American external debt was initiated when several loans were extended from London to the new republics, including Chile and Peru.[7] Furthermore, given Frederick Huth's personal experience in Corunna (as part of which he had to travel several times to South America), there is no doubt that by this time Huth & Co. had extensive expertise in South American produce and knew many local markets well.

Given the parlous state of both transport and communications during this time, however, Huth & Co.'s decision was a risky one. Controlling a branch house thousands of miles away from London would not be easy, but Huth and Gruning were nonetheless ready for the challenge. Indeed, in 1822 Daniel Wadsworth Coit was dispatched by them to Lima to open a house there (to be followed by a similar branch in Valparaiso). Huth, Coit & Co., as the office was styled, which had Frederick Huth as its main partner, but Coit was active too, and was in turn supported by one Samuel Frederick Scholtz,[8] a senior (German) clerk, and C. Hellman,[9] the junior clerk. At this point it is interesting to note that rather than employing Coit on a salary, Huth & Co. offer complied with his request for a substantial share of the new business as incentive for his move to Peru: Huth London retained 50 per cent ownership (of which 75 per cent belonged to Frederick Huth, the other 25 per cent to Gruning), while the other 50 per cent was taken by Coit and Scholtz (two-thirds for Coit, and the remaining third for Scholtz).[10] These establishments were branch houses controlled from the London headquarters, and although they were legally a separate business from the London firm, in real terms they were very much an extension of it. Indeed, both Huth and Gruning remained the principal partners in these overseas offices throughout their lives.

Yet again, Huth & Co. was defying the norm: as Chapter 1 explained, Frederick Huth has already diverted from the standard path of employing family members in order to expand a merchant bank when he hired John Gruning as a partner in 1816. By making Daniel Coit a partner of the branches in South America, Frederick Huth was sticking with that strategy.[11] That said, Coit was not even from Germany, as Gruning was, so the 'ethnicity' link was broken this time round. So who was this Coit, and why was he chosen by Frederick Huth to lead such an important mission and share potentially handsome profits with him?

Daniel Wadsworth Coit was born in Norwich, Connecticut, in 1787. He worked for five years as apprentice to Aspinwall Brothers, wealthy New York merchants,[12] before opening his own commission business in 1808, aged 21. After ten years as his own master, and because of the many wars affecting small businesses in the US during that period, he decided to work instead for his cousins G. G. and S. S. Howland, who were also well known New York's merchant community.[13] While Coit did not make his fortune during this period, he did gain valuable commercial experience, not only in the US but also in South America. For example, around this time Peru was fighting for independence from Spain, and was regarded by US merchants as a good market for arms and munitions – so much so, in fact, that Howland Brothers chartered a whole vessel and sent a full cargo of these to Lima thanks to a favour obtained from a Spanish minister, and dispatched Coit as supercargo for the *Boxer*, the ship chosen to take the military merchandise.[14]

But luck was not on Coit's side: he landed in Callao just a few hours before Lord Cochrane (1775–1860) began his famous blockade of the Peruvian coast in 1820. Cochrane was part of a combined liberation force coming from Chile and the River Plate, led by General José de San Martín, whose aim was to liberate Peru.[15] Even though Coit managed to sell the whole cargo to the Spanish authorities upon arrival, the turmoil resulting from the naval blockade meant that the Spaniards had no cash with which to make the payment, and Coit had to wait in Lima until he was able to complete the transaction.

Meanwhile, and fortunately for Howland Brothers, Coit managed to send the *Boxer* back to New York partially loaded with a cocoa cargo which formed a small part of the proceeds due to his employers in the US. In turn, as the Spanish government in Lima stumbled on for a while with an empty treasury because of the Cochrane-enforced blockade, the Spanish authorities allowed Coit to export another cocoa cargo (to be taken from Guayaquil by Coit himself) this time to Gibraltar – notably free of export duties – and sell it there, charging a commission to all interested parties. This second cocoa operation, although involving a complex trip to Guayaquil (now known as Ecuador) and an uncertain sale in Europe, would potentially allow Coit to settle his account with Howland Brothers. After spending more than eight months trapped in Peru, it was an offer he had no option but to accept. Furthermore, to complete the payment due to the Howlands, the Spanish Viceroy in Lima granted Coit a special licence to introduce expensive merchandise into Peru free of duty, at any time in the future.

In all Coit spent over a year between Callao, Lima and Guayaquil. This was enough time to learn Spanish quite well, and to enable him to become acquainted with the local society and the market, all of which undoubtedly helped to convince both Huth and Gruning that he was the right man to direct the prospective Huth & Co.'s establishments in the Pacific. The experience Coit had gained in New York would have been in his favour too: apart from the obvious bilateral trades between Peru/Chile and Britain, one of the firm's main plans for the branches in South America was to promote trade between them and the United States (a point discussed further below).

Having disposed of the cocoa cargo in Gibraltar (on very good terms), and sending the due remits to the Howlands in New York, in 1820 Coit was a free man with some capital and an ostensibly valuable licence to import merchandise into Peru once peace had returned to the region. Thus, before prosecuting his business career, and given that this was his first and perhaps last visit to Europe,[16] he decided to tour Spain and France before eventually landing in England, where he intended to encourage a UK merchant house that was conversant with South America to make profitable use of that licence.

Of all London merchant houses to be offered the deal (and there were quite a few), Coit chose none other than Huth & Co., via a connection brokered for him by Philip Mercier of Paris, a merchant he had met in Lima a few months before arriving in Europe, and who happened to be on good terms with the London firm.

That Huth knew many Parisian merchants – some of whom were extremely influential – was not surprising given the strong connections it had established with so many quarters of continental Europe by the early 1820s. But being unknown in London, as Coit was, was a major handicap for any one who wanted to enter British business. Indeed, Coit himself confessed to a relative that 'this was my only chance for making my antecedents known aside from my own representation',[17] and he certainly made the most of this unique opportunity.

After meeting with Coit and analyzing his prized import licence, Frederick Huth's opinion was that the permit was of less value than originally believed, since foreign vessels could now enter Callao freely. In fact Huth thought that Coit's knowledge of the Peruvian market was far more valuable than the licence itself, and advised him to select a cargo of British and colonial produce to be sent to Peru, for which he would be paid a handsome commission. Coit agreed, selected the cargo,[18] but declined a subsequent extra offer made by Huth & Co. to go and act as their supercargo for the journey to Callao. Coit wanted to instead establish himself in Gibraltar, it then being an important European entrepôt[19] with great commercial potential, particular in terms of Atlantic trades in which Coit could exploit his US connections and his knowledge of the American market.

However, while en route to Gibraltar, Coit received to his great surprise an urgent letter from Frederick Huth asking him to return to London immediately. Huth now made Coit an offer he could not possibly refuse: a co-partnership in Huth & Co.'s branches in Chile and Peru. The renewable arrangement was to last for six years, and Coit would receive 32 per cent of profits.[20] This was almost too good to be true, and Coit immediately accepted the offer. After all, Huth & Co. had already gained the reputation of being a robust, well-funded and trustworthy London merchant house.

It is unclear from the extant evidence whether Huth and Gruning had already decided to open a branch in South America before shaking hands with Coit. We have no way of knowing whether Coit accelerated an ongoing process or if, instead, meeting him was all the London financiers needed to convince themselves that opening branches in Chile and Peru was indeed possible if a reputable and trustworthy man with local market knowledge could be sent there as a partner. In any case, there is reason to believe that Mercier's recommendations aside, Coit made a positive impression on Huth and Gruning while in London and during their trip to the textile districts.[21]

Having returned promptly to London, signed the partnership contract and made the arrangements for the trip to Peru, Coit left the UK and in late 1822 arrived in Buenos Aires in order to avoid the hazardous passage around Cape Horn. He then decided to cross to Valparaiso through the Andes and eventually arrived himself in Lima in 1823, where the first Huth Coit & Co. house was opened just a few months before Peru achieved a definitive independence. The Lima house was followed by branches in Tacna, Valparaiso[22] and subsequently Arica, and South American operations quickly began to prosper. Indeed, less than six years later, Frederick Huth wrote to one of his sons in exuberant terms and in decent Spanish: 'Our establecimientos in Lima and Valparaiso continue prospering. All the news we get from those quarters are very good and they come together with large remittances of gold and silver.'[23]

Nonetheless, notwithstanding the profitability of the business, in 1828 the partnership was not renewed, despite Huth's inducements to Coit.[24] Having been away from the US for more than ten years, Coit yearned to return home and the potential future earnings in South America were not enough to convince him to stay in South America. He did, however, continue to work with Huth & Co. for years, as Huth's ledgers show.[25]

But Coit's departure did not mean that Huth and Gruning had necessarily to retire from these markets. Coit had excelled in his duties and laid the foundations of a very solid business. Thus, rather than closing the branches, the London partners decided to continue with the South American adventure and the establishments in the Pacific were now styled Huth, Gruning & Co. Even though Coit had moved on, they had retained the services of Scholtz, and several well-trained clerks in both Chile and Peru, and had gained good local market knowledge. Furthermore, as soon as new partners were incorporated into the London headquarters (see Chapter 4), they were also invited to take shares in the South American branches, injecting further energy into this side of the business.[26]

All in all, it is quite remarkable that given Coit's key role during the foundational period from 1823 to 1828, his involvement has been overlooked, in particular by scholars who had previously worked on Huth's activities in Chile or Peru. Indeed, all we have been (wrongly) told is that the West Pacific houses started as Huth, Gruning & Co.,[27] even though it is possible that Huth and Gruning would never have attempted to open branch houses in the Pacific without Coit's assistance. Following Coit's departure in 1828, Augustus Hermann Kindermann (1806–1852)[28] was made managing partner of these establishments, on a similar arrangement to that enjoyed by Coit. Around this time, another key man appointed by Huth in Valparaiso was H. V. Ward, who visited Britain regularly to meet face to face with their textile suppliers.[29] Furthermore, when in 1839 Kindermann was sent to Liverpool by Huth (to open a branch there, see Chapter 4), Ward became 'the principal partner of Messrs. Huth's house' in South America, thus becoming the main man in the Pacific for the following two decades.[30]

Operating from Chile and Peru during the 1820s–1840s

Once the Pacific branches had been established, Huth Coit & Co. initially devoted its main energies towards conducting bilateral trades between Britain, Chile and Peru. Having branches in South America, and having Coit as an in-country managing partner, allowed Huth & Co. to gain a profound knowledge of the market, in particular of the local demand for British manufactures at a time when Britain was the world's biggest manufacturer and exporter. As one might imagine, Huth Coit & Co. (and later on Huth, Gruning & Co.) soon specialized in importing British textiles, becoming one of the main textile traders on the West Coast of South America: textiles became the backbone of the business at a time when they were the most commonly traded manufacture world-wide. During the

1820s–1840s, over 70 different British textile manufacturers supplied Huth's houses in the Pacific,[31] as did many more from continental Europe. In exchange for British, German and French textiles, remittances were typically made in silver and gold at first, but other forms of payment were accepted subsequently, including copper, alpaca wool and hides.[32] Finally, as a result of Coit's and Huth's connections in North America, bars of Chilean copper were also sent to the US,[33] as I explain in more detail below. It should be noted that during the 1820s–1840s, copper emerged as the first globally integrated heavy industry centred in Britain, predominantly in Wales. In fact the Welsh copper industry developed into a truly global phenomenon by importing raw copper ore supplies from the many countries rich in this natural resource and then exporting the end product to an even wider geographical area.[34] But Huth's dealing in copper did not originate in their involvement in South America. Indeed, in the extant evidence, it is possible to find confirmation of Huth's shipments of British and Norwegian refined copper to Spain from 1817.[35] These kinds of operations surely cemented Huth's future expertise in the 'red' metal, which was enhanced after opening the branches in South America, a consequence of Chile's integral role as one of the main international suppliers of copper.

As part of the support provided to these bilateral trades, Huth actively provided marine insurance to Chilean and Peruvian exporters, as well as to British exporters to the region. This is not surprising given that there were few insurance facilities in Chile and Peru at this time, and therefore British merchant houses in Valparaiso acted as intermediaries between London insurance companies and Chilean or Peruvian exporters and importers. Indeed the marine insurance behind most of the West Coast's imports and exports was effected in Britain, even for trades that never touched on British ports.[36] From the 1810s, Frederick Huth established strong connections with several Lloyds underwriters, among them John Dubois and his brother Edward, who managed the insurance of Huth's consignments to many parts of the world. As a result, when Huth opened its South American branches in the 1820s, it was able to use the underwriters they already knew at Lloyds for exports to and imports from Valparaiso and Callao.[37]

Huth London was similarly happy to provide fire insurance in Chile and Peru, both for merchandise stored in Valparaiso and Callao ports or buildings in the vicinity.[38] At this point I should stress that although marine insurance was the most common branch of international insurance during the first half of the nineteenth century, fire insurance began to gain traction during this period and became international quickly. But London was not the only insurance market used by Huth & Co. for its activities in Chile and Peru: Petersen Huth & Co. of Hamburg (see below) also provided fire insurance in connection with the Pacific, as for example when they insured some houses belonging of Don Ambrosio Sanchez at Valparaiso because it was cheaper than doing so in London,[39] or when they insured textiles stored in Huth, Gruning & Co.'s premises.[40]

Another essential service provided by Huth & Co. to the bilateral trades between Britain and Chile was that of advancing funds to British consigners of manufactures to Valparaiso and Callao, to Chilean and Peruvian exporters of local produce directed to London or Liverpool, as well as to local producers in South America. As part of this enterprise, the firm entered the copper market decisively by advancing monies to local producers (Chileans and foreigners alike) in exchange for future consignments. For example, from the 1820s (when Coit was still in Chile), Huth Coit & Co. signed many agreements relating to the delivery of refined copper in the ports of Coquimbo, Huasco or Copiapó. Among the suppliers were the famous houses of Sewell & Patrickson and Nixon, Ariztia & Co., who in turn received advances from Huth.[41] A typical contract would involve Huth advancing in cash 30 days after signing the contract, with roughly 50–55 per cent of the agreed value of the copper to be delivered in, say, four to five months' time (after contract signature), then another 25 per cent advance a month later, and the remainder upon delivery of the whole cargo.[42] Likewise, Huth & Co. later began to issue advances to the Mexican and South American Company, one of the largest copper smelters in Chile during this period, and which had in the London firm its principal source of credit in Chile. The shipments in question were sizeable ones (i.e. advances associated with cargoes worth £15,000–£18,000).[43]

Huth & Co., like other British merchant bankers of the period, provided credit facilities that would have been otherwise unavailable in peripheral countries, and that credit played a vital role in national production and facilitated engagement in international trade given the high dependence of these countries upon the export sector. Without it, most Chilean and Peruvian foreign trade operations could not have taken place. And although capital was abundant in Britain, British exporters also had to rely on firms like Huth & Co. to finance their export operations to distant and emerging markets, primarily because these had a very slow turnover, particularly when compared with exports to nearby markets such as continental Europe.[44]

But the establishments in the Pacific did not limit themselves to bilateral trades with Britain, as most (smaller) British merchant houses operating in Chile and Peru did at that time. For a branch of a prominent merchant banker such as Huth & Co., there were many other ways of making money unconnected to Britain, even if that branch was in a pretty remote location. For example, the houses on the West Coast imported a wide range of goods from continental Europe. The case of Adolphe Roux deserves some closer attention here. During the early 1830s Huth & Co. formalized a partnership with Roux of Paris[45] in order to supply the West Coast establishments with cottons, silks and other products directly from France (Le Havre) or via Liverpool/London.[46] In exchange, Roux received advances for part of these shipments, provided that the invoice and bills of lading were endorsed to Huth & Co., and that marine insurances were entrusted to the same as a further means of protecting Huth & Co.'s credit. Roux was also an enthusiastic consumer of Chilean and/or Peruvian copper, nitrate[47] and silver, which were sent to him as remittances. Copper in particular was the preferred return for Roux, which was sent either to Britain or directly to France.[48]

Furthermore, Adolphe Roux visited Valparaiso during 1833–1834 to improve his knowledge of the market.[49] As a result of this visit and the good profits the association with Huth & Co. was generating, Adolphe would send one of his

Expansion of the firm during the 1820s–1830s 37

younger brothers to Chile to foster their business there. Proving the solid foundations of this partnership, young Roux was given shelter at Huth, Gruning & Co.'s premises in Valparaiso. These are both clear indications of the importance accorded by Roux to his trades with Chile and Peru via Huth London. Roux's brother began to engage in other trading operations from his Pacific base: he went to Brazil to procure sugar for the Chilean market, for example, and these undertakings were also supported by Huth & Co.[50]

But Roux was not the only merchant in continental Europe supplying Huth's houses in the Pacific and receiving advances for these shipments. Indeed, in the partnership agreements of Huth, Gruning & Co. (at least from 1838 onwards), it was clearly stated 'that in order to promote consignments to Frederick Huth, Gruning & Co. from European correspondents, Frederick Huth & Co. of London will make advances on goods to their address to such extent as they may consider safe and prudent',[51] to the benefit of many continental European merchants. For example, Anton Jancke of Bohemia[52] and Mayer & Fils (St Gall, Switzerland) also supplied Huth houses in the West Coast,[53] as did H. L. Detmering from Bordeaux, Hartoq & Denker from Hamburg, Mutzenbecher & Co., also from Hamburg,[54] not to mention other firms from Germany[55] and the Netherlands.[56] The case of Detmering is quite interesting because the French-made products dispatched from Bordeaux could be paid for by Huth with Chilean copper sent directly to France or even to India and China, according to the proposal made by Detmering himself.[57]

In addition, from the mid-1840s, Frederick Huth's son Henry entered into partnership in Hamburg with a Mr Ludolf Petersen to create Petersen, Huth & Co.[58] This is a classic example of the youngest son of a rich family having to go elsewhere to make his fortune, albeit supported by his family's connections. This new Hamburg firm intended to devote itself to a general commission business, which included trade with Chile and Peru, either directly from Germany or indirectly from elsewhere, such as via Huth & Co. of London. In other words, German products were sent to Chile and Peru with the assistance of Huth & Co. By the same token Petersen, Huth & Co. was happy to provide fire insurance for goods stored in its South American branches, as noted above. Finally, it is worth mentioning that Petersen Huth & Co. became partners of William de Drusina & Co. of Mexico City and Vera Cruz, which strengthened Huth & Co.'s already strong and enduring with this firm (a point developed further below). Indeed, Henry Huth had previously worked for the Drusinas in Mexico from the early 1840s, upon Frederick Huth's recommendation.

These two examples illustrate how the branches in Chile and Peru were easily and quickly connected with merchants in continental Europe, Asia and the Caribbean thanks to Huth's active global networks. Finally, it is worth mentioning that in London Huth & Co. also procured many other European products from countries such as Italy, Belgium and Spain, among others. These were then re-exported to Chile and Peru, as was for instance the case with Italian silks,[59] French silks produced by the firm of Blanc, Dupont & Co. of Savoy, 'one of the largest and most important silk manufactory on the continent of Europe'[60] and

Belgian woollens and worsteds.[61] In this case there were no direct connexions between suppliers and the branches in South America, but these other trades flowed between continental Europe and Chile or Peru via London anyway.

Moving beyond Europe, from Valparaiso and Callao strong connections with Asia, Australia and the United States were also promoted, all of which were directed from London, thereby weaving a complex network of interlinked contacts with the Chilean and Peruvian branches.[62] Huth London had established strong connections in these locations during the 1810s–1830s, usually after appointing confidential agents in key foreign ports. In China, for example, Bibby & Co. and Russell Sturgis were key collaborators, as were Nye Parkin & Co., Hathaway & Co. and Kennedy McGregor & Co. These houses happily provided tea and silks for Huth & Co.'s branches in South America in exchange for copper or silver.[63] For example, sateens and shawls were sent from China to the West Coast, and they 'met a very good sale and satisfactory prices were paid'.[64]

At this point it should be noted that many trade operations between China and Chile or Peru did not necessarily occur on either the China house account or Huth, Gruning & Co.'s account. Indeed, many Chinese exports to Chile or Peru and Chilean or Peruvian exports to China were at the US's account and risk, although Huth & Co.'s credit was typically used to finance these 'American' trades between Chile or Peru and China.[65] This system was called the 'China business'[66] by Huth London, which further added that these 'adventures between China and the West Coast … [it is] a branch we are anxious to encourage for the benefit of our establishments in the latter quarter'.[67] In addition, Huth London would also connect merchants in Germany with Huth's branches in Chile or Peru and their friends in China, as occurred in 1836 when the Royal Prussian Maritime Company of Berlin dispatched a ship to Chile and Peru loaded with German manufactures to be exchanged for silver, which was then to be taken to China to buy Chinese or Philippines produce intended for the German market.[68]

But many Yankees were also interested in trading directly *from* the US with Chile and Peru, and Huth & Co. was also content to support these branches of intra-regional trade, especially as the firm had appointed two crucial US general agents,[69] namely John W. Perit of Philadelphia and Goodhue & Co. of New York. Interestingly enough, Perit was one of the junior partners of Russell Sturgis's establishments in China and the Philippines,[70] which undoubtedly promoted business between Huth's West Coast branches, the US and China. But more important for us here, given that both Perit and Goodhue were mainly concerned with promoting Anglo-American trades, is the fact that Thomas Russell of New York was appointed by Huth as its exclusive US 'agent for the South American houses'.[71] Interestingly, Huth, Gruning & Co. had a direct line of communication with Thomas Russell in New York, which implied a deviation from Huth London's standard policy of not allowing their branch houses in the Pacific to have direct correspondence with any of their agents or contacts outside South America.[72]

Perhaps the main reason behind this concession was that in order to secure Thomas Russell's services and full commitment, he was made a junior partner of the Pacific West Coast establishments.[73] Huth London wanted to 'have a general

& confidential agent who might take such a lively interest in their concerns that the advantage their [USA] rivals [in Chile and Peru] possessed over them by having their parent houses in the [United] States might be greatly counterbalanced'.[74] We must remember that there were, apart from the British, many American houses operating in both Chile and Peru after independence.[75] Thomas Russell's task of focusing completely on American trades with Chile and Peru illustrates on the one hand the potential of a branch of a powerful London merchant banker with interests in the US, and on the other the prospective networks that could be woven from South America by belonging to a global enterprise.

Unfortunately, for reasons unclear from the extant evidence, Russell's appointment lasted only a few years, despite the fact that he had been appointed Chilean consul to New York, which undoubtedly increased his influence within the Chilean economy and US–Chilean relations more generally. In any case, after Russell's dismissal Huth started to rely successfully on new agents, Grinnell Minturn & Co., of New York. This was a respected firm of commission merchants, which enjoyed an excellent reputation within the business community,[76] so much so that they were once described by Huth & Co. of Liverpool as 'the best supporters our [West Coast] friends have in the US'.[77] Likewise, Huth, Gruning & Co. decided to rely more heavily than before on Huth London's general agents in the US (i.e. Perit and Goodhue). This back up plan yielded good results, to the extent that the end of Russell's agency was not seen as a great blow for Huth, Gruning & Co.'s interests in the US. As steam communication had brought London and New York closer together in one sense, Huth London was now better able to control and support the dealings between the US and Chile or Peru, and therefore a New York agency operating solely to support trades between these locations became less relevant, in particular considering the agency fees that had to be paid.

From their North American base, Huth's agents and other contacts procured US produce (e.g. textiles) for the houses in Valparaiso, Lima and Tacna;[78] insured cargoes from Chile and Peru to the US or Britain (if it was more convenient or quicker than insuring in London);[79] and often received Huth London's advances for these operations, provided the cargoes consisted of 'goods well assorted for the markets of the Pacific', in particular staple products such as domestics (a coarse cotton), cotton prints and quicksilver.[80] Thus, Huth & Co.'s contacts in the US would draw a bill of exchange against Huth London, which would be accepted without demur if: the bill of lading was made on behalf of Huth, Gruning & Co.; insurance were effected by Huth London for an amount exceeding 50 per cent of the sum advanced; and the return remittances were sent to Huth & Co. in London, thereby further protecting the latter against any risk of bankruptcy or embezzlement.[81] In London, Huth & Co. would liquidate the remittances sent from Chile, discount the same on account of the advances given, and send the remainder to the US. In addition to the agents named above, among the firm's other contacts in the US undertaking this sort of business was, for example, Pope & Aspinwall of Philadelphia, who sent American produce to Chile and Peru in exchange for copper sent to Liverpool.[82] (This, incidentally, was a connection inherited from Daniel W. Coit.)

On occasion, however, the parties in the US would also ask Huth, Gruning & Co. to send remittances in copper directly to them rather than to Britain, even if advances from Huth London were involved. Such was the case for the above-mentioned Pope & Aspinwall[83] but also for McCrea & Co., the latter being of the firm conviction that investing the proceeds of the outward cargo in copper was 'a more advantageous return than bullion'.[84] As Huth London advances would be compromised in these scenarios, Huth London allowed the branches in Chile and Peru to send remittances directly to the US if the copper was sent to either Grinnell Minturn & Co. of New York or to John Perit in Philadelphia, who would sell the copper, send the amount due to Huth & Co. in London and hand the rest to the American trader, who would also pay Grinnell Minturn's or Perit's agency costs for these London-financed triangular operations.[85]

US houses often wanted to buy copper in Chile or Peru but they did not have either local produce to give in exchange or cash to purchase copper. In these cases Huth London would also grant advances to the Americans to purchase copper, but in return requested that: the Valparaiso or Callao houses charged a commission of 2.5 per cent for purchasing the copper; the drafts on Huth London would not exceed 75 per cent of the invoice cost; the whole of the copper bought under this arrangement was to be shipped directly to Grinnell Minturn & Co.; and Huth London was entitled to charge a commission of 2 per cent on their acceptances. Finally, another alternative proposed by American traders was that Huth & Co. send the copper purchased in Chile directly to China and exchange it there for silks and tea to be remitted directly to the US, further complicating multilateral trades involving Chile or Peru, Britain, the US and China.[86] To understand the success of these multilateral operations, it is worth noting that Thomas Russell was well connected with Gideon Nye of Canton,[87] and even after Thomas' dismissal, they remained on good terms with Huth & Co. Once again, the unlimited trading potential of Huth, Gruning & Co. would have been unthinkable without the backing of a global merchant banker in London such as Huth & Co.

Beyond the US and Europe, Huth London also had important connections in Australia which happily engaged with the houses in the Pacific. For example, Meinertzhagen & Co. and Lamb & Parbury, both of Sydney, were in the habit of receiving local produce from Chile and Peru, which was paid for with drafts or produce sent from Australia to London, since Australia had little to offer Chile or Peru at this stage.[88] Indeed, in the Huth papers at UCL and the Guildhall Library there is plenty of evidence of wheat, flour and other goods such as horses, mules and jerked beef being sent by Huth, Gruning & Co. from Valparaiso and Callao to Sydney during the 1840s.[89] And although thanks to previous studies we were aware of the commercial relations between Chile and Australia during the 1820s–1840s, we were not aware of Huth, Gruning & Co.'s importance in this trade and the fundamental role played by Huth London in supporting these flows. Indeed, only one of the previous studies on the subject mentioned Huth, Gruning & Co. as an important player in this trade, but this was a mention made in passing only and without reference to the London headquarters.[90]

But more important than trades with Australia is the fact that Huth London also promoted intra-regional trades between their houses in Chile and Peru and other Latin American quarters such as Central America, Cuba, the River Plate and Brazil. For example, sugar was extensively shipped to Valparaiso from Rio de Janeiro or Bahia by merchants such as Vogeler & Co., often thanks to the intervention of US merchants such as Bevan & Humphreys and John Perit, both of Philadelphia but well connected in Brazil. Another important sugar supplier from Rio de Janeiro to the West Coast market was Limpricht Brothers,[91] and in turn Huth London would grant advances to the likes of Vogeler and Limpricht for these shipments.[92] Likewise, Pedro Blanco & Co. of Havana was in the habit of sending tobacco to Huth, Gruning & Co., drawing against Huth London for these cargoes, which were eventually settled with silver sent from the Pacific to London.[93] These are only a few examples of intra-regional trades being supported by Huth London; there were many others.[94]

But advances were not the only credit facility offered by Huth London to finance intra-regional trades from Chile or Peru. Indeed, the company also granted letters of credit to finance shipments of Latin American produce to Chile and Peru. For instance, while Thomas Russell was Huth, Gruning & Co.'s agent in New York, he was typically granted letters of credit for up to £3,000–£5,000 to buy sugar, wax and tobacco in Cuba to be shipped to Huth, Gruning & Co. of Valparaiso and Callao. Thomas Russell was also allowed to use letters of credit to procure sugar and yerba mate in Brazil for consignment by Huth & Co.'s houses in Valparaiso and Lima.[95] Evidently not only were Huth's connections in the US important by themselves, but so was the credit provided from London to finance these intra-regional trades. Huth & Co. also provided from London the insurance needed to back many of these operations even though they did not involve British ports at all.

In the River Plate, Zimmerman, Frazier & Co. of Buenos Aires and Montevideo were also very close to Huth London. As a result of this connection, many products were sent from the River Plate region to Chile and Peru and vice versa. For example, soap from Buenos Aires was shipped regularly to Valparaiso in exchange for gold or silver, while Chilean wheat often reached the River Plate markets, and in most of these operations Huth London's advances came into play once more.[96] Interestingly enough, the relationship with Zimmerman, Frazier & Co. was brokered for Huth by Daniel W. Coit as early as 1823.[97] It is therefore not surprising that Huth & Co. also supported flows of trade between the River Plate and the US, and that during the mid-1840s J. C. Zimmermann decided to move temporarily to New York to foster business there, after which a house styled Leland, Zimmermann & Davidson was opened and this too had regular correspondence with Huth & Co.[98]

The quicksilver trade

Another crucial connection developed by Huth London, and one which was particularly relevant for the Pacific houses, was that with Rothschild & Sons of London, and yet it has received little attention in the historiography on

Anglo–Latin American trade. For example, there is no mention at all of this profitable association in either Cavieres' or Mayo's main works on British merchants in Chile.[99] Only very recently have we been reminded about the important links between Huth & Co. and Rothschild & Sons,[100] in particular thanks to the opening of Rothschild's archives to researchers. This connection is important not only because of the profitability and extent of the collaboration it involved, but also because it illustrates how two rivals could put aside their differences and work together to promote a particular trade, complementing each other's competitive advantages in the process.

The leading London merchant banker of the period, Rothschild & Sons' earliest interest in Chile and Peru dates from at least 1825, when it started to import significant quantities of gold and silver from Valparaiso and Callao via Huth & Co. of London. By this time the Rothschilds were important world traders of bullion and specie (one of the few commodities they were interested in after gradually abandoning their mercantile activities in favour of purely financial endeavours),[101] and the Chilean and Peruvian markets did not escape their notice. Chile was becoming an important producer of silver, a development accelerated by Chañarcillo's silver mine discovery, while Peru had long been one of the most important world suppliers. To put Chilean figures in a wider context, Chile's silver production in the 1820s and 1830s was 55 per cent and 39 per cent respectively of that produced in mighty Peru,[102] so by no means a negligible amount.

But more important for this study, during the 1830s the Rothschilds adopted the role of intermediaries in the international mercury market. From 1835 the Rothschilds were the sole buyers of quicksilver or mercury from Almadén in Spain,[103] which gave them a powerful position within Latin American silver-producing countries, since Mexico, Peru, Bolivia and Chile relied heavily on this source of mercury for their silver production.[104] Indeed, the Almadén mercury mines, together with the nearby deposit in Almadenejos, were 'one of only two major sources of the metal in the world at this time'.[105] Other less important mercury suppliers during this period were Peru (Huancavelica) and Idria (now Slovenia). The high concentration of world's supply in just a handful of places gave those producers and intermediaries that controlled the trade a privileged position from which to impose selling prices.

Mercury was intensively used in silver mining during my period of study.[106] So important was this product that during the first decades of the nineteenth century, quicksilver became one of the fastest-growing products within Spanish exports.[107] Lacking agents in Mexico, Peru, Bolivia and Chile, which were all important silver-producing countries, the Rothschilds decided to sell their quicksilver there through a house they could trust. The chosen one was of course Huth & Co., which according to a Rothschild's agent visiting Valparaiso was 'considered as being the first house [in Chile and Peru] & have the reputation of being very careful',[108] in the South Pacific.

From the mid-1830s then, Huth & Co. was in charge of selling Rothschild's mercury in the West Coast, mainly on consignment.[109] Remittances to Rothschild were preferably in the form of silver bars or silver specie.[110] In exchange, the firm charged diverse commissions and fees amounting to some 13 per cent,[111] by any standard a handsome rate and for a very secure trade. Indeed, it was seen as a worryingly high charge by the Rothschilds, to the extent that in 1848 they sent an agent to the West Coast to see whether it was possible to operate without Huth & Co. as intermediary. But this option was rejected in a report sent by their agent:

> I cannot yet state whether I shall be able to take charge of the quicksilver ... without the intervention of ... Huth or some other house. I think however ... that I shall not be able to do so. As far as the sale is concerned it will be necessary to become acquainted with the purchasers, their means, and then as there is no bank or paper currency here and all payments are effected in various coins or in bar silver, it becomes necessary to have some proper place for the reception of the money, besides a certain knowledge of the different sorts in circulation.[112]

The Rothschilds were forced, therefore, to rely on Huth & Co. for mercury consignments to the Pacific. Furthermore, Huth London also bought on own account from Rothschild and sent the mercury to Valparaiso, Lima and Potosi.[113]

Huth & Co.'s interest in quicksilver pre-dated the mid-1830s, though, and in fact the firm had expressed an interest in the product some 20 years earlier. Huth journals contain plenty of evidence about the company's dealings in Spanish quicksilver during the 1820s,[114] an interest which was further enhanced when Huth opened its branch houses in Peru and Chile. Indeed, in 1829 Frederick Huth sent one of his sons (Frederick Huth Junior) to Spain to (among other tasks) procure consignments of mercury, and advised him that the firm wanted to have permanent stocks of this product for their houses in Lima and Valparaiso.[115] Such was Huth & Co.'s interest in this product that, even though during this time the firm traded mainly on commission, for this particular commodity it was willing to operate on own account, buying quicksilver in Spain for cash. In addition, if advances were required for these operations, Frederick Huth would have gladly made them available, as he explained to an influential trader in Cadiz called Pedro del Corral y Puente, who was negotiating at the time with the Spanish government for the supply of this product.[116] This deviation from the firm's general rule of operating only (or mostly) on commission is better explained by the huge profitability of this product and the price stability of the markets in South America, given the lack of a substitute for the increasing silver production. In 1829, for example (before the Ezpeleta's or Rothschild's monopoly), it could be bought in Spain at $37 per quintal[117] and sold in Chile at $57, thus giving a gross (and almost certain) profit of 35 per cent.[118]

And indeed, for a decade and a half the merchant banker's quicksilver dealings with the Rothschilds provided substantial profits in Chile and Peru: 'our mining districts in Copiapó are flourishing', reported an exuberant clerk at Huth, Gruning & Co. in Valparaiso to the Rothschilds during the mid-1840s.[119] Regarding the other silver-producing countries in the region, it is worth mentioning that Huth's branches in Peru and Chile redistributed quicksilver to Bolivia too, and in vast quantities.[120]

Beyond South America but still within the Americas, Huth & Co. was also the bridge between Rothschild and Mexico's silver producers, all thanks to the fruitful connections between it and William de Drusina & Co., which were further fostered after this house was appointed as Huth & Co.'s agents in Mexico, and even more so following the creation of Petersen, Huth & Co., as outlined above.

However, following the quicksilver discoveries in California in 1846 (at the Nueva Almadén mines), the quicksilver market in Latin America became more competitive and profit margins narrowed. California displaced Spain (i.e. the Rothschilds) as the main world producer of mercury, and although most of Californian mercury was consumed locally, Mexico, Bolivia, Chile and Peru now had access to a different and cheaper quicksilver supply, thereby ending the Rothschild quasi-monopoly in South America.[121] Indeed, so low were the prices of Californian mercury that they even halted quicksilver mining at Huancavelica. Unfortunately for Huth London, one of Huth, Gruning & Co.'s main competitors in the West Coast (Gibbs & Sons, now far more powerful than they were in the 1820s–1830s) managed to secure the representation of California's mercury suppliers (Forbes) in the South Pacific, which had catastrophic consequences for both the Rothschilds and Huth, at least as far as this trade in particular is concerned. In early 1851, Rothschild's agent in San Francisco reported that 'I am convinced that if Messrs. Forbes find that they can dispose of any quantities readily on the South Coast, they will not fail to make large shipments, which would interfere materially with the market'.[122] These fears materialized, and Forbes started to consign quicksilver to the West Coast in large quantities and at very low prices, vastly undercutting those that had been offered for more than a decade by Huth, Gruning & Co.[123] Rothschild's initial reaction to this new market entrant was to continue its attempts to enforce prices in the South Pacific markets, but Gibbs' reach became so strong that they had no option but to instruct Huth, Gruning & Co. in Valparaiso to sell at market rates 'as there is no prospect whatever of a rise, in the contrary I should not be astonished if the prices go still lower in consequence of the production of this country [the USA]'.[124]

Another option tested by Huth London on behalf of Rothschild was to create a cartel and collude with Gibbs, an offer rejected by Forbes' agents, as is dramatically reported by Huth, Gruning & Co. to Rothschild: 'we tried to come to an agreement with them [Gibbs] regarding sales & prices, but they preferred to be independent. Under such circumstances, we can hardly expect to be able to uphold prices',[125] further adding that 'their object evidently is not the price, but the quantity, & in order to monopolise sales & supply the whole of the wants of our miners, they would, if necessary, immediately lower the rates'.[126] This idea of cartelization was not uncommon for Rothschild. Indeed, in a recent article it has been shown that the Rothschilds' most common strategy in the non-ferrous metals markets was to limit competition pursuing monopolistic practices and cohesive agreements.[127]

In order to understand the impact generated by the fall in quicksilver prices on Huth–Rothschild business, we should note that before the Californian quicksilver discoveries in 1848, Huth had been able to sell Rothschild's quicksilver for as much as $135 per quintal, but in June 1852 Gibbs was selling this product in

Expansion of the firm during the 1820s–1830s 45

Valparaiso for as little as $50 per quintal: 'under such circumstances we can of course not make sales at higher prices, we must either sell at the same rates or be content not to sell at all', reported Huth, Gruning & Co. to Rothschild.[128] Only in late 1853 did Huth & Co. manage somehow to convince Gibbs to set a cartel price of $55, which would ensure that Huancavelica's production remained on hold. Nonetheless, despite the verbal agreement, Huth, Gruning & Co. constantly complained that Gibbs & Sons were not respecting the deal, and were often underselling them for $54, which eventually led to the dissolution of the cartel in mid-1856, although during 1857 and 1858 it is reported that new price agreements were reached again several times. It was all to no avail, however: with the Californian discoveries, the golden days of easy sales at high prices were gone forever, and equally importantly Huth–Rothschild's share of the market declined markedly. In fact, during 1852–1854 Britain (i.e. mainly Rothschild) did not re-export any Spanish quicksilver to either Chile, Peru or Bolivia (and only very little to Mexico), as can be seen in Figure 2.1. In the same vein, in 1850 Britain imported only a tenth of the volume of quicksilver she had imported from Spain the year before, and in 1851 there are no records of any Spanish quicksilver entering the British market (Figure 2.2). We might assume that Spanish quicksilver could have been exported directly from Spain to Valparaiso or Callao during this period (as had often happened before), but the Chilean custom records also show that between 1849 and 1853 little Spanish quicksilver entered Chile from Spain (indeed, none was exported in 1850, 1852 and 1853).[129]

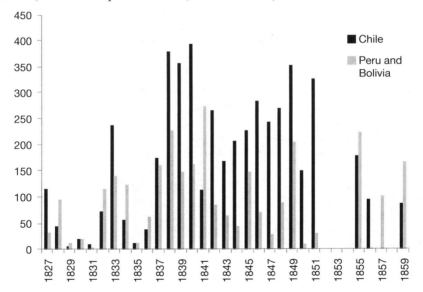

Figure 2.1 UK re-exports of quicksilver to Chile, Peru and Bolivia, 1827–1859 (thousand of lbs)
Source: British Parliamentary Papers, several numbers for 1828–1860.

46 *Expansion of the firm during the 1820s–1830s*

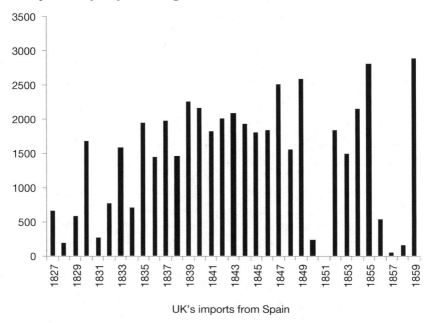

UK's imports from Spain

Figure 2.2 UK imports of quicksilver from Spain, 1827–1859 (thousand of lbs)
Source: British Parliamentary Papers, several numbers for 1828–1860.

Finally, according to the same source, in 1853 Chile re-exported to Britain as much as 150,000 lbs of quicksilver, an unusual (i.e. reversed) trade flow, which was surely on account of mercury previously imported from either Spain or Britain itself now being returned to London because the Chilean market was saturated with Californian produce. Nonetheless, the many problems that cropped up between 1848 and 1854 did not mean that Rothschild's quicksilver disappeared from Chile forever; there was actually some recovery during the second half of the 1850s but that period lies beyond the scope of this monograph.[130]

As this chapter has explained, from its London base Huth & Co. was behind a wide range of trade operations and financial services that linked Chile and Peru with so many regions of the Americas, Europe, Asia and Australia. The firm often orchestrated complex multilateral trades from London, even if these flows involved goods that never saw a British port. This was not unique for the West Coast of South America: Huth & Co. replicated this same strategy in many other places where the company was strong. This was certainly the case in Spain, as we shall see in the next chapter.

Notes

1 Confidential agents were agents as described in Chapter 1: businessmen who performed a business task for another businessman in a different location. The 'confidential' element was a terminology used by Huth & Co. themselves, in reference to those agents with whom the firm had long-lasting and very close relations, and with

whom they shared sensitive information on critical aspects of the business, often relating to the standing of other firms and particular markets. Confidential agents were a permanent source of information on a wide range of subjects, and also acted as advisors.
2   Strictly speaking, when Huth & Co. decided to open the branch in Peru, this country was still in Spanish hands, gaining definitive independence just a few months after the Lima business opened.
3   Gibbs & Sons 1958, p. 27.
4   See for example, Cavieres, *Comercio Chileno*; Mayo, *British Merchants*; C. W. Centner, *Great Britain and Chile, 1810–1914: a Chapter in the Expansion of Europe*, PhD Thesis (Illinois: University of Chicago, 1941); C. W. Centner, 'Relaciones Comerciales de Gran Bretaña con Chile, 1810–1830', *Revista Chilena de Historia y Geografía*, 103 (1942); C. W. Centner, 'Great Britain and Chilean Mining, 1830–1914', *Economic History Review*, 12 (1943); J. R. Couyoumdjian, 'El Alto Comercio de Valparaíso y las Grandes Casas Extranjeras: 1880–1930. Una aproximación', *Historia*, 33 (2000); D. Amunátegui, 'Origen del Comercio Inglés en Chile', *Revista Chilena de Historia y Geografía*, 103 (1943); H. Ramírez, *Historia del Imperialismo en Chile* (Santiago: Empresa Editora Austral Limitada, 1960); Salazar, Dialéctica de la Modernización'; M A. Fernández, 'Merchants and Bankers: British Direct and Portfolio Investment in Chile During the Nineteenth Century', *Ibero-Amerikanisches Archiv*, 9 (1983); J. Kinsbruner, 'The Political Influence of the British Merchants Resident in Chile during the O'Higgins Administration, 1817–1823', *The Americas*, 27 (1970); W. M. Mathew, 'The First Anglo-Peruvian Debt and its Settlement, 1822–1849', *Journal of Latin American Studies*, 2 (1970); W. M. Mathew, 'Peru and the British Guano Market', *Economic History Review*, 23 (1970); J. Deustua, *La Minería Peruana y la Iniciación de la República, 1820-1840* (Lima: IEP, 1986); C. Wu, *Generals and Diplomats: Great Britain and Peru, 1820–1840* (Cambridge: Center for Latin American Studies, 1991).
5   Cavieres, *Comercio Chileno*, p. 179.
6   Llorca-Jaña, *The British Textile Trade* (2012); R. Miller, *Britain and Latin America in the Nineteenth and Twentieth Centuries* (Essex: Longman, 1993).
7   Mathew, 'The First Anglo-Peruvian Debt'; C. Véliz, 'Egaña, Lambert, and the Chilean Mining Associations of 1825', *Hispanic American Historical Review*, 55 (1975); F. G. Dawson, *The First Latin American Debt Crisis: the City of London and the 1822–25 Loan Bubble* (New Haven, Yale University Press, 1990); F. J. Rippy, 'Latin America and the British investment "Boom" of the 1820's', *Journal of Modern History*, 19 (1947). This is not surprising: Britain was the largest capital exporter at that time (perhaps the only country with a large surplus of capital), as well as the first industrial nation. As a consequence, during the early 1820s there was an investment boom in Britain, through which thousands of Britons invested huge sums in the bonds of foreign governments, including many of the new Latin American republics.
8   HPSL-159, Huth & Co. to Bertram Armstrong & Co. (Buenos Aires). London, 7 June 1822. It is worth mentioning that Samuel Frederick Scholtz founded the first Protestant cemetery in Chile, intended to bury deceased members of Chile's German and Anglo-Saxon community. J. P. Blancpain, *Les Allemands au Chili, 1816–1945* (Colonia and Vienne: Böhlau Verlag, 1974), p. 820.
9   HPJ-224, December 1823.
10 HPJ-224, pp. 443 and 451.
11 It was only when Frederick Huth's sons came of age that one of them – John Frederick Huth – was sent to Valparaiso. Freedman 1968, p. 15. Furthermore, we must be aware of the fact that employing relatives as distant agents 'guarantees neither competency nor honesty'. Pearson and Richardson, 'Social Capital', p. 766.
12 Incidentally, the Aspinwalls were related to direct ancestors of the president of the United States, Franklin Delano Roosevelt; John Aspinwall was Roosevelt's

48 Expansion of the firm during the 1820s–1830s

       great-grandfather. R. F. Cross, *Sailor in the Whitehouse: The Seafaring Life of FDR* (Annapolis: Naval Institute Press, 2003).

13 In turn, later on, Howland and Aspinwall joined forces and formed an establishment styled Howland & Aspinwall, who after Coit's return to the USA became valuable contacts for Huth & Co. HPEL-22, Huth & Co. to Huth & Co. (Liverpool). London, 10 January 1839.

14 All the information on D. W. Coit from these years, unless otherwise specified, was obtained from W. C. Gilman, *A Memoir of Daniel Wadsworth Coit of Norwich, Connecticut, 1787-1876* (Cambridge: Cambridge University Press, 1909).

15 Thomas Cochrane joined the British Royal Navy in 1793. He participated actively in the Napoleonic Wars and quickly rose to high office in the Navy. After a long, albeit problematic career, in 1817 he accepted an invitation of the first fully independent Chilean government to organize and command its fleet in the war of liberation from Spain. After having gained an impressive military reputation in Chile, Cochrane was asked to lead the large combined expedition to liberate Peru in 1820. A. Lambert, 'Cochrane, Thomas, Tenth earl of Dundonald (1775–1860), Naval Officer'. (Oxford: Oxford Dictionary of National Biography, 2004), pp. 1–9.

16 At this stage there were no commercial steamships plying the routes between Europe and the Americas. Travel between the two therefore took several weeks. It was very expensive to travel to Europe for leisure, in particular on account of the huge opportunity cost of being effectively 'trapped' aboard a sailing vessel for so long.

17 Quoted in Gilman, *A Memoir*, p. 62.

18 As part of the cargo selection, Frederick Huth himself took Daniel W. Coit on a trip to Leeds and Manchester to visit potential textile suppliers. HPJ-224, April 1822.

19 L. Prados de la Escosura, 'El Comercio Hispano-Británico en los Siglos XVIII y XIX. I. Reconstruccion', *Revista de Historia Económica*, 2 (1984); Cuenca-Estevan, 'British "Ghost" Exports'.

20 That is, two-thirds of the 50 per cent profit share of the South American branches. HPJ-24, p. 443.

21 An alternative was to send one of Huth's sons to South America, but Huth's eldest son (Charles Frederick) was just 16 by 1822, perhaps too young to take such a responsibility. That said, people of similar age had positions in British merchant houses in South America even before this period. For instance, in 1809, John Parish Robertson, aged just 17 and then an unknown young Scot, was made clerk of the Buenos Aires branch of Wylie & Co. Robertson later on became internationally famous because of his role in trying to open Paraguay to British trade and more importantly for arranging the 1824 bond issue by Baring Brothers for the Buenos Aires government, as well as other issues for the Peruvian government. Llorca-Jaña, 'British Merchants in New Markets' (2014).

22 In turn, the Valparaiso house had a branch office in Santiago de Chile. On the role of this agency, see HPEL-9, Huth & Co. to John Halliday (Sanquhar). London, 14 May 1832.

23 Original in Spanish: 'nuestros establecimientos en Lima y Valparaiso siguen prosperando cada vez mas. Todas las noticias que recibimos de aquellos puntos nos son muy satisfactorias y nos vienen acompañadas de muy buenas y fuertes remesas de plata y oro'. HPSL-161, Fredrick Huth to Fredrick Huth Jr. (Madrid). London, 13 November 1829.

24 HCP, Notice on expiration of partnership between Huth & Co. and Daniel W. Coit, signed by Huth, Gruning & Co. Lima, 12 April 1828. See also Gilman, *A Memoir*, pp. 94–96. I could not gather evidence on the annual profits made by Huth Coit & Co. before 1828, but evidence for the year running from April 1834 to March 1835 shows that the houses in the Pacific reported net profits of £32,400. HPJ-228, April 1835.

25 During the late 1820s and early 1830s Coit remained very active according to Huth's journals. Being based in New York, he often drew against Huth & Co., while he also

received British manufactures on consignments from London. See for instance, HPJ-226; HPJ-227; and HPBP for the 1830s.

26 For instance, in 1835, Frederick Huth reduced its personal shares in the 50 per cent of the South American establishments (which was Huth London's total participation) from 75 per cent to 55 per cent, while Gruning did likewise (from 25 per cent to 22 per cent), thus giving Meinertzhagen and Huth junior a 15 per cent and 7 per cent share, respectively. HPJ-228.

27 Cavieres, *Comercio Chileno*, pp. 177–179.

28 It is worth mentioning that Kindermann was the future husband of Manuela Huth (b.1814), one of Frederick Huth's daughters.

29 HPEL-6, Huth & Co. to H. H. Stansfeld (Manchester). London, 18 September 1830. They were both supported by a Mr Reidner (a senior clerk) and other junior clerks brought from England.

30 BDP, XI/38/81B, Benjamin Davidson to Rothschild & Sons (London). Valparaiso, 28 February 1848.

31 M. Llorca-Jaña, 'Knowing the Shape of Demand: Britain's Exports of Ponchos to the Southern Cone, *c*.1810s–1870s', *Business History*, 51 (2009); Llorca-Jaña, 'The Organization of British Textile Exports' (2011).

32 See for example, HPEL-42, Huth & Co. to Edward Rawson (Halifax). London, 18 January 1844; HPEL-45, Huth & Co. to Foster & Son (Bradford). London, 8 January 1845.

33 HCP. Loose papers. For an example, see 'Contract between Sewell & Patrickson and Huth, Coit & Co. for twelve hundred quintals of cooper'. Valparaiso, 27 November 1827.

34 C. Evans, and O. Saunders, 'A World of Copper: Globalizing the Industrial Revolution, 1830–1870', *Journal of Global History*, 10 (2015).

35 HPIL hereafter, R/38. Entries in Account Current, December 1817.

36 Apeseg, *100 años en la Historia del Seguro* (Lima: Asociación Peruana de Empresas de Seguros, 2004); M. Llorca-Jaña, 'The Marine Insurance Market for British Textile Exports to the River Plate and Chile, *c*.1810–1850', in R. Pearson (ed) *The Development of International Insurance* (London: Pickering & Chatto, 2010); M., Llorca-Jaña, *La Historia del Seguro en Chile, 1810–2010* (Madrid: Fundación Mapfre, 2011); M. Llorca-Jaña, 'To be Waterproof or to be Soaked: Importance of Packing in British Textile Exports to Distant Markets. The Cases of Chile and the River Plate, *c*.1810–1859', *Revista de Historia Económica-Journal of Iberian and Latin American Economic History*, 29 (2011).

37 For some examples, see HPEL-5, Huth & Co. to John Du Bois (Lloyds, London). London, 4 February 1830; HPEL-6, Huth & Co. to John Du Bois (Lloyds, London). London, 28 October 1830. See also HPIL-261; HPINL-262.

38 For some examples, see HPJ-227 and HPJ-228.

39 HPEL-54, Huth & Co. to Petersen, Huth & Co. (Hamburg). London, 13 August 1847.

40 HPEL-57, Huth & Co. to Petersen, Huth & Co. (Hamburg). London, 14 July 1848.

41 HCP, 'Contract between Sewell & Patrickson and Huth, Coit & Co. for twelve hundred quintals of cooper'. Valparaiso, 27 November 1827. A demurrage fee was also agreed, in case of any delay in the delivery of the copper to the ports above mentioned.

42 HCP, 'Contract between Nixon Aristia & Co. and Huth, Coit & Co. for 2500 quintals of copper'. Valparaiso, 3 November 1827, Box 1, folder, 81.

43 HPEL-62, Huth & Co. to the Mexican & South American Company. London, 16 October 1849; HPEL-63, Huth & Co. to the Mexican & South American Company. London, 30 January 1850; HPEL-66, Huth & Co. to the Mexican & South American Company. London, 5 October 1850. See also L. Valenzuela, 'The Chilean Copper Smelting Industry in the Mid-Nineteenth Century: Phases of Expansion and

50   Expansion of the firm during the 1820s–1830s

Stagnation, 1834–58', *Journal of Latin American Studies*, 24 (1992), pp. 524, 542–543.
44   The credit side of Huth's activities is covered in further details in Chapter 6.
45   For the terms of the agreement, see HPEL-11, Huth & Co. to Adolphe Roux (Valparaiso). London, 18 April 1833; GLHP, MS 10700-5, 'Agreement between Mr. Adolphe Roux from Paris and Messrs. Frederick Huth & Co. of London'. London, 1 June 1839. See also Cavieres, *Comercio Chileno*, p. 179.
46   HPEL-26, Huth & Co. to Huth & Co. (London). Liverpool, 2 March 1839. French manufactures could be sent directly to Chile or indirectly from Havre to London (or Liverpool) and from Britain re-shipped to Chile and Peru. For some examples, see GLHP, MS 10700-5, 'Invoice of 115 packages shipped at Havre to address Frederick Huth & Co. of London to be re-shipped for Callao for account of Roux of Paris'. Paris, February 1846.
47   See for example, HPEL-28, Huth & Co. to Huth & Co. (Liverpool). London, 11 May 1840.
48   For some examples, see HPEL-22, Huth & Co. to Huth & Co. (Liverpool). London, 5 February 1839; HPEL-26, Huth & Co. to Huth & Co. (London). Liverpool, 5 January & 15 February 1839.
49   HPEL-11, Huth & Co. to Adolphe Roux (Valparaiso). London, 18 April 1833; HPEL-13, Huth & Co. to Adolphe Roux (Valparaiso). London, 25 February 1834.
50   HPEL-17, Huth & Co. to Thomas Russell (New York). London, 31 January 1837. Furthermore, through Huth London, Roux also supplied De Drusina & Co. of Mexico, who was Huth's agent there.
51   GLHP, MS 10700-5, Renewal of Partnership agreement of Huth, Gruning & Co. 1838, 1843, 1848 and 1853.
52   This was one of the very first suppliers of Huth's houses in South America from continental Europe, in their case sending glassware via Hamburg. HPJ-224.
53   HPEL-3, Huth & Co. to Mayer & Fils (St Gall). London, 5 and 20 January 1829.
54   Mutzenbecher was an important supplier of *platillas*. HPEL-31, Huth & Co. to Huth & Co. (Liverpool). London, 7 February 1841.
55   VJP-321-9, Hallmann against Huth, Gruning & Co. Valparaiso, 20 February 1856.
56   For imports of refined sugar from Amsterdam, see VJP-417-8, Norman Brothers against Huth, Gruning & Co. Valparaiso, 25 May 1853.
57   HPEL-26, Huth & Co. to Huth & Co. (London). Liverpool, 31 May & 28 June 1839.
58   BT 1/1/2, Printed circular. Hamburg, 1 October 1844.
59   HPEL-26, Memorandum of a cargo from the Mediterranean to Chile & Peru. Liverpool, 16 January 1830.
60   HPEL-36, Huth & Co. to Huth & Co. (Liverpool). London, 14 October 1842.
61   HPEL-38, Huth & Co. to Huth & Co. (Liverpool). London, 17 May 1843; HPEL-44, Huth & Co. to Huth & Co. (Liverpool). London, 10 December 1844.
62   GLHP, MS 10700-6.
63   For some examples see HPEL-17, Huth & Co. to F. S. Hathaway (Canton). London, 14 March 1837; HPEL-23, Huth & Co. to F. S. Hathaway (Canton). London, 13 April 1839; HPEL-30, Huth & Co. to Huth & Co. (Liverpool). London, 29 October 1840; HPEL-45, Huth & Co. to Nye Parkin & Co. (Canton). London, 24 January 1845.
64   HPEL-45, Huth & Co. to Nye Parkin & Co. (Canton). London, 24 January 1845.
65   HPEL-9, Huth & Co. to Russell & Co. (Canton). London, 19 April 1832.
66   HPEL-31, Huth & Co. John W. Perit (Philadelphia). London, 3 March 1841.
67   HPEL-31, Huth & Co. John W. Perit (Philadelphia). London, 9 March 1841.
68   HPEL-16, Huth & Co. to Russell & Sturgis (Manila). London, 18 October 1836; HPEL-21, Huth & Co. to Huth, Gruning & Co. (Valparaiso). London, 13 November 1838.

Expansion of the firm during the 1820s–1830s 51

69 'General agents' was a term used by Huth & Co. in reference to those agents that performed a wide range of tasks on its behalf, as opposed to those 'ordinary' agents, who performed specific tasks only.
70 HPEL-14, Huth & Co. to H. H. Stansfeld (Leeds). London, 17 July 1835.
71 HPEL-22, Huth & Co. to Huth & Co. (Liverpool). London, 10 January 1839. For more details, see HPEL-17, Huth & Co. to Thomas Russell (New York). London, 22 April 1837.
72 HPEL-17, Huth & Co. to Thomas Russell (New York). London, 13 May 1837.
73 HPEL-21, Huth & Co. to Thomas Russell (New York). London, 13 December 1838.
74 HPEL-26, Huth & Co. to Huth & Co. (London). Liverpool, 13 May 1839.
75 For Anglo-American rivalry after independence, and in particular for USA merchant houses in Chile, see D. B. Goebel, 'British-American Rivalry in the Chilean Trade, 1817–1820', *Journal of Economic History*, 2 (1942); L. M. Méndez, *El Comercio entre Chile y el Puerto de Filadelfia en los Estados Unidos de Norteamérica: Estudio Comparado Binacional* (Valparaíso: Universidad de Playa Ancha, 2001); J. Rector, *Merchants, Trade and Commercial Policy in Chile, 1810–1840*, PhD Thesis (Indiana University, 1976); E. Pereira, *La Actuación de los Oficiales Navales Norteamericanos en Nuestras Costas* (Santiago: Universidad de Chile, 1935); E. Pereira, *Los Primeros Contactos entre Chile y Los Estados Unidos, 1778-1809* (Santiago: Editorial Andrés Bello, 1971).
76 Hidy, *The House of Baring*, pp. 249–250. The Barings went so far as to maintain that by 1848 this house had become 'the first commercial house in the United States'. Hidy, *The House of Baring*, p. 561.
77 HPEL-26, Huth & Co. to Huth & Co. (London). Liverpool, 15 May 1839.
78 For procuring consignments from the USA to Chile, Huth paid a commission of 1 per cent for direct consignments without advances, 0.75 per cent if advances were given, and 0.5 per cent for indirect consignments (e.g. from China). HPEL-23, Huth & Co. to Henry Ward (Baltimore). London, 16 May 1839.
79 HPEL-17, Huth & Co. to Thomas Russell (New York). London, 21 January 1837.
80 HPEL-17, Huth & Co. to Thomas Russell (New York). London, 30 January 1837. According to Harley, US coarse cottons were widely sold in Chile, to such an extent that it was in Chile that the United States 'had their greatest relative success' for these products. C. K. Harley, 'International Competitiveness of the Antebellum American Cotton Textile Industry', *Journal of Economic History*, 52 (1992, p. 578). Such was their success, that according to Huth, these rough cottons were underselling British textiles and pushing prices down at Valparaíso. HPEL-13, Huth & Co. to Philips Woods. London, 10 February 1834.
81 HPIL, Huth, Gruning & Co. to Huth & Co. (Liverpool). Valparaiso, 24 June 1838. For example, when in 1841 Pope & Aspinwall were in serious difficulties, Huth remained calm: 'We observe by the papers that Messrs. Pope & Aspinwall of Philadelphia have suspended their payments. We do not see that we run any risk of losing by this event as our Valparaiso friends had ample means to cover us for all our advances on shipments to South America according to our instructions.' HPEL-31, Huth & Co. to Huth & Co. (London). Liverpool, 8 March 1841.
82 HPEL-31, Huth & Co. to Pope & Aspinwall (Philadelphia). London, 7 and 9 February 1841.
83 HPEL-31, Huth & Co. to Huth & Co. (London). Liverpool, 17 February 1841.
84 HPEL-26, Huth & Co. to Huth & Co. (London). Liverpool, 1 April 1839.
85 HPEL-23, Huth & Co. to H. V. Ward (Baltimore). London, 6 April 1839; HPEL-31, Huth & Co. to John W. Perit (Philadelphia). London, 3 March 1841.
86 HPEL-26, Huth & Co. to Huth & Co. (London). Liverpool, 30 March 1839.
87 HPEL-21, Huth & Co. to Thomas Russell (New York). London, 18 October 1838.
88 HPEL-31, Huth & Co. to Meinertzhagen & Co. (Sydney). London, 17 February 1841.

Expansion of the firm during the 1820s–1830s

89 For some examples, see MS 10700-6, loose papers, 1841; HPEL-33, Huth & Co. to Huth & Co. (Liverpool). London, 6 January 1842.
90 T. Bader, 'Before the Gold Fleets: Trade and Relations between Chile and Australia, 1830–1848', *Journal of Latin American Studies*, 6 (1974), p. 42. For other studies, which ignore Huth's role in supporting Chilean exports to Australia, see Anonymous, 'Las Harinas Chilenas en Australia', *Revista Chilena de Historia y Geografía*, 120 (1952); E. Pereira, 'Las Primeras Relaciones Comerciales entre Chile y Australia', *Boletín de la Academia Chilena de la Historia*, 53 (1955); E. Pereira, 'Las Primeras Relaciones Comerciales entre Chile y el Oriente', *Boletín de la Academia Chilena de la Historia*, 39 (1948).
91 For some examples, see HPEL-22, Huth & Co. to Huth & Co. (Liverpool). London, 10 January 1839; HPEL-60, Huth & Co. to Limpricht Brothers (Rio de Janeiro). London, 2 April 1849.
92 HPEL-31, Huth & Co. to John W. Perit (Philadelphia). London, 3 March 1841. For typical cargoes of sugar from Brazil to Valparaiso, see also VJP-77-10. Valparaiso, 13 July 1837; HPEL-24, Huth & Co. to Huth & Co. (Liverpool). London, 26 August 1839.
93 HPSL-178, Huth & Co. to Pedro Blanco & Cia (Havana). London, 1 January and 1 March 1848.
94 For example, sugar was regularly brought from Havana into Valparaiso by Huth's branches there. See for example, VJP-319-23. Huth, Gruning & Co. against Riofrio. Valparaiso, 3 September 1847. Likewise, for Huth's imports of coffee from Costa Rica into Chile, see VJP-87-14. Huth, Gruning & Co. against Thompson Watson. Valparaiso, 28 October 1850.
95 HPEL-17, Huth & Co. to Thomas Russell (New York). London, 30 January 1837.
96 For some illustrative examples, see HPEL-5, Huth & Co. to Zimmerman, Frazier & Co. (Buenos Aires). London, 17 March 1830; HPEL-9, Huth & Co. to Zimmerman, Frazier & Co. (Buenos Aires). London, 18 January 1832; HPEL-13, Huth & Co. to Zimmerman, Frazier & Co. (Buenos Aires). London, 8 January 1834; HPEL-24, Huth & Co. to Zimmerman, Frazier & Co. (Buenos Aires-Montevideo). London, 3 July 1839.
97 HPEL-183, Huth & Co. to Zimmerman, Frazier & Co. (Buenos Aires). London 7, April 1823.
98 From the late 1840s, this house started to use credit from Huth & Co. to fund trading ventures between the USA and the River Plate. Freedman, *A London Merchant Banker*, p. 332.
99 Cavieres, *Comercio Chileno*; Mayo, *British Merchants*. See also J. Mayo, 'British Merchants in Chile and Mexico's West Coast in the Mid-Century: the Age of Isolation', *Historia*, 26 (1991); J. Mayo, 'Before the Nitrate Era: British Commission Houses and the Chilean Economy, 1851–80', *Journal of Latin American Studies*, 11 (1979); J. Mayo, 'Britain and Chile 1851–1886. Anatomy of a Relationship', *Journal of Inter-American Studies and World Affairs*, 23 (1981).
100 See in particular the works of Platt, 'Spanish Quicksilver'; T. Platt, 'Container Transport: from Skin Bags to Iron Flasks. Changing Technologies of Quicksilver Packaging between Almadén and America, 1788–1848', *Past & Present*, 214 (2012); Platt, 'Espacios Económicos'; Llorca-Jaña, 'The Economic Activities' (2012).
101 M. A. López-Morell and J. O'Kean, 'Rothschilds' Strategies in International Non-Ferrous Metals Markets, 1830–1940', *Economic History Review*, 67 (2014), p. 722.
102 Own calculations from J. R. Couyoumdjian, 'Portales y las Transformaciones Económicas de Chile en su Epoca: una Aproximación', in B. L. Bravo (ed.), *Portales, el Hombre y su Obra* (Santiago: Editorial Jurídica de Chile, 1989); and C. Contreras, 'El Legado Económico de la Independencia en el Perú', *Documento de Trabajo* No. 301 (Lima: Departamento de Economía. Pontificia Universidad Católica del Perú, 2010).

103 From 1830, the Spanish Crown decided to grant the production of Almadén to a sole buyer. The first contract was given to Iñigo Ezpeleta of Bordeaux, and lasted for five years, before passing in 1835 to Rothschild & Sons. Yet even before 1835, Rothschild had already associated with Ezpeleta in order to control the mercury trade. Platt, 'Spanish Quicksilver'; López-Morell and O'Kean, 'Rothschilds' Strategies'. This near monopoly-monopsony left Huth & Co. with few options of trading directly in this product.
104 We must remember that the production of Huancavelica quicksilver mines started to decline during the eighteenth century, recovering only partially during the next century. See Platt, 'Spanish Quicksilver'; Platt, 'Container Transport'. A. Pearce, 'Huancavelica 1563–1824: History and historiography', *Colonial Latin American Review*, 22 (2013), pp. 422–440.
105 Ferguson, *The House of Rothschild*, pp. 358–362; López-Morell and O'Kean, 'Rothschilds' Strategies', pp. 726–727.
106 Subsequently it started to be used in gold-plating, physical instruments, paints, mirrors and other applications. López-Morell and O'Kean, 'Rothschilds' Strategies', p. 726.
107 Prados de la Escosura, 'Comercio Exterior y Cambio Económico', p. 183.
108 BDP, XI/38/81B, Benjamin Davidson to Rothschild & Sons (London). Valparaiso, 29 April 1848.
109 RHL, XI/38/149-50.
110 RHL, XI/38/149/A, Huth, Gruning & Co. to Rothschild & Sons (London). Valparaiso, 2 March 1841; Huth & Co. to Rothschild & Sons (London). London, 19 January 1843.
111 RHL, XI/38/149/A, Huth, Gruning & Co. to Huth & Co. (London). Valparaiso, 20 July 1838; 29 January 1840; and 15 February 1840. It was made up as follows: 7.5 per cent general commission; 2.5 per cent commission for guaranteed accounts; 1 per cent commission for Santiago agency; storage fee of 1 per cent; port agency fee of 0.5 per cent. These combined commissions and charges amounted to 12.5 per cent. The rest was on due to: stamped paper & postage; freights rates; insurance against fire; and landing fees.
112 RHL, XI/38/81B, Benjamin Davidson to Rothschild & Sons (London). Valparaiso, 28 February 1848.
113 RHL, XI/38/149/A, Huth & Co. to Rothschild & Sons (London). London, 17 December 1839.
114 Juan Francisco Barrié, Manuel Yñigo, J. C. de Bernales & Co. and Gabriel Balez were some of the middle-men they used to acquire this product. For some examples, see HPJ-224, p. 480, January 1824; and HPJ-225, for operations during 1825.
115 HPSL-160, Huth & Co. to Frederick Huth Jr. (Madrid). London, 26 October 1829. Subsequently, another of Frederick Huth's sons (Louis), was sent permanently to Spain as an agent. Freedman, *A London Merchant Banker*, p. 15.
116 Years later, Pedro del Corral y Puente became Cadiz's *regidor* (mayor) in 1833 and 1836. Corral y Puente was the godson of Martín de Aramburu, another influential merchant of Cadiz, and once also its *regidor*. G. Butrón, 'Elite Local, Poder y Cambio Político en Cádiz, del Antiguo Regimen al Liberalismo, 1823–1835', in D. Caro (ed) *El Primer Liberalismo en Andalucía, 1808–1868: Política, Economía y Sociabilidad* (Cádiz: Universidad de Cádiz, 2005), p. 76.
117 During this period, mercury was usually packed in iron flasks (Platt, 'Container Transport', p. 241), which were equal to 34.5 kg of mercury. López-Morell and O'Kean, 'Rothschilds' Strategies', p. 727.
118 HPSL-161, Huth & Co. to Pedro de Corral y Puente (Cadiz). London, 4 December 1829 and 1 January 1830; HPSL-160, Huth & Co. to Fredrick Huth Jr. (Madrid). London, 22 December 1829.
119 RHL, XI/38/149/A, Huth, Gruning & Co. to Rothschild & Sons (London). Valparaiso, 6 September 1845.
120 Platt, 'Espacios Económicos'.

121 And indeed, between 1847 and 1850 the Rothschilds could be said to have retired from the Spanish market, and did not participate in the government auctions. Spanish production was given to Banco de Fomento and then to Banco de San Fernando during this period. Only between 1850 and 1857 did the Rothschilds regain control of the Spanish production. López-Morell and O'Kean, 'Rothschilds' Strategies', p. 727.
122 BDP, XI/38/82/A, Benjamin Davidson to Rothschild & Sons (London). San Francisco, 31 March 1851.
123 BDP, XI/38/82/A, Benjamin Davidson to Rothschild & Sons (London). San Francisco, 31 July & 31 August 1851.
124 BDP, XI/38/82/A, Benjamin Davidson to Rothschild & Sons (London). San Francisco, 4 December 1851.
125 RHL, XI/38/149/B, Huth, Gruning & Co. to Rothschild & Sons (London). Lima, 9 January 1852.
126 RHL, XI/38/149/B, Huth, Gruning & Co. to Rothschild & Sons (London). Lima, 11 May 1852.
127 López Morell and O'Kean, 'Rothschilds' Strategies'.
128 RHL, XI/38/149/B, Huth, Gruning & Co. to Rothschild & Sons (London). Valparaiso, 10 June 1852.
129 Chile, *Estadística Comercial de Chile* (Santiago, 1850-1854).
130 Furthermore, it is worth mentioning that between 1857 and the late 1860s, the Rothschilds once again retired from the Spanish market, after the Spanish government recovered the Almadén sales from 1857 to the late 1860s. López-Morell and O'Kean, 'Rothschilds' Strategies', pp. 727–728.

3 Huth & Co.'s Spanish and German connections during the 1820s–1840s

Why a separate chapter on Huth & Co.'s activities in Spain? The answer is clear: Frederick Huth himself was initially trained by Spanish merchants; his first independent business was opened in Spain; his wife was Spanish and she was well connected to the Spanish crown; and perhaps more importantly, together with Germany, Spain remained the main focus of Huth & Co.'s activities from London for the entire period covered by this book. No other prominent London merchant banker was as enthusiastic as Huth & Co. about Spain's foreign trade and finance.[1] Indeed, between 1812 and 1851 the firm sustained correspondence with at least 870 merchants or businessmen in Spain, who were located in about 75 different cities or towns (Table 3.1), although most of them were concentrated in Madrid, Corunna, Santander, Cadiz, Barcelona, Santiago de Compostela and Seville. Many of these were business partners or agents, as defined in Chapter 1.

In addition, the few available studies of Spanish foreign trade covering the period from the end of the Napoleonic Wars until the mid-nineteenth century largely concentrate on the following 'macro' topics: Spain's colonial trade and the impact of the collapse of the Spanish empire on the Spanish economy; the long-term impact of foreign trade on economic growth; general trends of the overall performance of Spanish imports and exports; the changing composition of Spanish exports, in terms of products and geography; the impact of the industrial revolution on Spanish foreign trade; and bilateral trades with selected destinations. Furthermore, studies of Anglo-Spanish trade and financial connections for this period focus mainly on the overall value of exports, re-exports and imports.[2]

Despite the importance of these studies in improving our understanding of Spanish foreign trade and Anglo-Spanish economic relations immediately following the collapse of the Spanish American empire and until the mid-nineteenth century, the available historiography for this short period does not cultivate a global history approach or provide a 'micro' analysis of the main actors behind Spain's external trade, including London merchant bankers. In particular, the important role played by trading and financial intermediaries behind Spanish foreign trade has been neglected. Particularly striking is the lack of research on the service sector: for example, the use of London intermediaries by Spanish international traders is fully understandable in terms of transaction cost theory but there is little (if any) mention of this factor in extant studies of Anglo-Spanish economic relations.

Table 3.1 Geographical distribution of Huth & Co.'s correspondents (*C*) in Spain: a sample for 1812–1851

Location	No. of C.	Location	No. of C.	Location	No. of C.	Location	No. of C.
Alcala	1	Castropol	2	Molina de Aragon	2	San Sebastian	22
Alcoy	1	Cordoba	1	Mondoñedo	3	Santander	85
Algeciras	1	Corunna	113	Moreda	2	Santiago de Compostela	29
Alicante	1	Cudillero	2	Mugardos	1	Santoña	1
Almazan	1	Cuenca	1	Muros	1	Segovia	2
Almeria	1	Estella	8	Ocaña	2	Seville	29
Amposta	1	Ferrol	5	Olaveaga	1	Soria	5
Aranda de Duero	1	Gijon	30	Orense	10	Tarragona	3
Asturias	1	Gines	1	Oviedo	8	Tenerife	4
Avila	1	Guernica	2	Padron	1	Valencia	8
Barcelona	32	Jerez	5	Palencia	2	Vega de Rivadeo	1
Bejar	1	Llerena	1	Pamplona	12	Vigo	20
Betanzos	2	Logroño	1	Pontevedra	2	Villoslada de Carneros	1
Bilbao	101	Luarca, Asturias	1	Puerto Cesures	1	Vitoria	6
Burgos	7	Madrid	158	Puerto de Santa Maria	2	Vivero	8
Caceres	3	Mahon	1	Puerto Real	1	Zaragoza	1
Cadiz	59	Malaga	21	Reus	2	Zarauz	1
Candamo, Asturias	1	Meira	1	Rivadeo	17	Grand Total	870
Carril	2	Merida	1	Salamanca	1		

Source: HPSL and HPEL, several volumes.

Thanks to the general literature on merchant banking,[3] we do know that London was financing British foreign trade, including bilateral trade between the UK and Spain. However, the important role played by London merchant bankers in financing Spanish trades that avoided British ports is less familiar. Take, for instance, the main works by Chapman and Jones, in which there is little mention of Spain.[4] It will be shown in this chapter that Huth, and other London merchant bankers, provided important 'market-making' and financial services that helped promote Spanish trade, whether it involved British ports or not. This situation is quite different to the picture provided in the classic work of Chapman,[5] for whom London merchant bankers 'preferred to allow credit to agents permanently resident in Britain ... because experience had taught them that the legal process of recovering debts abroad was impossibly expensive'.[6]

Likewise, Chapman himself provided evidence showing that the earliest development of British merchant banking was so closely connected to the US that in the late 1830s about half of British acceptances related to Anglo-American trade.[7]

Not surprisingly acceptances for other markets have been neglected by most colleagues working on merchant banking. More importantly, this is of consequence for the purposes of this volume because credit from London was crucial in supporting trade between Spain and her remaining colonies. It also underpinned commerce between Spain and other quarters of the world before 1850 at a time when Cuba, for example, ranked third amongst Spain's principal export destinations and import origins.[8] This backing from London was particularly crucial for Spanish traders operating during my period of study because the 1820s–1840s were particularly harsh times for the Spanish economy following the demise of its empire in the Americas: Spanish foreign trade (in particular that beyond Europe) declined substantially; investment slumped; local industries suffered from the loss of a captive market (i.e. the colonies); and state finances withered.[9] In short, most areas of the economy were impacted, including financial markets.

Overall, we know little about the relationship between London's merchant bankers and Spain before 1850, not just in terms of trade-related issues but also with regard to the movement of securities. For example, important London houses such as Huth & Co., Darthez Brothers, Gower & Co., Sadler Whitmore and Mathiesen & Co. provided critical support to Spain's foreign trade and capital flows, but few of their archives have survived. Of these merchant bankers, the only major collection available for the period 1810–1850 is Huth & Co.'s. According to Chapman, this situation is mainly due to the fact that merchant bankers have been strangely reluctant to commit their stories to print.[10] It is, therefore, unfortunate that we are not able to compare the experiences of these London houses in order to explain why so many merchants in Spain preferred to use Huth & Co.'s services rather than those offered by their competitors.

This dearth of information is important because a select number of London merchant bankers provided crucial services to Spanish merchants and other Spanish businessmen before 1850, and were not only important vehicles for Spanish foreign trade but also for Spanish short-term foreign investment. Note that many of the services provided by the elite London financiers were not available in Spain, or at least not on better terms than they were in Britain, as was the case in many of the world's emerging markets before 1850. But why was this happening in Spain? Why were Spanish merchant bankers (or their equivalents) unable to compete effectively with their peers in London for some of these services?

The answers I suggest below draw on transaction cost theory as a useful theoretical frame, and are supported by the literature on the theory of trading companies, merchant banking and the relationship between trade and trust. It is also worth noting that some important Spanish merchants did compete with Huth & Co. and other London merchant bankers in the provision of a few services such as the granting of advances and shipping services, and thus this chapter does not argue that London held a monopoly over all the services offered by Huth & Co. to its Spanish connections. And although it would be interesting to know why so many of Huth's Spanish clients preferred Huth & Co. over, say, Ybarra of Bilbao, to answer this question fully we would need to dig deep into Spanish merchants' archive collections, which would take several years of research and lead this investigation in a different direction. That said, with the evidence available to us we can make some conjectures, which I also outline below.

While this chapter focuses on Spain, the nature of Huth & Co.'s activities in that country can be easily extrapolated to the other markets in which it had strong connections (such as Germany), and there were many of them. To that end, this chapter's findings apply not only to Spain, but also to Germany, France, the Netherlands, and many other places in continental Europe. That said, given Germany's prominence within Huth & Co.'s business, I have also included a short section dealing specifically with the German connection below.

Consolidating bilateral trades with Spain

Chapter 1 established that business with Spain was a critical part of Huth's early operations from London. Being based in Britain but having lived, married and operated in Spain for several years gave Frederick Huth an edge over potential competitors. Being able to tap into so many sources of information for both British and Spanish markets meant that his grasp on them was much more thorough than most of his peers. We must be aware that London merchant bankers not only handled flows of goods and securities, but also handled large amounts of information[11] in a world where information asymmetries paid off. Indeed, it was the advantage provided by this data, together with their significant capital, which gave London merchant bankers an edge over potential rivals.

In turn, because Huth & Co. was trusted by merchants at both ends of the market chain (thanks to regular reciprocal exchanges over long periods of time), it was in a better position than most competitors to reduce transaction costs and thus provide the necessary means of linking the buyers and sellers who could not otherwise trade easily among themselves. It was too costly, for instance, for Spanish wool exporters to find a buyer in Britain and to agree on a selling price; they preferred to use the services of trading companies based in Britain, including merchant bankers such as Huth & Co., as 'market-making' intermediaries.[12] Similarly if a merchant in Spain wanted to act as a 'bridge' between British consigners and Spanish consignees, he would need either to open a branch in London (at a significant incremental cost) or to pay a commission to a broker based there. Given that this was probably the same commission Huth charged their Spanish clients, it would have made little sense to become involved in that kind of transaction.

In the same vein, when a seller was consigning to a foreign market during the 1810s–1840s, he usually needed credit and this was usually provided by merchant bankers. The provision of credit was an intrinsic part of any international merchant's activities during this period, in fact, and Huth & Co. (like many of its peers) was quick to enter this market. For example, its Spanish connections would draw against it for exports from Spain. Without these advances, most Spanish consignments would not have been possible since Spanish exporters usually lacked the working capital so abundant in a vibrant financial centre like London, a point further developed in Chapter 6.

As part of Huth & Co.'s strategy of product diversification (described in detail in Chapter 5), it had now become a major player in the British textile export trade. As noted, for the period covered in this book, textiles were the principal import in Spain and Britain the most important supplier to that Spanish market.[13] As a logical consequence of these processes, Huth & Co.'s textile exports to Spain also increased importantly during this period, as did the number of the company's clients in the country. It also started to send vast quantities of other British products to Spain, such as iron and coal, both of which could easily be catered for thanks to its expertise in international trade, as seen in Chapter 1.

This in part explains why so many Spanish importers receiving consignments from Britain preferred to use the services of Huth & Co. rather than using the services of in-country merchants. We do not know what level of commission a merchant in Spain would need to charge in order to obtain consignments from London of many British or colonial products for other Spanish merchants also resident in Spain, but we do know that Huth & Co.'s 2.5 per cent commission was very low. Furthermore, if a local Spanish merchant wanted to compete with the London firm, not only would he require the same level of product-related expertise, but he would also probably need either to establish a branch in Britain or to pay a confidential agent there, which would surely increase his costs well above Huth & Co.'s.

Even the mighty Ybarra & Co.[14] used the intermediary services of Huth & Co. to purchase products in Britain.[15] Crucially the latter had a sound knowledge of most products widely transacted between Britain and Spain, and most Spanish-based merchants would struggle to match that. Huth & Co. also had a good reputation in London, having survived all the financial crises affecting merchant bankers during *c.*1810-1850, so that those British companies consigning to Spain preferred to do so through Huth & Co. (and other British merchants) rather than via an unknown and untested Spanish trader. Using modern parlance, Huth & Co. had built up massive social capital, understanding this concept as connections among individuals, whose value 'is the direct result of the time and effort invested in nurturing and expanding those connections'.[16] Finally, the British legal framework, which applied to those consigning through London merchant houses, was certainly preferred by UK consigners over the Spanish legal framework when things went wrong.

Frederick Huth's connections with the Spanish monarchy

Frederick Huth's marriage had important consequences for his company's future commercial dealings with Spain. His wife, Manuela, was well connected with the Spanish monarchy as it is thought that her father was a senior courtier to the Spanish king, and following his death she became the ward of the influential Duke of Veragua.[17] Thanks to these connections, Manuela became acquainted with the Princess of Asturias, Maria Antonia (1784–1806),[18] and they became very close friends. Maria Antonia was the first wife of the heir to the throne (her cousin), the Infante Don Ferdinand (future Ferdinand VII, 1784–1833), and was herself a daughter of King Charles's brother, King Ferdinand of Naples and Sicily. When Frederick left Spain for Britain in 1809 he and his wife took with them jewels belonging to Ferdinand (who had now acceded to the Spanish throne) and Maria Antonia for safe-keeping, as Maria Antonia had feared before her death that they could be lost, given the political instability in Spain during the Napoleonic Wars.[19] The jewels were returned by Huth in person once Ferdinand was restored although sadly Maria Antonia had already passed away.[20]

But Maria Antonia's early death (from tuberculosis) was not the end of Frederick Huth's connections with the Spanish monarchy. He and his wife remained on good terms with Ferdinand VII but in particular with the future queen of Spain, Maria Christina (1806–1878).[21] Indeed, in 1829 Frederick was appointed as her financial adviser and private banker in Britain. Furthermore, after her husband's death in 1833, Maria Christina further relied on Frederick for private financial operations in London. That same year she secretly married Agustín Fernando Muñoz (1808–1873), who happened to be the son of one of Huth's earliest connections in Spain, Juan Antonio Muñoz, and who was subsequently appointed Duke of Rianzares. Indeed, during the first Carlist Wars (1833–1840),[22] Maria Christina regularly channelled private funds to London via Huth in order to invest them in British and American securities.[23] The nature of these operations should not surprise us given the high level of corruption in Spain at that time.[24] The key men behind these operations were Fernando Muñoz, Funez y Carrillo and Manuel de Gaviria. It is worth mentioning that the latter had been a very close friend of Ferdinand VII and his widow, so much so that in 1833, when he was already the quartermaster of the *Casa Real*, he was also entrusted with the royal family's treasury.[25]

By purchasing American securities, Spanish investors (including the Crown) were looking for the potential high returns to be made by tapping into territorial and economic expansion of the United States as new states were created.[26] During the first decades of the nineteenth century, money could be borrowed in Britain for as little as 5 per cent, while in the US interest rates were some 7–8 per cent. US stocks were therefore associated with higher returns than their European equivalents and American securities were widely introduced into Europe by institutions such as the Bank of the United States (BUS of Philadelphia) in association with London merchant bankers such as George Peabody and Huth & Co.[27]

As part of this process, in 1836 Huth & Co. sold British consols belonging to Funez y Carrillo, which fetched over £309,000 on the London market. This sum was 250 per cent of Huth's capital at that time, and this sizeable sum of money eventually ensured Huth's entry into the American securities market. Following the consol sale, Funez y Carrillo asked Huth & Co. to invest some of these funds in American securities. After assessing several options, Huth & Co. decided to invest most of the Spaniards' money with the infamous Bank of the United States, in the middle of the 1836–1837 financial crisis (see also Chapter 4). This decision was taken off the back of a recommendation from John W. Perit of Philadelphia, one of Huth's US agents. Despite the ongoing economic turmoil, Perit still viewed the Bank of the United States as a reputable institution.[28] The operation involved a £200,000 loan from Huth & Co. (using Funez y Carrillo's funds) to the Bank at a 5 per cent annual interest, and with the entire capital to be reimbursed ten years later. The Bank was also to pay a commission, which was distributed between Funez y Carillo, Huth & Co. and Perit.[29] In addition, £25,000 was invested by Funez y Carillo in Morris Canal & Banking bonds (of New Jersey).

Several years later, in 1839, Huth & Co. bought more American securities for its Spanish clients, and this time the chosen instruments were state bonds of the Union Bank of Mississippi, worth over £120,000. Among the final buyers were Gaviria (£79,000), Funez y Carrillo (£42,000) and a lesser-known Spanish investor called Miguel Alava.[30] In addition, Gaviria acquired Alabama bonds for some £44,000 and Arkansas bonds for another £60,000. It is believed that as part of these operations, Gaviria and Funez y Carrillo subsequently transferred these bonds to Fernando Muñoz, now the secret husband of Queen Maria Christina, and that in turn Muñoz was actually buying on her behalf.[31]

At this stage the reader may wonder why Spanish investors needed Huth & Co.'s services to buy American securities or why American sellers needed London merchant bankers' intermediation to sell their securities on the Spanish market. The answer is clear: transaction costs would otherwise have been too high, in particular due to the lack of trust between parties and poor market information. In intermediating financial flows, a merchant banker used the same principles needed to intermediate commodity flows, procuring funds from an investor 'with whom it has built up a reputation for sound judgement'.[32] In our case, if a Spanish investor wanted to invest in American securities, he needed to have reliable information about the securities being offered at that time in the market. Few Spaniards could have had a good working knowledge of the American market during this early period (many had probably never previously heard about the establishment of new states); Huth, on the other, had very important financial connections with the US and the information provided by confidential agents resident there was a key part of that. In other words, most potential Spanish competitors were excluded from this profitable business because emerging American states and companies preferred to use the services of trustworthy London merchant bankers who were widely known not only in the US and Britain, but also in the various quarters of continental Europe where many of the US securities usually ended up.

Huth & Co.'s preeminence continued and from the mid-1830s the company became very active in floating US securities on the European market,[33] at a time when not even Baring Brothers or Rothschild & Sons had explored this option.[34] As discussed in Chapter 2, by this stage it had two important confidential agents in the US: Goodhue & Co. of New York and the John Perit of Philadelphia also mentioned above. Both provided invaluable information for Huth & Co.: the firm trusted them and this fact was known to Huth's friends in Spain who in turn fully trusted Huth. Trust and information were thus readily and cheaply provided by the London company, in particular if compared to other alternatives available in Spain. From the American sellers' point of view, they needed a reputable house to offer their securities (otherwise no one would buy them, in particular those belonging to lesser known states) and Huth & Co.'s reputation was beyond reproach.[35] This is important because before the transport and communications revolutions of the second half of the nineteenth century 'a good reputation, built on past behaviour, was often the only reliable antidote to the effects of distrust'.[36]

As a result, the commission Huth & Co. charged Spanish investors for buying American securities was extremely low. If a Spanish merchant banker wanted to compete with London merchant bankers in this market he would need high-quality confidential agents in the Unites States – such as Huth & Co. had in Goodhue and Perit – to whom a commission also had to be paid. This was not only a challenge, but expensive. Furthermore, the Spanish merchant banker wanting to buy American securities needed to be trusted by the American states who wanted to float their debt in Europe, and thus they would need to be perceived as reputable and attractive not only to Spanish investors but to other investors across Europe. This Spanish merchant banker would also need networks of clients who wanted to buy the securities, and those clients would have to trust him. Building an international reputation takes time, though, and as Spanish financiers of the time did not often deal directly with the United States, they were little known there.

And yet despite Huth & Co.'s impeccable credentials, the Bank of the United States suspended specie payments in 1839, eventually closed its doors in February 1841 and eventually went into liquidation.[37] Likewise, in 1840 the Morris Canal & Banking failed to provide dividends and later also collapsed;[38] the Philadelphia Loan Company also failed.[39] In addition, in 1841 the Union Bank of Mississippi failed to pay dividends on its bonds, and subsequently the legislature of that state repudiated the bonds altogether. Other states (including Arkansas) also failed to pay dividends on their debts due to lack of funds. Not surprisingly, American securities started to have a very bad reputation within Europe, and few transactions took place on the London market during this period. As a consequence, Huth & Co.'s Spanish clients saw an important part of their investments heavily compromised. This was perhaps the worst error of judgement the London firm ever made. It had advised its Spanish friends poorly and public opinion was quick to rubbish those merchant bankers who recommended that their customers invest in risky and uncertain ventures. After all, Huth & Co., like many other intermediaries disposing of securities, did not lose any money; they lost their *clients* money.

The Times in particular launched a ferocious attack on merchant bankers, which no doubt was applauded in Madrid. *The Times* even called for an enquiry

> into the manner in which they [USA securities] first obtained circulation here; into the conduct of the mercantile or banking firms who first introduced them, more especially as regards the preliminary investigation by which they satisfied themselves of the resources and the means of credit of the borrowing states, which induced them to offer shares in the loans to their friends … It is hoped, therefore, that something may be done in the matter, particularly as it has been insinuated that enormous commissions … have been allowed to

mercantile firms for assistance in getting this rubbish into circulation and defrauding ... innocent holders.[40]

Spanish investors were doubtless top of the list of these 'innocent holders', among them members of the royal family.

For several years Huth & Co.'s Spanish clients did not see a single penny from their investments in the Morris Canal, the Union Bank of Mississippi and the Bank of the United States. Such was Funez's anguish (and surely the queen's), that in the early 1840s Funez moved to the US to try to recover part of their capital.[41] Painful negotiations followed, but the Spanish investors only recovered just a fraction of their money.[42] The Spaniards' most important concern was undoubtedly the £200,000 invested in the Bank of the United States. Thomas Dunlap, a former president of the bank, was assigned to recover the monies due, which seemed like a strategy that would benefit Huth & Co. The banker León Lillo, financial adviser to Queen Maria Christina in Paris, was also sent to support Dunlap's efforts,[43] but even after the bonds matured in 1847, it proved nigh on impossible to recover anything. At one point it was even suggested that in order to recover the Union Bank of Mississippi's bonds, it would have to be disclosed that 'the Queen of Spain was the owner of a large amount of bonds represented by Huth ... [and] that a foreign royal personage could sue a state in the United States Supreme Court',[44] although this idea was eventually disregarded given all the secrecy surrounding these operations.

Frederick Huth's bad advice to Spanish investors did not seem to affect his reputation in Spain, however, not even among royalty. It is unclear what sort of explanations the firm gave to their Spanish clients, but what is certain is that in 1847 Frederick was made Knight Commander of the Order of Charles III.[45] The partners of Huth & Co. were similarly rewarded: they were appointed as Paymasters Abroad for the Spanish state, which meant that they were responsible for paying Spanish consular agents and diplomats worldwide. By having so many correspondents in a wide variety of locations globally, Huth & Co. was in an ideal position to accomplish the task entrusted to the firm by the Spanish Crown. As will be shown in Chapter 5, no other London merchant banker of his time had diversified geographically as Huth & Co. did before 1850, let alone any Spanish merchant banker.

All Huth & Co. had to do was to instruct Spanish diplomats and consuls abroad to present their receipts for their salaries to one of the company's nominated connections in the location where that consul resided, as this letter shows: 'being now instructed to have the following payments effected on account of the Spanish Government to Don Jose de Bivanco, Spanish Consul General at Hamburg, viz. two months salary or "sueldo" at the rate of ___ Marcos Corrientes ... we request you will have the goodness to make these payments against Mr de Bivanco's receipts in duplicate.'[46] Huth & Co. would, for example, pay the salaries of several dozen Spanish government employees, including: Francisco Baguer y Rivas (Consul in Odessa); Enrique Luis Belman (Consul in Elseneur-Denmark); Manuel Castillo (Consul in Athens); Juan Jimenez Sandoval (Minister to the Low

Countries, The Hague); Ysidro Lopez de Arce (Consul in Malta); Jose de Malagamba (Consul in Tunes); Jose Moreno (Chargé d'affaires, Stockholm); and Juan Mazarredo (Consul in Liverpool).[47]

Ultimately Huth & Co.'s connections with the Spanish authorities were spread further afield. For example, for a while the firm was well connected to José Safont, who was one of the agents of the contractors to the Spanish government procuring tobacco for the country. Thus, Huth & Co. arranged a deal between Clason & Ules of New Orleans (at times Huth's main connection in the southern US) and José Safont, for the former to supply tobacco to the latter. Safont represented the contractors supplying this commodity to the Spanish government. For these operations, Huth & Co. granted a substantial credit of £60,000, for which the company reserved the rights to charge a small commission (i.e. 1.25 per cent), and it was also happy to provide credit to support this trade.[48] All in all, it is clear at this point that Huth & Co.'s connections with Spanish royalty were surprisingly diverse, as demonstrated not only by this latter dealins but also by the company's indirect participation in the Spanish government's quicksilver monopoly, as was extensively described in Chapter 2.

Moving beyond bilateral trades: helping Spain to trade with the world

As the rest of this chapter will show, Huth & Co. grew exponentially after the 1820s. By 1850 it had an accumulated list of over 6,000 correspondents all over the world, in more than 70 countries across all continents. As part of this process, the company's connections in Spain could now profit from their counterparts all over the world. Indeed, Huth & Co. not only participated actively in the bilateral trades between Spain and Britain, but was also happy to help supply Spanish merchant establishments in Spain, Spanish colonies or former Spanish American colonies from beyond Britain. Upon its intermediation and recommendation, the London firm's business 'friends' in continental Europe, Asia and the Americas regularly supplied many of its 'Spanish' connections anywhere in the world. For example, glasses from Bohemia were sent to Buenos Aires thanks to Huth London's intervention.[49] From Cuba, Layseca of Havana coordinated shipments of sugar and tobacco to northern Spain,[50] while Groning of Hamburg used to send German glasses regularly to Spain, to the likes of Rochelt Brothers (Bilbao), just as Huffel of Hamburg supplied Antonio Prado from Rivadeo with many German manufactures. Beyond Germany, cheese from Amsterdam was often sent by Van Veen & Son to Rochelt Brothers of Bilbao and Adalid of Corunna.

In this vein, the Riga connection deserves a mention. From the 1810s, Huth & Co. was an instrumental player in the flax-fibre trade from Riga – the capital of present-day Latvia, but then part of the Russian Empire – and other Russian regions to Galicia and Bilbao at times when this product ranked amongst the most important raw materials imported by Spain.[51] So vital became this trade that Riga's exports to Spain constituted one of the most important trades connecting Huth & Co. and Spain. In a letter from Frederick Huth to one of his sons, it was revealed that 'Riga's flax fibre is one of our main occupations, a trade about which there are many jealous fellow traders, in particular Spanish ones'.[52]

This flax fibre was used in Galicia for the production of the famous Galician linens.[53] From the 1810s, Riga trading houses consigned vast cargoes to Huth & Co.'s contacts in Galicia and the Basque country. Mitchell & Co. became its main connection in Riga, but many other houses also became involved,[54] with the volume of trade increasing significantly and remaining high during the 1820s–1840s. By 1829, for example, 12–15 cargoes of flax fibre linked to Huth & Co. left yearly from Riga for Spain.[55] Amongst the principal houses in northern Spain receiving lino from Riga were: Jugo & Norzagaray (Bilbao);[56] Bobo e Hijos (Orense); Torres & Co. (Santiago de Compostela); Varela & Co. (Santiago de Compostela); Garcia & Co. (Santiago de Compostela); Cabello e Hijos (Santiago de Compostela); Cora & Polo (Vivero); Garcia-Fernandez (Corunna); Marzal e Hijos (Corunna); Santos & Co. (Corunna); and Bengoechea & Co. (Rivadeo). Finally, the Riga connection also supplied wheat and corn for the Spanish market, and to Britain if needed.

But Spain's exports to destinations beyond Britain also benefited from Huth & Co.'s global contacts. For example, wine was consigned by Sierra & Hermanos (Santiago de Compostela) and the likes of Vilardaga (Barcelona) to connections in Buenos Aires.[57] Likewise, once Huth & Co. had opened branch offices in both Peru and Chile (Chapter 2), many of its connections in Spain were happy to supply its establishments on the West Coast. For example, Vilardaga & Reynals of Barcelona happily supplied wine to Callao and Valparaiso upon Huth's request. It is tempting to think that independence abruptly cut off all commercial ties between the new Latin American republics and Spain,[58] but the patchy evidence available suggests otherwise. Many Chilean and Peruvian merchants were actually Spanish nationals, or if Chilean and Peruvian by birth, they still had strong family connections in Spain and these promoted bilateral trades after independence.

But what was the reason for this Spanish dependence on Huth & Co.'s intermediation and contact networks, not to mentipn that of other London merchant bankers? Why could these Spanish merchants not trade directly with those foreign merchants beyond Spain and Britain? Why were the services provided by merchant bankers in Spain itself shunned? This is a key theoretical question concerning the existence of merchant bankers and of multinational trading companies in general.[59] The lack of research on the functions performed by merchant bankers may be a result of the neoclassical economic theory that treats firms (including merchant bankers) as 'black boxes' within a world in which there is no role for intermediaries due to the assumed existence of perfect information and enforcement.[60] But the first half of the nineteenth century was not a neoclassical world. Indeed, Spanish merchants used Huth & Co. (and other British merchants) as intermediaries rather than searching directly for contracting partners, because – as we have learned – international trade during this period was risky, and required trust and reliable information about the import and export markets. Chapman has already pointed to the fact that when communications were slow and difficult 'the ultimate problem of the overseas merchant was maintaining understanding, policy and trust with correspondents'.[61]

Huth & Co.'s unique global network and extensive product diversification provided trust and information at a lower cost than could be procured in Spain, thus reducing risks: the London firm reduced greatly search, negotiation and general transaction costs on behalf of Iberian businessmen. Huth & Co. specialized in overcoming these obstacles to trade on behalf of his correspondents in a world of informational asymmetries. Its impressive global network of contacts gave the firm at least a handful of trustworthy correspondents in every major port in which any Spanish merchant wanted to trade. This was known to Spanish merchants and they used Huth & Co. effectively. Furthermore, there were also linguistic and cultural barriers to overcome. For example: if a Spanish merchant wanted German manufactures, how would he contact a supplier in Germany? In which language should the Spaniard write? In contrast, Huth & Co.'s partners and clerks were conversant in German, Spanish, English, Portuguese, French and even Italian. More importantly, not only did Huth & Co. know hundreds of German manufacturers who trusted the firm, but the company was also trusted by hundreds of Spanish merchants requiring German manufactures, and thus acting as a bridge between buyers in Spain and sellers in Germany (for a commission) was easy for Huth but very challenging for a Spaniard directly. But perhaps equally importantly, these foreign trade operations required credit, and credit was scarce and expensive in Spain, as the following section explains.

Financial and other services provided by Huth to Spanish merchants

I have mentioned that one of the most important products traded between Spain and Britain during the period covered by this monograph was Spanish raw wool. To support this branch of trade, a great deal of credit was extended in London to Spanish suppliers. Wool trading also represented one of Huth & Co.'s most important Iberian commercial activities. Once the wool had arrived in Bilbao, San Sebastian, Santander or any other Spanish port, local wool suppliers were entitled to draw against Huth & Co. for a share of the value of the cargo at 90 days (a practice known as 'advances').[62] Likewise, Haurie's shipments of wine to Britain were also made possible thanks to Huth & Co.'s liberal advances, as was the case with so many other Spanish exports. Huth & Co. charged a commission of just 1 per cent on the value of the drafts before accepting them. The liberal credit facilities offered by the company were not available in Spain to merchants exporting to Britain because Spanish enterprises were less creditworthy for bills payable in London. As noted, the distinguishing feature of London merchant bankers of the period was a combination of large capital resources linked with intimate knowledge of a particular market.[63] In this regard, Huth & Co. was unrivalled in Spain.

The company also extended credit more liberally to British exporters to Spain than for most other markets. For example, a Manchester-based British textile manufacturer would draw against Huth & Co. for the shipment of cottons to one of its correspondents in, say, Galicia, and then probably discount the bill immediately after acceptance. Thus the British manufacturer benefited because he was less exposed to the risk of selling directly to a foreign market.[64] Huth & Co. would accept the draft in London because it trusted both the British exporter and the Spanish importer. In turn, the Mancunian exporter would not draw a bill against a merchant in Galicia (or in Madrid) because it was most likely not discountable in either Britain or Spain, and certainly not payable in sterling as he might have wanted. Put bluntly, a merchant banker resident in Spain would not be able to offer the same services offered by London merchant bankers because he would have been unknown to the British manufacturer.

But Huth & Co.'s advances were extended to support many other trades linked to Spain and her colonies, even those which never touched on London. These included trades:

1   between Spain and her colonies;
2   between former Spanish colonies and Spain;
3   between existing Spanish colonies and former Spanish colonies;
4   between Spanish colonies and other markets beyond the Americas.

As an example from the first category, sugar was sent from Cuba to Corunna, Cadiz and other Spanish ports thanks to Huth & Co.'s generous advances to the merchants in Cuba. Likewise, shipments of sugar from Manila to Spain received advances from Huth's London house. In the second category, cacao shipments sent from Venezuela to Santander or to other Spanish ports received advances from Huth & Co. In particular, Bermudez of Caracas would draw against Huth & Co. for cargoes sent to Porrua Egusquiza of Santander, with drafts of 90–120 days that had to be covered by Porrua Egusquiza at maturity. Cargoes of hides sent from Buenos Aires to Spain also received Huth's generous advances.

In the third category, extensive shipments of jerked beef from the River Plate to Havana received advances from Huth & Co. in London. Cuban sugar was also shipped to Chile and Peru using credit from the London firm. And finally Huth & Co. also funded trade operations between Spanish colonies and other markets beyond Spain or the Americas, such as continental Europe. For example, Miguel de Embil & Co. of Havana was in the habit of sending sugar cargoes to Antwerp and St Petersburg funded by Huth & Co.'s advances, as did Mariategui Knight & Co. and Drake & Co., while José Pastor of Havana consigned tobacco to Gaedechens of Hamburg after drawing bills of exchange against Huth & Co. as advances. To support these operations, Huth & Co. would open a credit account to the importer in (say) St Petersburg in favour of the consigner in (say) Havana, and the latter would draw against Huth & Co. to settle his account with the consignee.

The house of James Drake (Drake & Co.)[65] deserves discussion here. Located in the Cuban capital of Havana, this influential house (and its branch house at Matanzas, styled Drake & Pert) was for most of the period covered by this book amongst Huth & Co.'s main contacts.[66] Relations between the two companies began in the late 1820s, and grew to such an extent that in 1839 Drake enjoyed an open credit of as much as £10,000 for shipments of sugar to Huth & Co. in

London.[67] However, this was only one side of the business, probably the less important. Drake consigned far more frequently to a wide range of Huth & Co.'s friends in Russia,[68] Spain,[69] Germany,[70] the Netherlands,[71] Belgium[72] and France, many of whom also enjoyed credit with Huth & Co.[73] The connection with continental Europe became stronger after Drake & Co. incorporated as partners Messrs. Joseph M. Morales, Ulric Zellweger and Charles Respinger and as of 1839 the firm became known as Drake Brothers & Co.[74] By the 1830s Drake & Co. had been appointed Huth's agents in this largest of the Caribbean islands, performing many standard duties but also undertaking some special tasks: the firm was a key intermediary when Huth & Co. decided to invest in the Cardenas Railroad by buying shares in the said enterprise, for example.[75]

So Cuba was the main connection in the Caribbean but it was not the only one: E. & A. Weber of Haiti (and Antwerp) were 'very good friends' of Huth & Co.,[76] and were even signalled by Baring Brothers as one of Huth's main connections in the world for the consignment of coffee.[77] Also in Haiti and Cuba, Balbiani proved to be an enduring connection, one that was cultivated from the early 1820s. Puerto Rico in turn was a rich source of cocoa for Huth's friends in Spain. Houses such as Capetillo, O'Kelly, and Ezquiaga were amongst the main Boricua connections, and drew extensively against Huth for cocoa cargoes sent to Spain.[78]

Returning to the topic of supplying credit to finance Spanish foreign trade, I outlined above that most of the strategic Riga flax-fibre trade was made possible thanks to credit supplied by Huth & Co. The latter's agents in Riga would buy flax fibre, ship it to Spain and draw against Huth & Co. In London Huth & Co. would immediately accept these drafts. The merchant banker was in this way indirectly extending credit to the Spanish merchants in Galicia who received the flax fibre. For example, Stresow & Sons and Jacobs & Co. would buy in Riga for Bengoechea (Rivadeo) or for Garcia in Santiago de Compostela. Before shipping the products they would draw against Huth & Co. on account of this flax fibre, usually for up to two-thirds of the invoice value of the cargoes. The Spanish recipient of the flax would pay back to Huth & Co. the monies 'lent' by Huth & Co. to the Riga merchants, ideally covering the drafts before maturity.

At this point an obvious question arises. Why were Spanish merchant bankers unable to offer the same credit services as those provided so extensively by London merchant bankers? Or, alternatively, why did Spanish traders prefer Huth & Co.'s credit to Spain's own credit facilities during the period covered by this book? To answer these questions we must remember that during the 1810s–1840s Britain was the world's largest trading nation as well as the largest capital exporter. As a consequence, a great deal of the finance underpinning global trade 'was orchestrated in London and sterling was the main currency of international finance'.[79] London had already overtaken Amsterdam as the premier centre for international finance and payments.[80] Therefore, London merchant bankers' credit facilities could not be matched by their Spanish counterparts because capital was more expensive in Spain and the local financial sector was less developed than the British sector. We also know that during the first half of the nineteenth century, the financing of overseas trade within Europe and beyond was an elite activity because of the large amount of capital required to operate in this sector.[81] In this respect, Huth & Co.'s capital and international reputation easily out-stripped those of most merchant bankers resident in Spain.

The provision of credit aside, the dealing of bills was another valuable role performed by London merchant bankers during the first half of the nineteenth century, and this activity did not escape Huth & Co.'s enthusiasm. In order to fulfil this role, the firm obtained acceptance in London for bills of exchange drawn anywhere in the world if they were drawn on a London house. If drawn in a currency different to sterling, Huth & Co. also negotiated exchange rates on behalf of their correspondents, including many Iberian establishments.

Among Huth & Co.'s principal Spanish customers was the Banco Español de San Fernando of Madrid (predecessor of the Bank of Spain, and previously called Banco de San Carlos),[82] whose director was none other than Joaquin de Fagoaga, who had facilitated many Spanish wool exports to Huth & Co. Although Baring Brothers did not think highly of Fagoaga (he was seen as 'elevated by circumstances more than by his merits'),[83] this did not stop Huth & Co. from engaging extensively with him. At this point it is worth noting that in 1840 (when Maria Christina's regency ended) Fagoaga succeeded Gaviria as quartermaster of the Casa Real, while keeping the directorship of the Banco de San Fernando, and thus becoming even more influential within Spanish financial and political circles.[84]

Furthermore, in 1844 Huth & Co. secured another important Spanish deal in bills of exchange after being appointed by the Banco de Isabel II as their representative on the London market. For a 0.25 per cent commission, Huth & Co. would obtain acceptance and negotiate exchange rates on this bank's behalf.[85] Unfortunately this bank lasted only for a few years, failing during the financial crisis of 1847. The Banco de Cadiz was another important Huth & Co. client and again, as for many other contacts in Spain, Huth obtained acceptance of bills in London, negotiated exchange rates, collected London bills endorsed in the Banco de Cadiz's favour and credited them into its account.[86] Huth & Co.'s connections in Spain also performed reciprocal services locally for Huth regarding bills of exchange drawn on Spain: for example, Serra Hermanos of Barcelona were entrusted to gain acceptance in Catalonia for any bill of exchange drawn in Huth & Co.'s favour,[87] as were Hermanos Urtetegui & Colom of Cadiz.

Why did these Spanish banks need financial intermediation from London merchant bankers on the bills of exchange market? Yet again, the answer lies in commercial reach. In order to obtain acceptance of bills in Britain on behalf of Spanish merchants, Huth & Co. could draw on the expertise available in its London headquarters in London as well as (from 1839) a branch in Liverpool, confidential agents in many other British locations and dozens of experienced clerks (many of them specialists on Spain, such as C. L. Vidal, M. de Pedrorena and J. B. Cabanyes). Its positive reputation also helped them to represent their Spanish friends to British banking institutions. Similarly, in negotiating exchanges between London and Madrid, Huth & Co.'s expertise in both markets was unmatched by most competitors in either Spain or Britain, and the company's friends in Spain could make use of its information at a low commission.

The connections between Huth & Co. and Spanish businessmen lead us once more to the securities market. Here two other important facts should be highlighted. First, not only was the Spanish Crown interested in buying securities via Huth & Co. on the London market, but many more Spanish businessmen used it to buy (and to sell) securities in the English capital. These typically included British and US securities, but there was also an interest in their Spanish equivalents, which were widely transacted in London. For example, in the 'Spanish panic' of May 1835, Spanish securities lost 30 per cent of their value on the London market, bringing ruin to many investors. Thereafter, many Spanish securities were also liquidated on British soil by Huth & Co. on behalf of Spanish businessmen.[88] Yribarren & Sobrinos often asked Huth & Co. to sell on their behalf shares of the '*empréstito nacional*', and Gaviria was also in the habit of requesting the company to liquidate in London '*títulos españoles*' and '*cupones*',[89] many of which either belonged to the royal family or to Gaviria himself, given his proclivity for mixing government and private business.[90] This is not surprising: after the restoration of Ferdinand VII, Spain's debt was issued in both France and Britain by eminent bankers, and therefore 'Spanish' bonds were widely transacted in both London and Paris.

Beyond the financial sector, Huth & Co. was also happy to provide any other reasonable service upon request. For example, in 1828 Spain imposed a very high import duty on linen coming from Riga if brought in foreign vessels (if imported in Spanish vessels, the duty was just half that amount). Around this time, exports of flour from Spain to Havana in foreign vessels had also to pay very high import duties in Cuba, but if carried in Spanish vessels they were free of duties. Thus, many of Huth & Co.'s contacts in Spain and Cuba asked it to buy British ships and send them to Spain to sail them under the Spanish flag. A ship was eventually bought for Francisco A. Varela of Santiago de Compostela and used solely for the Riga linen trade.[91]

Huth & Co. provided a raft of other services to its connections, notably important postal services which were vital at a time when mail packet companies were not in operation on many international routes and communications were slow, expensive and unreliable. Many foreign merchants sent letters to Huth in London to be forwarded to diverse destinations. For example, merchants in Spain would send letters intended for the Americas to Huth & Co. in London, to be forwarded to their final destination. Such was the case of Porrua e Hijos of Santander, who sent letters to La Guayra via the English capital. Merchants on the periphery of the world economy would send letters in the opposite direction so that they could be forwarded on from Huth & Co.'s HQ: Nicolas Galceran of Havana, for instance, used to send letters to Manila via Huth in London,[92] while Muñoz & Funes of Caracas used to send letters regularly to the same office to be forwarded to many destinations in Spain,[93] and so did Ezquiaga & Nephews in Puerto Rico and Pons & Ziegler of Santiago de Cuba among many others. Huth also offered many other smaller services, from buying lottery tickets for Sebastian de Lasa of Havana[94] to purchasing a silver watch for his friends Manuel de Gaviria[95] and Juan Francisco Barrié,[96] or buying London newspapers regularly for many merchants in Spain. It is clear from these latter examples that Huth & Co. was eager to cultivate friendly relations with selected correspondents. We are clearly talking here about non-economic motivations behind several of Huth's actions, or as Lamikiz put it, very often 'merchants' actions were socially embedded, and therefore responded to motives other than purely economic'.[97]

Huth as insurance broker for Spanish merchants

It is well known that multinational merchants engaged in overseas trade were usually involved in marine insurances during the period covered by this book. In previous chapters we have already seen that Huth & Co. did not conform to this trend, and participated actively in insurance broking for trades connecting Britain and South America. This was replicated for Spain. Indeed, marine insurance was one of the many commercial activities connecting Huth & Co. in London with Spanish merchants. They had requested Huth & Co.'s insurance broking services because marine insurance could be procured in London on more favourable terms than those available in Spain. London's market for this product was unrivalled across the world during the 1810s–1840s and here again, since Huth & Co. was based there, asymmetrical information was in its favour. Spanish traders would rather pay the London firm a small commission (0.5 per cent) to effect marine insurance on their behalf than use the intermediary services of Spanish merchants based in Spain in a relatively underdeveloped market, as was the case until 1850.[98] Sooner or later a Spanish merchant offering insurance in Spain needed the services of an intermediary in London if he wanted to remain competitive, or would have to bear the cost of establishing a branch of his own there.

Judging from Frederick Huth's business correspondence, it is clear that he was extremely risk-averse, and throughout his career used to insure all trade operations in which he (or his company) had any interest, and against all risks. In turn, and perhaps because of the founder's very cautious approach, Huth & Co. managed to build a healthy reputation among London underwriters that gave rise to a vast network of insurers to which Spanish merchants operating from Spain had no access. Huth & Co. worked with at least 150–200 different names in Lloyds during the late 1810s and early 1820s. The value of policies taken by these names varied between as little as £50 to as much as £20,000, although the modal rates were £100–£300.[99] These were times when the British insurance market was dominated by Lloyds and by two companies chartered in 1720, namely the London Assurance Corporation and the Royal Exchange Assurance Corporation. For over 100 years, the British marine insurance market consisted of these two firms and the private underwriters operating mainly at Lloyds. By law, no other corporation could enter the market. Freedom to establish new companies was not granted until 1824, when Nathan Rothschild's Alliance Marine Insurance Company was created as part of the repeal of the 1720 Act. In the same year, Indemnity Mutual entered the market, and other companies would follow.[100] As part of this development, from the mid-1820s Huth & Co. started to use the services of a variety of suppliers, including the Royal Exchange Assurance Company, the

Marine Insurance Company, the Alliance Assurance Company, the Neptune Assurance Company, they Indemnity Assurance Company and the Atlas Insurance Company.

Thus Huth & Co. arranged most, if not all, of the marine insurance of shipments between Britain and Spain in which it had any interest, either as a consignee or as a distant intermediary advancing funds. These included shipments of wool, wine and many other products from Spain to Britain and vice versa. Huth was also happy to provide insurance brokerage for shipments between Britain and the Spanish colonies: the sugar cargoes sent by Vazquez Falcon Echarte of Havana to Britain were always insured by Huth in London, as were sugar shipments from Puerto Rico.[101] If advances given by Huth & Co. were involved, then as prerequisite for this financing, Huth & Co. brokered the insurance too. And because Spanish merchants used so much of the London firm's credits, its insurance brokerage had to be widely used too. In addition, Huth & Co. effected marine insurance for a number of Spanish merchants shipping consignments from locations outside Britain to Spain (and her colonies) and vice versa. We are talking here about trades which never touched on British ports but which were nonetheless insured on the London market.

Overall, Huth & Co.'s marine insurance services were of great consequence for Spanish foreign trade: without them, many Spanish traders would have been reluctant to enter into international commerce at all. Huth & Co. not only advanced insurance premiums to Spanish merchants, but also made available their vast network of contacts at Lloyds in order to effect the insurances requested from Spain. Several Spanish merchants avoided ruin thanks to this cover: seawater damage was very common during this period, in particular for cargoes such as textiles, sugar and tobacco.[102] Perhaps more importantly, shipwrecks happened more often than merchants would have liked, and often ships, crews and cargoes alike were wholly lost. Such was the case of the Spanish ship *San Jacobo*, which sailed from Havana to Corunna and Riga loaded with sugar, but fortunately was insured by Huth & Co. on behalf of many merchants, and for which it claimed £6,000 from the underwriters.[103] Huth & Co. also arranged fire insurance for merchandise en route to Spain, including flax stored in Riga and subsequently headed for Iberia.[104]

The German connection

Chapter 1 explained that Frederick Huth's German connection became more important than ever following the Napoleonic Wars, and was further enhanced by Gruning's incorporation as a partner. By the late 1820s Huth & Co. had more correspondents in Germany than in Spain. It is difficult to tell whether or not this was the result of Germany's increasing significance for firm's overall revenues, but it certainly shows the growing value of this connection for the company's total profits (see Table 3.2). Around 1830, 36 per cent of the firm's German correspondents were concentrated in Hamburg, which together with Bremen accounted for half of all correspondents in the country that year. Leipzig and

Berlin too were important hubs for Huth, and during the 1830s other centres such as Wuppertal, Konigsberg and Frankfurt became increasingly important, perhaps as a result of the diffusion of industrialization across Germany.

The nature of Huth & Co.'s connection in Germany was quite similar to that of Spain (as well as France, the Netherlands and other European countries), and therefore I will not enter here into further detail which ultimately would only repeat the main arguments put forward above. Indeed, Huth & Co. provided similar services from London, Liverpool and other quarters to their correspondents in Germany as they did to those in Spain. Germany exported more manufactures than Spain, but both countries exported and imported primary products, and many of these trades were supported by Huth & Co., whether they passed through Britain or not.

Huth & Co.'s principal contacts in Germany deserve a mention. Apart from the names already provided (that is, Brentano Bovara & Urbieta (Hamburg),[105] Justus Ruperti (Hamburg), J. C. Godeffroy (Hamburg), L. A. Huffel (Hamburg), J. F. Scheinert & Co. (Hamburg), Chapeaurouge & Co. (Hamburg), Groning & Co. (Hamburg), G. Loning & Söhne (Bremen) and J. G. Schutte & Co. (Bremen), other important contacts included: Preusser & Co. (Leipzig); Trinius & Co. (Leipzig);[106] Frege & Co. (Leipzig); Seehandlung Societat (Berlin); J. W. Bastian & Söhne (Bremen); C. J. Johns (Hamburg); H. J. Merck & Co. (Hamburg);[107] B. J. Poschaan (Hamburg);[108] Hinck & Co. (Hamburg); Ross Vidal & Co. (Hamburg); H. H. Meier & Co. (Hamburg); G. Simons Achenbach (Wuppertal); and Matthaei (Magdeburg).

Table 3.2 Geographical distribution of Huth & Co.'s correspondents in Germany: a sample for the main cities, c.1812–1848

Location	1812	1815	1822	1830	1838-1839	1846-1848
Hamburg	1	24	71	85	108	146
Bremen	0	1	20	32	35	49
Leipzig	0	0	12	22	17	20
Berlin	0	0	3	11	11	30
Wuppertal	0	0	0	6	22	32
Konigsberg	0	0	0	0	17	25
Frankfurt	0	0	1	5	10	20
Nuremberg	0	0	8	7	4	8
Cologne	0	0	0	0	5	18
Magdeburg	0	0	5	7	4	6
Lubeck	0	1	1	2	5	10
Dresden	0	0	7	3	3	5
Braunschweig	0	0	3	5	1	1
Top-13	*1*	*26*	*131*	*185*	*242*	*370*
Share top-13 within Germany	100%	93%	81%	79%	82%	70%
All other cities	0	2	30	50	54	158
Total Germany	1	28	161	235	296	528
Share of Germany in world	1%	15%	24%	29%	26%	29%
All countries	*113*	*192*	*665*	*804*	*1,142*	*1,850*

Source: HPEL, HPSL, HPGL, several volumes.

Notes

1. It is probably true that the Rothschilds exerted more influence upon the Spanish economy, but their activities were mainly linked to issuing rather than to trade. At this point it is worth mentioning that it was not only Spain that escaped the radar of most prominent London merchant bankers of the 1820s–1840s; other European markets were largely ignored too. For instance, according to the biographers of the Hambros, 'the map on which the older British merchant bankers had divided up Europe showed that none of them was as yet displaying the slightest interest in Scandinavia. From the beginnings this was Hambro's territory'. Bramsen & Wain, *The Hambros*, p. 262.
2. L. Prados de la Escosura, *Comercio Exterior y Crecimiento Económico en España, 1826–1913* (Madrid: Banco de España, 1982); Prados de la Escosura 'Comercio Exterior y Cambio Económico'; Prados de la Escosura, 'El Comercio Hispano-Británico'; L. Prados de la Escosura, 'Las Relaciones Reales de Intercambio entre España y Gran Bretaña Durante los Siglos XVIII y XIX', in P. Martin Aceña and L. Prados de la Escosura (eds.), *La Nueva Historia Económica en España* (Madrid: Tecnos, 1985); L. Prados de la Escosura, 'Una Serie Anual de Comercio Exterior Español, 1821–1913', *Revista de Historia Económica*, 4 (1986); L. Prados de la Escosura and G. Tortella 'Tendencias a Largo Plazo del Comercio Exterior Español, 1714–1913', *Revista de Historia Económica*, 1 (1983); J. Fontana-Lazaro, 'Colapso y Transformaciones del Comercio Exterior Español entre 1792 y 1827. Un Aspecto de la Economía del Antiguo Régimen en España', *Moneda y Crédito*, 115 (1970); J. Cuenca-Estevan, 'Statistics of Spain's Colonial Trade, 1792–1820', *Hispanic American Historical Review*, 61 (1981).
3. Chapman, *The Rise*; Chapman, *Merchant Enterprise*; Jones, *Merchants to Multinationals*; Jones, *International Business*.
4. Chapman, *The Rise*; Chapman, *Merchant Enterprise*; Jones, *Merchants to Multinationals*; Jones, *International Business*.
5. Chapman, *The Rise*, pp. 8–9, 14–15.
6. Chapman, *Merchant Enterprise*, p. 135.
7. Chapman, *The Rise*, p. 105.
8. Prados de la Escosura, 'Comercio Exterior y Cambio Económico', pp. 211 and 221.
9. L. Prados de la Escosura, 'La Pérdida del Imperio y sus Consecuencias Económicas en España', in L. Prados de la Escosura, and S. Amaral. (eds.), *La Independencia Americana, Consecuencias Económicas* (Madrid: Alianza Editorial, 1993).
10. Chapman, *The Rise*, p. 169; Chapman, *Merchant Enterprise*, p. xiii.
11. Casson, 'The Economic Analysis', pp. 34–35.
12. Jones, *Merchants to Multinationals*, pp. 27–28; Casson, 'The Economic Analysis', pp. 22–24.
13. Prados de la Escosura, 'Comercio Exterior y Cambio Económico', pp. 215–217.
14. On the Ybarra family business, see P. Díaz Morlán, *Los Ybarra. Una Dinastía de Empresarios, 1801-2001* (Madrid: Marcial Pons, 2002); M. Sierra, *La Familia Ybarra, Empresarios y Políticos* (Sevilla: Muñoz Moya Editores, 1992).
15. See, for instance, HPIL, R48, Ybarra & Co. to Huth & Co. (Liverpool). Bilbao, 27 November 1839.
16. Lamikiz, 'Social Capital, Networks', p. 19.
17. Jones, 'Huth, Frederick Andrew', pp. 1–3.
18. Murray, *Home from the Hill*, pp. 72 and 77.
19. Freedman, *A London Merchant Banker*, pp. 11–12.
20. Murray, *Home from the Hill*, pp. 77–78, 108.
21. Maria Christina was the fourth wife of Ferdinand VII and the daughter of Francis I (1777–1830), brother of Maria Antonia. She was queen of Spain due to her marriage to Ferdinand VII. She was Queen consort of Spain (1829 to 1833) and Regent of Spain (1833 to 1840) after Ferdinand's death.

22 The Carlist Wars (*carlistadas*) were civil wars that took place in Spain during 1833–1840, when several contenders fought to establish their claim to the throne.
23 The first investments made on behalf of the queen were made in British consols. It is striking that many operations were made through Funez y Carrillo. For examples, see HPJ-228, May 1835, p. 160; July 1835, p. 242 (consols bought for a value of £130,000); more consols bought for £100,000 in August 1835; yet again in October 1835, this time for £33,000; and another operation worth £40,000 in November 1835. In all, Huth bought over £300,000 in British consols for Funez y Carrillo.
24 M. A. López-Morell, *La Casa Rothschild en España* (Madrid: Marcial Pons, 2005), p. 89.
25 López-Morell, *La Casa Rothschild*, p. 88.
26 Louisiana was created in 1812, it was followed by Indiana (1816), Mississippi (1817), Illinois (1818), Alabama (1819), Maine (1820), Missouri (1821), Arkansas (1836), Michigan (1837), Florida and Texas (1845), Iowa (1846), Wisconsin (1848) and California (1850). All these states needed to invest in infrastructure, including railways, canals, public buildings, port facilities, etc.
27 McGrane, *Foreign Bondholders*, pp. 8-9; Kynaston, *The City of London*, pp. 116–117; Chapman, *The Rise*, pp. 46–47; Freedman, *A London Merchant Banker*, p. 7.
28 It is fair to mention, in defence of Perit's judgement, that despite the disruptions in the Anglo-American trading system as a result of the 1836–1837 financial crisis, 'the reputation of the BUS still stood high in Europe'. Freedman, *A London Merchant Banker*, p. 42.
29 HPEL-17, Huth & Co. to J. Perit (Philadelphia). London, 29 April 1837; HPJ-228, for 1836; and HPJ-229B, for operations in 1837.
30 HPJ-229, 1839, p. 408.
31 Freedman, *A London Merchant Banker*, p. 343.
32 Casson, 'The Economic Analysis', pp. 37–38.
33 L. H. Jenks, *The Migration of British Capital to 1875* (London: Nelson & Sons, 1963), chapter 3; McGrane, *Foreign Bondholders*, p. 9. But Huth sold securities not only for European clients, but for anyone who wanted to buy them. For instance, Drusina & Co. of Mexico also purchased securities, from Mexico, via Huth & Co. of London.
34 Barings and Rothschild entered this market in 1852 only. Chapman, *The Rise*, p. 92.
35 Chapman, *The Rise*, p. 72.
36 Lamikiz, *Trade and Trust*, p. 10.
37 Kynaston, *The City of London*, pp. 116–117. This bank had been created in 1816, and it soon emerged as the leading element in bills of exchange connected to the raw cotton trade. Freedman, *A London Merchant Banker*, p. 4.
38 In defence of Huth & Co., it is worth mentioning that Jonathan Goodhue (i.e. Huth's agent in the US) had been an official of the Morris Company, and had in turn recommended that Huth & Co. invest funds in bonds of this company. Freedman, *A London Merchant Banker*, p. 34.
39 This later incident cost John Perit his agency services with Huth & Co. Indeed, after 1839 correspondence between Huth & Co. and Perit became far less intense than it used to be, or at least less significant than before.
40 *The Times*, 14 April 1842, 'Money-Market and City Intelligence'.
41 HPSL-175, Huth & Co. to Funez y Carrillo (New Orleans). London, 8 January 1843; HPIL, S/SP/2, Funez y Carrillo to Huth & Co. (London). Philadelphia, 27 September 1844; HPEL-46, Huth & Co. to Funez y Carillo (unknown place). London, 3 June 1845.
42 Business correspondence in the Huth papers ends abruptly in 1852. After this year, little is known about what Spanish investors recovered.
43 HPEL-54. Huth & Co. to Thomas Dunlap (Philadelphia). London, 3 August 1847. According to George Francis Train, writing in the mid-1850s, Lillo was probably the son of Queen Christina, by the Duke of Rianzares. G. F. Train, *My Life in Many States*

and Foreign Lands. Dictated on my Seventy Four Fear (New York: Library of Alexandria, 1902). This, unfortunately, I have not been able to corroborate.
44 McGrane, *Foreign Bondholders*, p. 216.
45 Previously, Huth was appointed a Knight of the Order of Charles III of Spain.
46 HPEL-59, Huth & Co. to Petersen Huth & Co. (Hamburg). London, 24 January 1849.
47 For some examples, see HPSL-182.
48 HPEL-53, Huth & Co. to Clason & Ules (New Orleans). London, 3 and 18 June, 19 July 1847.
49 HPSL-156, Huth & Co. to Llano Brothers (Buenos Aires). London, 5 November 1814.
50 HPSL-159, Huth & Co. to Francisco Layseca (Havana). London, 30 July 1822.
51 Prados de la Escosura, 'Comercio Exterior y Cambio Económico', p. 184.
52 Original in Spanish: 'linos de Riga que como Vmd sabe es el que nos ocupa esencialmente y respecto del cual tenemos muchos envidiosos entre nuestros vecinos en este comercio, principalmente Españoles.' HPSL-160, Huth & Co. to Fredrick Huth Jr. (Cadiz). London, 30 October 1829.
53 On the Galicia linen industry see Carmona-Badía, *El Atraso Industrial*.
54 These were Garry Curtis Hay; Stresow & Co.; Querfeldt Wittkowsky; Kaull & Co. For some examples, see HPEL-6, Huth & Co. to Kaull & Co. (Riga). London, 20 August 1830; HPSL-177, Huth & Co. to Stresow & Co. (Riga). London, 16 and 20 April 1847.
55 HPSL-160, Huth & Co. to Huth Jr. (Cadiz). London, 6 November 1829.
56 HPEL-5, Huth to & Co. Jacobs & Gordon (Riga). London, 7 January and 12 February 1830.
57 HPSL-159, Huth & Co. to Dickson Montgomery & Co. (Buenos Aires). London, 21 June 1822.
58 See, for example, for the Chilean case, J. L. Rector, 'El Impacto Económico de la Independencia en América Latina: el Caso de Chile', *Historia*, 20 (1985), p. 298: after independence Spanish merchants abandoned the country and were immediately replaced by British and American merchants.
59 Jones, 'Multinational Trading Companies', pp. 16–17.
60 Jones, *Merchants to Multinationals*, p. 4.
61 Chapman, *Merchant Enterprise in Britain*, p. 45.
62 HPSL-160, Huth & Co. to Huth Jr. (Cadiz). London, 9 October 1829.
63 Chapman, *Merchant Enterprise in Britain*, p. 70.
64 Chapman, *Merchant Enterprise in Britain*, pp. 68–71.
65 James Drake (1763–1838), born in Devon, was the son of a British merchant resident in Cadiz. In 1792 he was allowed by the Spanish king to establish himself in Cuba, after obtaining a warrant. He was one of the first foreign merchants allowed to open houses in a Spanish colony. Subsequently he married Carlotta Nuñez del Castillo, niece of the third Marquez de San Felipe y Santiago, who owned some of the largest plantations in Cuba. This gave him his passport into Cuban aristocracy. Curry-Machado, 'Running from Albion'; J. Curry-Machado, 'Rich Flames and Hired Tears: Sugar, Sub-Imperial Agents and the Cuban Phoenix of Empire', *Journal of Global History*, 4 (2009); R. T. Ely, 'The Old Cuba Trade: Highlights and Case Studies of Cuban-American Interdependence during the Nineteenth Century', *Business History Review*, 38 (1964).
66 This was the same house in which the founder of Kleinwort London (i.e. Alexander Friedrich Kleinwort) worked as a clerk during the 1830s, and was made a partner in 1845. Wake, *Kleinwort Benson*, p. 73.
67 HPEL-22. Huth & Co. to Huth & Co. (Liverpool). London, 10 January 1839.
68 Such as Louis Wachter of St Petersburg or Ponomaroff & Co. of the same city.
69 To houses such as Santos e hijos of Corunna, Oneto & Co. of Cadiz, Lopez Doriga of Santander.

Huth & Co.'s Spanish and German connections 77

70 For example, to the likes of Hartog & Denker of Hamburg.
71 For instance to De Bruyn & Sons of Amsterdam.
72 Joachim Neyt & Fils of Ghent, or A. Reusens of Antwerp, amongst many others.
73 Elsewhere in Cuba, the German house of Clauss Witt was also attached to Huth for consignments to England and Germany. For example, in February 1836, Clauss Witt drew several drafts against Huth for £5,000. See HPBP-193. Other useful German houses linked to Huth's connections in Hamburg and Bremen were those of Godeffroy and Bastian. Likewise, Torrientes (of Havana and Matanzas) did a large amount of business with Huth, operating in a similar fashion to Drake. Via Huth & Co., Torrientes consigned sugar to Bolado. HPSL-170; and HPSL-175. Huth & Co. to Bolado Hermanos (Santander). London, 3 and 13 January 1843.
74 After James Drake's death, his eldest son and a brother took the reins of the firm. BT 1/1/2.
75 HPEL-45. Huth & Co. to Drake & Co. (Havana). London, 16 January 1845 and 15 March 1845. The first railway in Latin America was laid in Cuba using British capital (Havana-Bejucal, in 1837), followed by many other similar projects, such as this project of Cardenas.
76 HPEL-22. Huth & Co. to Huth & Co. (Liverpool). London, 10 January 1839. See also HPJ-229B.
77 HC 16/1.
78 HPSL-178. Huth & Co. to Ygnacio Ezquiaga (San Juan, Puerto Rico). London, 1 April 1848.
79 Chapman, *Merchant Enterprise in Britain*, pp. 4–5, 41–42; Jones, *Merchants to Multinationals*, pp. 2-3, 19–20.
80 Chapman, *The Rise*, p. 9.
81 Chapman, *Merchant Enterprise in Britain*, pp. 27–28; Jones, *Merchants to Multinationals*, p. 6.
82 For some examples, see HPSL-177, Huth & Co. (London) to Banco Español de San Fernando (Madrid), any letter for this volume.
83 HC 16/21. April 1848.
84 López-Morell, *La Casa Rothschild*, p. 105. There is some agreement in the literature that Fagoaga, like Gaviria and Maria Christina herself, was of dubious reputation. López-Morell, *La Casa Rothschild*, p. 124.
85 HPSL-176, Huth & Co. to Banco de Isabel II (Madrid). London, 14 and 16 May 1844.
86 HPSL-180, Huth & Co. to Banco de Cadiz. London, 8 February 1851.
87 HPSL-181, Huth & Co. to Serra Hermanos (Barcelona). London, 28 January 1851.
88 The evidence available shows that Huth & Co. was offering Spanish bonds on the London market from at least 1822. For example, Lopez Hermanos, Adalid & Hijos, A. Martinez, Vilardaga & Co. and Yribarren & Nephews sold Spanish bonds in London through Huth. HPJ-224, transactions for 1822 and 1823.
89 HPSL-175, Huth & Co. to Manuel Gaviria (Madrid). London, 1 January 1843.
90 López-Morell, *La Casa Rothschild*, p. 88.
91 HPSL-160, Huth & Co. to Fredrick Huth Jr. (Cadiz). London, 6 November 1829.
92 HPSL-177, Huth & Co. to Nicolas Galceran (Havana). London, 1 April 1847.
93 HPSL-178, Huth & Co. to Juan Gregorio Muñoz & Funes (Caracas). London, 16 February 1848.
94 HPSL-159, Huth & Co. to Sebastián Lasa (Havana). London, 28 September 1822.
95 HPJ-224, p. 411, November 1823.
96 HPJ-229B, May 1839.
97 Lamikiz, 'Social Capital, Networks', p. 26.
98 J. Pons-Pons, 'Spain: International Influence on the Domestic Insurance Market', in P. Borscheid and N. V. Haueter (eds), *World Insurance: the Evolution of a Global Risk Network* (Oxford: Oxford University Press, 2012), pp. 189–190.

99 See also HPINL-261; HPINL-262. As early as 1819, Huth insured cargoes for over £160,000.
100 Llorca-Jaña, 'The Marine Insurance Market' (2010).
101 HPSL-177, Huth to Elzaburu (Puerto Rico). London, 16 January 1847.
102 Llorca-Jaña, 'To be Waterproof or to be Soaked' (2009).
103 HPEL-6, Huth & Co. to Du Bois (London). London, 9 July 1830.
104 For some examples, see HPJ-224, June 1822, p. 79; HPJ-228, June 1835, p. 184; HPJ-229B, p. 957.
105 Interested in particular in saltpetre.
106 Supplier of raw wool.
107 Enthusiastic consumer of pepper and pimento.
108 Great consumer of rum.

4 The Liverpool branch, agents in Britain and the US connection

Huth & Co. was born in London, and the headquarters of the firm remained there until its dissolution in 1936. In its early days, the business was simple enough to operate without other branches in Britain. As we have learned, much of the company's focus was on Spain and subsequently Germany, and both countries channelled their trade with Britain mainly via London. Nonetheless, Frederick Huth understood that for the business to reach its full potential, agents in other British ports would be necessary.

At this point it would be useful to distinguish between the different types of Huth & Co.'s correspondents. A branch was obviously part of Huth & Co. London and acted as an extension of the firm, as was the case with (for example) Huth, Gruning & Co. Huth London would share in the ownership of the said branch, controlling at least 50 per cent of its capital, and would have direct control over its activities and daily operations. Profits and losses arising from the branch's activities would be shared between the partners at headquarters and associates of the satellite office. Exclusivity was an important factor: the branch worked for headquarters alone. Branch partners and (most) employees were employed at headquarters' discretion too.

The scenario was quite different for formal agents, however. Formal arrangements would be put in place to share profits (or losses) arising from specific operations generated by mutually-agreed business, or commission paid on selected operations, products or services. An agent could also be employed on a salaried basis, or on a combination of a fixed salary and variable commissions. Most of these arrangements lasted for considerable periods. Usually the agent charged a fee or commission to Huth & Co. (or the latter charged a fee or commission to the agent) but for specific branches of trade. Agents tended to be specialists and were allowed to have dealings with firms other than Huth & Co. Indeed, most of its agents also performed many other duties unconnected with its business, working for other merchant bankers or mercantile houses if they wished. Needless to say Huth & Co. did not exert any control over the operations of these sorts of agents. That said, exclusivity contracts could be arranged if appropriate.

There was another category of correspondent that was neither a branch nor an agent, but rather a 'friend' or business partner. Again, no formal contracts were signed by either party to share profits (or losses) on a permanent or regular basis, but both sides were held together by mutual loyalty and both benefited from joint projects undertaken on case-by-case basis. Commissions and fees were (or could be) charged, but an agreement had to be reached every time the parties collaborated. Correspondents were employed on a non-exclusive basis and performed a wide range of activities: they could be brokers, producers, consignees and consignors, to name but a few, as the occasion demanded.

Since Huth & Co.'s initial operations were purely mercantile (and mainly linked to primary products), the first agents were appointed in southern England only, where some of Britain's key ports were located and from which Huth could connect with both intra-European trades (including re-exports of colonial produce) and long-distance Atlantic trades. As explained in Chapter 1, Fox & Co. acted as Huth & Co.'s agents in Falmouth, as George Edwards & Co. and Hill & Sons did in Bristol. G. C. & R. W. Fox were also appointed in Falmouth and other key agents included James Olver in Plymouth[1] and Day & Phillips[2] in Portsmouth. They performed similar duties to those already outlined for Fox & Co., assisting Huth & Co. by providing maritime intelligence, the forwarding of letters and samples of products, and handling of returns received from places such as Spain, Germany or the River Plate. They were the eyes and ears of the London firm in these vitally important British ports, reporting on any information deemed useful for business.

As discussed in earlier chapters, as time went on Huth & Co. started to operate more intensively in a range of British manufactures, including textiles, railway iron and other iron products. The list of the company's British correspondents began to rise exponentially, as did the number of cities (and regions) in which they were located. By 1830 Huth & Co. had around 130 correspondents in England and over 25 in Scotland (Table 4.1). Ever more agents were needed to co-ordinate dealings with these friends, not only in the prosperous south but increasingly in the north, home to the manufacturing industries and the principal exit port for their products – Liverpool. Huth & Co. began to realize that a new northern branch might be needed to cater for the expanding volume of business linked to the region and other places beyond Europe. Liverpool and Manchester were no doubt the locations most under consideration, given their relevance as port and manufacturing hub respectively.

Huth & Co.'s agents in the textile districts

We have already established that the export of British manufactures was fundamental to Huth & Co.'s business in Latin America, Asia and continental Europe. This is not surprising and it was not unique to Huth & Co, however: textiles in particular were the backbone of British exports during this period. According to Davis, between 1814–1816 and 1844–1846, textiles accounted for between 68 per cent and 74 per cent of the UK's international exports of produce and manufactured items (i.e. excluding re-exports of colonial produce).[3] Very evidently, just one industry accounted for a significant proportion of British exports.

Table 4.1 Huth & Co.'s correspondents in Britain. A sample for selected cities, c.1812–1848

Country and Period	1812	1822	1830	1838-1839	1846-1848
England	*37*	*100*	*127*	*125*	*278*
London	11	43	29	23	94
Liverpool	1	10	14	17	29
Manchester	1	4	17	21	28
Sheffield	1	2	1	5	11
Leeds	0	4	11	7	7
Bristol	3	5	3	1	4
Birmingham	2	5	4	6	4
Halifax	0	0	3	6	4
Trowbridge	0	0	6	3	3
Plymouth	4	1	1	1	2
Falmouth	3	0	1	4	2
Portsmouth	6	1	2	1	1
Huddersfield	0	1	6	0	1
Scotland	*0*	*10*	*27*	*29*	*26*
Dundee	0	1	1	4	4
Edinburgh	0	3	1	4	1
Glasgow	0	2	22	17	15
Wales	*0*	*0*	*0*	*1*	*12*
Ireland	*0*	*1*	*3*	*5*	*12*
Dublin	0	1	2	1	1

Source: HPSL, HPEL, several volumes.

Somewhat predictably, then, from 1812 to 1850 Huth & Co. was supplied by literally hundreds of different textile manufacturers or textile merchants. Amongst the most important ones were: John Anderton (Cullingworth, Bradford);[4] Longworthy Brothers (Manchester);[5] Edward Rawson (Halifax); Rawson & Saltmarshe (Halifax);[6] Webster & Sons (Morley, near Leeds);[7] S. & J. Waterhouse (Halifax); Du Fay & Co. (Manchester); Burton & Son (Manchester); Merck & Co. (Manchester); Birley Hornby Kirk (Manchester); Stewart & Wilson (Glasgow); Guthrie & Co. (Glasgow); and Dugdale & Brother (Manchester). For the Chilean and Peruvian market alone Huth & Co. had over 70 different textile suppliers from all over northern Britain during the 1820s–1840s. Some of these also supplied other Latin American countries, but many others specialized in European or Asian outlets.

As the selective list above demonstrates, these key suppliers were at least 100 miles from London, and this made it challenging for Huth & Co. to co-ordinate orders, particularly considering all the details underlying the production of textiles destined for so many different markets targeting very specific local demands. Co-ordinating orders, packing, insurance, freights, shipments and payments from hundreds of suppliers was never to be an easy task, and it was almost impossible to accomplish it from London. Huth & Co. had necessarily to rely on agents permanently stationed in Liverpool and the key textile districts. For example, in Glasgow, it used the agency services of houses such as Laurie & Hamilton,[8] from whom it obtained its own textile consignments but who also co-ordinated consignments from other merchants such as Guthrie & Co.[9] and Buchanan & Young[10] of the same city. Another Glasgow agent was Stewart & Wilson, and in time it proved the most successful Scottish connection for Huth & Co.[11] Stewart & Wilson specialized in textiles, and supplied Huth & Co. for the markets of the Philippines, United States, Chile, Peru, Brazil, Venezuela and Mexico, amongst others.[12] Likewise, in Ireland, Huth & Co. employed the services of J. S. Ferguson[13] and Andrew Mulholland,[14] both of Belfast, to acquire Irish linens. Finally, in Manchester Huth used the services of commission houses such as Burt & Son for purchasing cottons. In the same city, 'German' commission houses such as Merck and Passavant-Lemonitz also bought cottons.

But the most important of all textile agents was H. H. Stansfeld. It is unclear from the extant evidence how and why Huth & Co. selected this man as their key agent in the textile districts. All we know is that Stansfeld had previously worked as a lone commission merchant in Leeds, where he had good family connections, and that some of these connections worked for Huth & Co. as middlemen in the raw wool trade.[15] It may well be that they recommended Stansfeld to Frederick Huth. In any case, with this appointment H. H. Stansfeld probably became the Englishman of most significance within the firm. Having opened branches in South America, which were dependant on textile supplies, it was imperative for the company to have a full-time agent working for them close to the textile-producing centres. Indeed, from the mid-1820s, Stansfeld was the main middleman used by Huth & Co. in Lancashire and Yorkshire to procure consignments for its correspondents in many quarters, but in particular for the establishments in the West Coast of South America. In time Stansfeld became one of the most knowledgeable experts in Britain on the textiles consumed in Latin America, and even some niche markets in continental Europe. In this sense, communication with the likes of Coit, and at a later date A. H. Kindermann and H. V. Ward in Valparaiso and Callao, was crucial for Stansfeld's endeavours to supply Huth Coit & Co. and later on Huth, Gruning & Co.[16]

But in contrast to the other agents used by Huth & Co. in places such as Falmouth or Bristol (who probably provided services for many other merchants apart from Huth & Co., or at least performed other business activities unconnected to it), the Stansfeld scenario was very different. H. H. Stansfeld was employed by Huth & Co. on an exclusive basis. That is, Stansfeld solely represented the company's interests in the textiles districts and he worked for no other merchant. Stansfeld's main tasks consisted of: finding new suppliers;[17] visiting established suppliers and advising them on the textile patterns needed for Latin America, Europe[18] or Asia; co-ordinating packing and shipping operations for Valparaiso, Callao, Buenos Aires, Mexico and other quarters, including close liaison with Huth & Co.'s agents in Liverpool; negotiating advances on consignments and forwarding correspondence; assessing the standing of merchants and producers;[19] and other diverse agency tasks. For these services, Stansfeld was furnished with a handsome commission.[20]

Stansfeld's range of operations was immense and not limited to Lancashire and Yorkshire, vast areas to cover in their own right. He spent most time in Leeds and Manchester (usually the former) but also made regular trips to Liverpool, Halifax, Glasgow, Ireland[21] and London when appropriate to hold face-to-face meetings with his bosses.[22] His brother George was also used by Huth & Co. as an agent in Leeds, but focused on the consignments of raw wool imported from Germany or Spain.[23]

Having a dedicated agent in the north had a massive positive impact on the work done at Huth & Co.'s London headquarters. Table 4.2 gives an idea of the speedy growth of Huth & Co.'s global networks during the 1820s and 1830s, when compared for example with the situation outlined in Table 1.4. Table 4.2 shows that nearly 1,000 correspondents were active during 1833 to 1835. This impressive number is matched by the spread of countries covered.

Table 4.2 Location of Huth & Co.'s correspondents. A sample for 1833–1835

Country	Number of Correspondents	Share	Country	Number of Correspondents	Share
North America	*33*	*3.4%*	*United Kingdom*	*244*	*25.1%*
Mexico	17	1.8%	England	216	22.2%
USA	16	1.6%	Northern Ireland	4	0.4%
			Scotland	22	2.3%
Caribbean	*13*	*1.3%*	Wales	2	0.2%
Cuba	10	1.0%			
Haiti	3	0.3%	*Europe*	*620*	*63.9%*
			Austria	8	0.8%
South America	*22*	*2.3%*	Belgium	9	0.9%
Argentina	4	0.4%	Croatia	1	0.1%
Brazil	7	0.7%	Czech Republic	12	1.2%
Chile	1	0.1%	Denmark	3	0.3%
Ecuador	1	0.1%	France	50	5.1%
Guyana	1	0.1%	Germany	224	23.1%
Uruguay	2	0.2%	Gibraltar	1	0.1%
Peru	4	0.4%	Ireland	2	0.2%
Venezuela	2	0.2%	Italy	6	0.6%
			Latvia	4	0.4%
Asia	*10*	*1.0%*	Netherlands	17	1.8%
China	2	0.2%	Norway	4	0.4%
India	7	0.7%	Poland	12	1.2%
Philippines	1	0.1%	Portugal	2	0.2%
			Spain	252	26.0%
Africa	*3*	*0.3%*	Sweden	1	0.1%
South Africa	3	0.3%	Switzerland	12	1.2%
Australia	*3*	*0.3%*	*No available*	*23*	*2.4%*
Australia	3	0.3%			
			Grand Total	*971*	*100%*

Source: HPSL-167; HPEL-14; and HPGL-90.

The diversity of Huth & Co.'s global networks meant that more partners needed to be taken on at headquarters in order to effectively lead operations. To that end in 1833, a fourth partner was taken into Huth & Co. of London:[24] he was Daniel Meinertzhagen, a German from Bremen who had valuable previous experience by working in Nantes and Bordeaux.[25] The Meinertzhagens were an old Bremen commercial family that been severely affected by the financial downturn of 1826. It is thought that the family were in some way connected to the Grunings, and when Daniel emigrated to London, he was taken on as a clerk by Huth & Co., apparently on the recommendation of Gruning and a former clerk, Jules Dufou.[26] Daniel's position was bolstered in 1832, just a few months before he became a partner, when he married one of Frederick Huth's daughters, thereby guaranteeing his entry not only to the firm, but also its first family.[27] He would remain an important figure at the company for many years, particularly following Frederick Huth's death.

The opening of the Liverpool branch

By the 1820s, most of the textiles intended for Chile, Peru and other Latin American quarters, as well as many important European ports, left Britain via Liverpool rather than London. This development was part of the meteoric rise of the northern city, which saw it become Britain's principal port during the nineteenth century,[28] a process further fostered by the completion of the Manchester–Liverpool railways in 1830. As noted above, effectively co-ordinating the many aspects of exporting goods (including but not limited to textiles) to the Americas, Europe and Asia from London was difficult, even though Huth & Co. had a full-time exclusive agent in the textile districts in the shape of Stansfeld. Huth & Co. had to rely on trusted Liverpool-based agents to handle crucial business information and valuable cargoes. It is striking that despite the huge level of business passing along the Mersey, Huth & Co. operated for many years – three decades, to be precise – without branches in northern England, instead employing forwarding agents in Liverpool until 1839, when a branch house was finally opened there.

During the 1810s–1830s, Huth & Co. was content to engage the services of other local agents, the first of which was Robert MacWilliam, a local general merchant, who was used during the 1810s and until the mid-1820s.[29] For reasons not made clear in the evidence (there is a gap in the business correspondence for the mid-1820s), Huth & Co. ended the commercial relationship with this house. At a later date Huth & Co. began to use instead the services of Castellain, Schaezler & Co.[30] and John Bibby & Co.[31] Judging from the extant sources, it is clear that before 1839 Huth & Co. of London did not want to become over-reliant on one agent in the Mersey area (i.e. Castellain, Schaezler & Co. or Robert MacWilliam before them), and preferred to engage at least two agents at a given time. Indeed, many of the duties performed by Castellain, Schaezler & Co. were simultaneously performed by Bibby & Co., even for the same markets.

These Liverpool houses performed many services for Huth & Co., including all the necessary arrangements needed to export to Latin America, Europe or Asia and import from there.[32] For example, they handled the firm's imports from the United States and many other countries, which involved sending to London samples of the produce received (e.g. raw cotton), as well as taking charge of unloading and storing the cargoes. They also: forwarded letters to Cuba, Mexico, the US, Chile Peru and other locations; reported on the market situation for a wide range of products; provided information on other merchants in Liverpool; negotiated the acceptance of bills of exchange; handled exports; and provided intelligence on ship arrivals and departures. Yet unlike Castellain, Schaezler & Co., Bibby & Co. was also entrusted with a service atypical for an agent in a port: the purchase of some manufactures – non-textiles, such as paints, glue, tar, mustard and iron[33] – for the houses in the Pacific and parties elsewhere. So exclusive was this service, in fact, that even after Huth & Co. opened the Liverpool branch in 1839, Huth London remained well connected to Bibby, in particular for trades with Asia.

For these various agency services, Robert MacWilliam, and later on Bibby & Co. and Castellain, Schaezler & Co., were paid a commission, and very often also benefited by getting new businesses from third parties linked to Huth. In turn, Huth & Co. also acted as Bibby & Co.'s agents in London, for which Huth & Co. was also paid a commission by John Bibby. As part of this reciprocal arrangement, Huth & Co. would sell London merchandise belonging to Bibby,[34] arbitrage prices between London and Liverpool for selected products or arrange for consignments of several products for Bibby & Co. to be sent to Asia, where Bibby was very well connected.[35]

Even though Bibby & Co. played an important role for Huth & Co., however, it is clear from the evidence available that by the late 1820s Castellain, Schaezler & Co. had become the London firm's preferred agent on the Mersey. This was probably due to Adolphus Frederick Schaezler's close links with Brentano & Urbieta, Frederick Huth's former employers.[36] Yet when in 1834 Castellain, Schaezler & Co. went into liquidation (following irreconcilable differences between the main partners), with Adolphus Schaezler and Alfred Castellain each going their separate ways,[37] Huth & Co. decided to use the agency services of Castellain and his new partners, rather than those of Schaezler.

This turned out to be a critical decision for Huth & Co.: in 1839 the company opened its Liverpool branch,[38] with Alfred Castellain as an active partner. The circular sent to fellow merchants and bankers at that time read:

> We ... have this day established a branch of our firm at Liverpool, into which we receive as partners, Mr Augustus Hermann Kindermann,[39] who has been for many years a managing partner of our establishments in South America, and Mr Alfred Castellain, whom his previous avocations have rendered familiar with the principal branches of the Liverpool trade.[40]

It was envisaged that the Liverpool branch would assume responsibility for many tasks, not least taking over all the agency services hitherto provided freelance operatives, but perhaps its most crucial role would be to become the main point of contact with Huth & Co.'s agents all over the world, and with the branches in Chile and Peru in particular.[41] This explains why Augustus Kindermann was brought from the West Coast of South America to Liverpool, despite being their key man in Valparaiso until 1839.[42] But before returning to England, Kindermann was asked to visit the United States to further familiarize himself with Huth & Co.'s dealings in that quarter.

Huth & Co. of Liverpool was also entrusted with managing several products, including indigo imports, cotton imports from the US (see below) and the sales of wool from Spain, Russia (specifically from Odessa, now in the Ukraine) and Australia. The Liverpool and London houses shared essential information about market intelligence in diverse products such as wheat, copper, flour, cotton and sugar, thus effectively arbitraging prices. Samples of products imported via either port were circulated between the two houses to see which one would get the best price.[43] Similarly, information on the standing of certain firms within each other's market was frequently shared.[44]

And so, after 30 years of operating in London, Huth & Co. finally had another branch in Britain. In fact many other London-based merchant bankers also opened branches in Liverpool, particularly during the 1830s:[45] Schroder & Co., for example, opened a Liverpool house in exactly the same year as Huth, and Brown Shipley & Co., and James Finlay & Co. had a presence there.[46] Having an office on the banks of the Mersey undoubtedly strengthened Huth & Co., although a proportion of the company's profits had to be divided between more partners than before. But perhaps more important than this financial aspect – after all, total profits were expected to increase for all involved – by incorporating Castellain as a new partner, Huth & Co. revealed many of its business secrets to them. Indeed, of the thousand business letters I went through, there is one sent by Huth & Co. London to Huth & Co. Liverpool soon after the latter's opening that could not be more revealing.[47] In any case, it seems it was worth taking the risk.

Although in 1839 the Liverpool branch was tightly controlled from London, five years later the Mersey office had 'developed in some ways as an independent entity'.[48] For instance, Huth & Co. of Liverpool engaged with clients for whom the London houses did not keep either correspondence or even accounts. Thus many drafts drawn on Huth Liverpool were drawn by parties unconnected to Huth London, and the Liverpool branch used agents not engaged by headquarters.[49] In effect, it had started to operate as an agent itself.

A sour note: the dismissal of Stansfeld

It was perhaps unavoidable that, having taken on the activities previously performed by Castellain, Schaezler & Co. and Bibby & Co., the Liverpool branch would also start to eat into some of the services provided by H. H. Stansfeld, and tensions built between the two. For instance, the Liverpool branch thought that Stansfeld was not active enough in securing consignments of cotton, and suggested to headquarters change its supplier for this product: 'Mr Stansfeld has tried in vain for a number of years to procure this article [prints].'[50] Worried about damaging relations with Stansfeld, the London house expressed some concerns, to which the Liverpool branch replied: 'Mr Stansfeld can lose nothing by the proposed agreement, for he has declared repeatedly that he cannot procure consignments of [cotton] prints, much less without advances, & as we on our part frequently told him that we could not do without this article, it follows as a matter of course that we must endeavour to procure them through other channels.'[51] Eventually the Liverpool branch's position prevailed. Having been based in Liverpool for so many years, Castellain *et al.* had valuable contacts in nearby Manchester and other textile districts, many of whom wanted to enter into business with Huth & Co., by now one of the most prominent British merchant bankers.

Unsurprisingly Stansfeld's answer did not take long to arrive: 'With regard to … your London house having formed an arrangement with another house here, whose name is not even mentioned, to procure consignments of [cotton] prints, I consider it quite inconsistent both in letter & spirit with the arrangement subsisting between us. I have written [to] your Mr Huth to this effect.'[52] Stansfeld felt that his position with Huth & Co. was being eroded. And although it was never part of the contract with Stansfeld that only he could procure textiles for Huth & Co., Stansfeld thought that the Manchester suppliers were encroaching on his exclusive domain.

But disputes between Huth & Co. and Stansfeld were not new, which perhaps explains why Huth London complied with the plan proposed by their Liverpool house. Huth & Co. of London had become increasingly unhappy with some of Stansfeld's services from as early as the late 1820s. Indeed, Frederick Huth frequently wrote to him in strong terms, complaining about his poor performance in getting consignments of some products for Valparaiso, Callao and other quarters.[53] At times, Huth & Co. of London was also unhappy with the lack of fluent and timely communication from Stansfeld, as can be seen in this extract:

> We must regret to continue deprived of your favours, we confess that this protracted silence on your part surprises us, for if some important reason prevents you from attending to our interests at Manchester at a moment which we deem particularly favourable for shipments to the Pacific we should at least have expected to be informed of the circumstance, and might in this case have written direct, to remind some of our friends of their promises, and stimulate others. The ships which leave Liverpool at this season of the year, arrive out in the spring when business is briskest and our houses [in Chile and Peru] will be greatly disappointed.[54]

Another, more recurrent, cause of dissatisfaction with Stansfeld was the fact that this agent did not want to live permanently in Manchester (or at least in Liverpool), as Huth & Co. would have preferred: 'The circumstance of your not having a fixed place of call at Manchester leaves always a doubt on our mind whether our correspondence to you is punctually received by you, which however is such an important point that we should wish to have all doubts removed on the subject.'[55] The point was made clearer in a subsequent letter: 'It is with regret that I perceive from your letter to our establishments [in the West Coast] that you do not intend to remain at Manchester, but to return to Leeds and only propose to make a stay at Manchester of a few months every year.'[56]

But Stansfeld was originally from Leeds and wanted to remain there most of the year, travelling only occasionally to Manchester, despite Frederick Huth's personal and persistent complaints: 'Feeling so fully convinced, and no argument to the contrary could shake my opinion, that a permanent residence of our [textile] agent at Manchester is absolutely necessary for bringing our business to that extent to which it is capable, and which after so many years patience and toil we have a right to request, I should be sorry indeed, if you should persist in returning to Leeds, instead of remaining at Manchester ... You will therefore, I trust, give the matter your best consideration.'[57] In a later letter, Huth added that 'I had a right to suppose that if you would not make Manchester your permanent residence, you would at least stay at Liverpool'.[58] Although Leeds was amongst the most influential wool manufacturing centres in Britain, cottons were now by far the most important branch of British textile exports,[59] and this explains Huth's interest in having Stansfeld stationed in Manchester rather than Yorkshire.

But despite the threats, Stansfeld did not feel under pressure, further adding that Huth's remarks were 'stronger than the case deserves'. What is puzzling is why it took Huth & Co. so long to get a new agent in either Lancashire or Yorkshire. Was there no one else already working from Manchester who could serve Huth's purposes, and whom they could fully trust? Apparently not: Stansfeld would surely have been fired otherwise. Indeed, three years later, in 1836, Huth & Co. was again complaining about its agent's performance: 'The sum total of consignments from Lancashire since the beginning of the year is we regret to observe extremely small, and it will require your utmost exertions to make the year at all remunerating to yourself and us; we hope you will make the best of the present favourable prospects, otherwise we foresee we shall be quite thrown into the shade by our neighbours.'[60]

Difficulties between the parties escalated to the point where Stansfeld made some consignments on his own account to Huth & Co.'s establishments in Chile and Peru without authorization, clearly in violation of business ethics and breaking previous agreements between the parties. Loyalty was the most important quality an agent could possess, and Stansfeld had clearly abandoned it. Frederick Huth felt betrayed, and the personal letter sent to Stansfeld eloquently illustrates the point:

> I have not been able until now to find the time for answering your private letter ... In doing so now I can only express my request that you should have ever thought of making shipments on your own account to our establishments [in the West Coast]. Whatever your inducements for so doing may have been, we have certainly never given any encouragement for it. On the contrary, we have always disauthorized any business from our agents, because in the first instance we know they cannot ship goods in fair competition with manufacturers, and secondly because it destroys the proper position &

connexion between Principals & Agents and leads to dissatisfaction, which in prudence should always be avoided ...[61]

Relations quickly deteriorated thereafter and mutual business declined, although it was only in 1841 that Huth & Co. eventually stopped using Stansfeld as an agent in Lancashire and Yorkshire altogether. Perhaps the only reason why Stansfeld was not immediately sacked was that his relations with Huth & Co. had lasted for over 15 years and he had an unpaid debt with it arising from funds advanced to him during that time.[62] Being unable to recover these monies, which amounted to £500, Frederick Huth decided to waive them, and eventually concluded Stansfeld's agency in a gentlemanly way, as is shown in the following extract, which confirms in writing the events of a personal meeting in London:

> Having mutually agreed at our interview this morning on the cessation of your agency in Lancashire and Yorkshire ... we beg to state in writing the terms upon which this arrangement has been concluded: 1) That your said agency ceases with the 30th of June next evening, but that you will be entitled to your agency commission on all consignments shipped before or up to the same date and what may come under the arrangement at present existing; 2) That in consideration of the long and satisfactory connection that has existed between us, and also that of the unfavourable result of part of the consignments which you were induced to make to our establishments on your own account, although contrary to our wishes, we agree to credit you with the sum of five hundred pounds.[63]

The £500 was not paid in cash but instead credited to Stansfeld's account – to his surprise, as we know he owed Huth & Co. roughly the same sum of money. In broad terms, then, this arrangement was at once a surrender of old debts and compensation for years of service.

Huth & Co.'s US connection

In his PhD thesis, Freedman maintained that the Liverpool branch was opened with the purpose of dealing with Huth & Co.'s Anglo-American interests, in particular to 'overcome previous disadvantages in competing for consignments of American produce [i.e. mainly cotton] and also to engage more widely in transactions with America securities'.[64] Although I disagree with this assertion, believing instead that the Liverpool branch was mainly opened to foster business with South America, this does not mean that the Mersey house was not concerned with the Anglo-American side of Huth & Co.'s operations: the firm had had dealings with the US well before 1839.

Indeed, from the early 1820s Huth & Co. of London began to cultivate American correspondents (such as Lucchesi & Co. of New York and Perit & Cabot of Philadelphia, who had connections in China), although these were not important for the overall business.[65] Before the 1830s, cotton exports from the US remained depressed in value given the low prices on international markets for this primary product. Likewise, American securities were not yet being exported to Europe in great quantities, although they would be later on. There was, therefore, ostensibly little else of interest for Huth & Co. in America. Yet by the early 1830s the number of the firm's correspondents there began to increase slowly, although it is true that its involvement in the US still remained relatively minor when compared to activities elsewhere. Nonetheless, the company developed important relationships with new correspondents, such as Charles Karthaus[66] of New York and F. W. Brune & Son of Baltimore.

It was only really from the mid-1830s that the US connection became stronger for Huth & Co. This was perhaps part of a broader phenomenon, namely an intensification of the economic relations between the US and Britain. Indeed, cotton exports from the US increased significantly during this period, as did British exports to America. British cotton imports from the US reached an annual average of 328 million lbs in 1835–1839, more than double the comparable figure of 159 million lbs for 1825–1829.[67] Conversely, if in the 1820s exports from the UK to the US averaged £5.8m per annum, in the next decade the average annual exports were £7.9m, and would remain at a similar level during the 1840s (in a context of falling export prices) before recovering in the next two decades, as is shown in Figure 4.1.

As part of this increasing Anglo-American trade, from around 1835–1836 Huth & Co. made a significant impact on the market in raw cotton imports from the US,[68] as well as in tobacco. They started to export textiles and iron rails to the US more extensively,[69] and became influential in these latter branches of trade. Due to this, the expansion of Huth & Co.'s business with the US merits attention in this monograph, despite the useful discussion of this topic by Joseph Robert Freedman over four decades ago.[70]

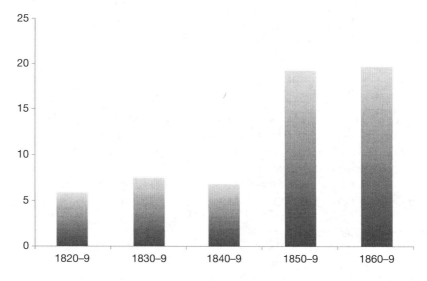

Figure 4.1 UK exports to the US, 1820s–1860s. Declared value of the produce of the UK, annual averages (£M).
Source: Own elaboration from BPP, several volumes.

By entering with such force into America, Huth & Co. joined the group of the so-called 'American Houses'. These were British enterprises with strong and enduring connections in the US: the likes of Baring Brothers and W. J. Brown & Co. top the list of these, but other houses such as George Wildes & Co., Timothy Wiggin & Co., Thomas Wilson & Co. (the famous 'Three Ws'), Morrison Cryder & Co., Lizardi & Co. and later Rothschild & Sons, amongst others, were also important. It seemed that these 'older' American houses were not able to cope on their own with the growing Anglo-American trade and capital flows, and new incumbents were able to enter these branches of trade without major barriers.

Huth & Co.'s main correspondents in the US at this time of great expansion were located in New York, Philadelphia, Boston, New Bedford, Baltimore, New Orleans and Virginia. As first noted in Chapter 2, their principal contact in New York was Jonathan Goodhue of Goodhue & Co., a wealthy commission merchant, who was in charge of disposing of consignments of British manufactures, as well as of obtaining cotton and tobacco consignments, for which extensive credit was provided.[71] Under Huth & Co.'s instructions, Goodhue & Co also entered into the securities market. They were appointed Huth & Co.'s first agents in the US, to the surprise of many, since they were also active correspondents of Baring Brothers, and the Barings more often than not preferred to have exclusivity deals with their most important contacts.[72] We should note at this point that Huth & Co. never had a sole general agent in the US supervising the entire Anglo-American relations, as Baring Brothers did in the person of Thomas Wren Ward. In any case, it was Goodhue who enjoyed the largest credit facilities with Huth, at least before the 1837 crisis (although by the early 1840s their importance diminished by some way). Other houses enjoying open credit with Huth & Co. in New York were Meyer Hupeden (a German house) and Nevins Townsend, a firm of bankers introduced and recommended to Huth by Jonathan Goodhue himself.[73]

The other key contact in the US was, as we have discussed above, John W. Perit of Philadelphia (who in turn was associated with Goodhue & Co. through his brother Peletiah Perit, a partner at the New York firm).[74] Perit also became Huth & Co.'s agent in America, fulfilling this role for c.1837–1843. He received a wide range of British goods from Huth & Co., including iron nails, rails and skins, and was also entrusted with securing consignments of cotton.[75] Perit became involved too in the trades between Huth & Co.'s houses in the Pacific, the firm's friends in Asia and other connections in the US, and entered the securities market as well. Yet even though Perit was an important agent, unlike his counterparts in other locations he did not receive a monthly salary from Huth & Co., but was instead paid via an attractive commission on all business he managed to sign up for it.[76]

From New Orleans Huth & Co. imported cotton and tobacco directly, relying on Fehrman as tobacco brokers, and for cotton supplies mainly on Merle & Co., Adams & Whitall (New Orleans),[77] Vogelsang & Co. (New Orleans) and Frey & Co. The case of Adams & Whitall is particularly interesting because once the Liverpool branch was opened, this New Orleans house was appointed as Huth & Co.'s agent in the southern states of the US on the recommendation of Samuel Jaudon,[78] then the London agent for the Bank of the United States (henceforth

92 The Liverpool branch

BUS, of Pennsylvania).[79] Nonetheless, the unexpected occurred: Perit discovered that Adams & Whitall were also agents for the rival firm of Humphreys & Biddle, and this was unacceptable to Huth & Co., who decided to cut all commercial dealings with this company immediately. Following the end of this agency's services, Huth & Co. decided to operate without formal agents in the south, but W. W. Frazier was in charge of monitoring its credit for cotton orders.

In all, Huth & Co.'s acceptances on American accounts reached on average £298,000 per annum between 1835 and 1850. Amongst those authorized to draw against Huth & Co. were mainly Goodhue & Co. (New York), John W. Perit (Philadelphia), the Bank of the United States,[80] Clason & Ules (New Orleans, in particular from 1840),[81] and Nevins Townsend & Co. (New York), but also a long list of less important companies such as Meyer Hupeden & Co. (New York), Manice Gould & Co., McCurdy Aldrich & Co., Cleveland & Lewis and Downes & Rogers. This credit went to fund the consignment of American commodities and British manufactures, but also of securities.

After roughly two years of fruitful relations with the US (c.1835–1836), however, there came an exogenous shock. 1837 was marked by a severe financial crisis linked to Anglo-American concerns. Indeed, credit was scarce from London, leading to the failure of several planters, speculators and many others connected to American cotton exports, which in turn led to the failure of several London 'American houses' who were heavily compromised in this branch of trade. Most famously, this 1837 crisis will be remembered for the resounding failure of the hitherto mighty 'three Ws'. As a consequence, during most of this year Huth & Co. decided to cut back their activities arising from the Anglo-American connection, and even made discreet enquiries about the financial health of their agents in New York,[82] once described by Huth themselves as their 'most intimate correspondents'.[83] Unsurprisingly Huth's American expansion had come to a stop by mid-1837.

The crisis was deemed to be over by the end of 1837, however, and Huth & Co. resumed business as usual in the US, this time with less competition than before given some competitors' failures, although newer firms did enter the market too (e.g. Reid Irving & Co., Palmer McKillop & Co., Magniac Smith & Co.).[84] 1838 and 1839 were then particularly brisk for Huth's Anglo-American set-up. The firm achieved great success in promoting greatly expanded shipments of raw cotton from the US to the Liverpool branch, in particular after the abandonment of the BUS's operations.[85] The prominent Bevan & Humphreys from Philadelphia played a crucial role in this: they had formerly channelled cotton to the UK via Humphreys & Biddle, but were now supported by Perit.[86]

Likewise, Huth & Co.'s involvements in American securities surpassed all previous levels during this intense period. Indeed, judging from the evidence available, by the late 1830s and early 1840s, the bulk of its involvements with the US was centred around the movement of securities. The situation would not last, however: the failures of several American states or companies linked to Huth & Co.'s securities business (as discussed in Chapter 3) brought the connection to a standstill, at least as far as the movement of capital was concerned. In early 1840

Huth & Co. reported that 'there is at this moment a total stagnation in our market for all American securities'.[87] In 1841 the crisis deepened when the BUS closed its doors, and during that year and early 1842, nine states of the Union ceased paying interest due on their stocks,[88] thus destroying American credit not only in Britain but in the rest of Europe too. The European market for American stocks was paralyzed. Of course, this situation also eroded the movement of goods, and Anglo-American economic relations continued to deteriorate until late 1843.[89]

In Chapter 3 it was mentioned that many of Huth & Co.'s clients lost some of their investments in American securities. As discussed, they had pursued these investments upon Huth & Co.'s recommendation, and in general its judgement was based on information received from Perit. Frederick Huth duly held Perit partly responsible for his clients' losses arising from this episode, so much so that Perit's agency is thought to have ended by 1843, thereby leaving Huth & Co. without any other general resident agent of their own in the US other than Goodhue & Co., whose relative importance was declining anyway.[90]

In fact, one could argue that by the mid-1840s Huth & Co. had no formal general agent in the US at all – perhaps an illustration of Huth & Co.'s declining interest in American business – and the firm began to rely on direct correspondence with several houses in the US, in some cases for many years. Among these friends, the most important American correspondent during the mid-1840s was J. E. Thayer & Brothers of Boston, to whom uncovered credit was even granted, and who replaced Goodhue & Co. They remained essential correspondents (if not the most intimate) in the US until the end of the period covered by this book, and even persuaded Huth & Co. to enter into joint-account operations in securities' operations during 1849–1850,[91] which was unusual for the company given the higher than normal risks involved.

Within Huth & Co., Daniel Meinertzhagen, who had been incorporated as a partner in the early 1830s but who had worked for the company for some years prior, was assigned the key role of the firm's specialist in the American side of the business. Daniel thus travelled to the US regularly, reporting back on a variety of issues. While the primary role of these trips was to foster business, he also stepped in when emergencies arose. In 1843, for instance, he was sent to Florida to assist Huth & Co.'s agent in that state (Mr Mercer), who had been appointed to manage debt-recovery in that part of the country.[92] Alfred Castellain of Huth & Co.'s Liverpool branch was also sent to the US on occasion, such as when in late 1843 he visited the country to in an attempt to revive Huth & Co.'s commercial operations there.

Overall, it can be concluded that Huth's Anglo-American business was a story of ups and downs, as it was for most London Anglo-American houses of the period. This was a consequence of the instability of the American and British economies, both of which were beset by a series of exogenous shocks. There was, for instance, the financial crisis of 1836–1837, the long American depression of 1841–1843, a financial crisis in Britain in 1845 and yet another one in 1847. Thus, for Huth & Co. in particular, the peak of its involvements in the US was reached in the late 1830s ($c.$1837–1840, but specifically in 1839), when the firm engaged

94 The Liverpool branch

enthusiastically both in trade and the movement of securities. The early 1840s were particularly poor (c.1841–1843), coinciding with a great decline in the securities' business, but by the mid-1840s the US regained some of the importance it had for the company in the late 1830s. Although in absolute terms the situation was never comparable to that in the late 1830s, in relative terms it certainly decreased in importance in favour of other quarters,[93] and 'the backbone of Huth's American activities was their function as an acceptance house'.[94]

Figure 4.2 accounts for this development, and it is perhaps worth noting that from the early 1840s Huth & Co.'s credit on American account was mainly linked to British imports of raw cottons (but some timber, flour and wheat too)[95] and to a lesser extent to exports of manufactures (e.g. textiles and iron rails).[96] Of all 'American' acceptances in 1844 (worth over half a million pounds sterling), none was linked to securities and 'thus were former practices sharply reversed'.[97]

In 1847 Anglo-American connections took another significant blow when a new financial crisis erupted.[98] But yet again, once the crisis was over the American economy expanded quickly, this time further aided by the discovery of gold in California. With that development, Huth & Co. began to increase its American engagements, as part of which the company resumed its interest in American securities. And indeed Huth & Co.'s acceptances on American account in 1850 were the highest of the company since the glorious heights of 1839, following a distinct improvement in the London market for US securities. It was not until 1848 that American stocks found their way into European markets again.

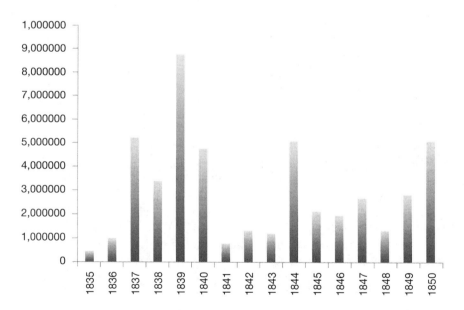

Figure 4.2 Huth & Co.'s acceptances on American account (£), 1835–1850 (London and Liverpool branches)
Source: Own elaboration from Freedman, *A London Merchant Banker*, appendix.

Notes

1. For some examples, see OHC. James Olver to Frederick Huth (London). Plymouth, 4 January, 14 January 1812 and 29 February 1812.
2. When the partnership between Day & Phillips was dissolved in late 1813, Frederick Huth started to rely on George Phillips as his agent in Portsmouth. See correspondence in HPSL-155.
3. R. Davis, *The Industrial Revolution and British Overseas Trade* (Leicester: Leicester University Press, 1979), p. 15.
4. John Anderton was both wool-stapler and wool manufacturer. J. Hodgson, *Textiles Manufacture, and Other Industries in Keighley* (Keighley: A. Hey, 1879), p. 169; P. Hudson, *The West Riding Wool Textile Industry: a Catalogue of Business Records form the Sixteenth to the Twenty Century* (Edington: Pasold Research Fund Ltd., 1975), pp. 362 and 368. Anderton supplied Huth with woollens and worsteds (e.g. cubicas, bonanza, serges, bombazetts and lastings) for Chile, Peru, Mexico, China and other markets. For some illustrative examples, see JAP, Volume 104. Huth & Co. to John Anderton (Cullingworth). Liverpool, 16 May 1845 and 12 December 1848. See also HPEL-7, Huth & Co. to John Anderton (Cullingworth-Bradford). London, 22 April 1831. It is worth noting that John Anderton even entered the business of tea imports from China under the Huth & Co. umbrella from the late 1840s.
5. Cotton manufacturers, spinners, printers and dyers. They were specialists in prints, muslins, nankeen, Florentins, drills, calicoes and domestics. They supplied markets in South America, Mexico, Cuba, amongst other outlets. For a representative example of normal dealings between the parts, see HPEL-26. Huth & Co. to Huth & Co. (London). Liverpool, 15 May 1839.
6. Important suppliers of wool baizes, carpet, ponchos, star-cloth and other products from Huth & Co.'s very early days, both for the Spanish and the Latin American markets. See for example, HPEL-1, Huth & Co. to Rawson & Saltmarshe (Halifax). London, 27 October 1827; HPEL-2, Huth & Co. to Rawson & Saltmarshe (Halifax). London, 11 June 1828. One of the main partners in this enterprise was Arthur Saltmarshe.
7. Suppliers of upper quality woollens and 'middling cloth', including products such as blue cloth, black cloth, carpets, cassimeres, toilanetts and striped nankeens, amongst others. This became important from the late 1820s. See HPEL-3. Huth & Co. to J. Webster & Sons (Morley, near Leeds). London, 20 April 1829; HPEL-7, Huth & Co. to Webster & Son. (Morley, near Leeds). London, 3 March 1831.
8. Once defined by Huth & Co. as 'our agents in your city [Glasgow] ... through whose intervention and approval we receive all our consignments'. HPEL-11, Huth & Co. to Buchanan & Young (Glasgow). London, 8 January 1833.
9. UGSC, MS Gen 533/2, Guthrie & Co. to Huth & Co. (London). Glasgow, 9 April 1832. Guthrie supplied goods such as madapolams and prints. For an illustrative example, see HPEL-11. Huth & Co. to Guthrie & Co. (Glasgow). London, 26 January 1833.
10. They were suppliers of merino shawls, muslins and other products. See for instance, HPEL-11. Huth & Co. to Buchanan & Young (Glasgow). London, 25 January 1833.
11. Originally, David Stewart and John Wilson were hired by Huth & Co. as agents in connection with South America only, as is seen in this letter: Stewart & Wilson 'will in future be the agents for our houses in the 'Pacific" in Scotland'. HPEL-13. Huth & Co. to H. H. Stansfeld (Leeds). London, 14 January 1834. Yet the remit of their operations expanded quickly after performing so well for Huth & Co., and more responsibilities accorded them.
12. UGSC. MS Gen 531/14. Stewart and Wilson to Huth & Co. (London). Glasgow, 25 April and 4 November 1836; 19 May 1836; 26 November 1836; 23 December 1836.

96 The Liverpool branch

13 See for instance, HPEL-8. Huth & Co. to J. S. Ferguson (Belfast). London, 15 August 1831, 27 September 1831.
14 For some examples, see HPEL-53. Huth & Co. to Andrew Mulholland (Belfast). London, 3 April 1847; HPEL-65. Huth & Co. to Mulholland & Son (Belfast). London, 1 and 19 July 1850.
15 For example, D. J. & W. Stansfeld were sundry tradesmen of Huth & Co. at least from the early 1820s (probably from earlier on). HPJ-224.
16 For some examples of the nature of the correspondence sustained with Stansfeld, see HPEL-9, Huth & Co. to H. H. Stansfeld (Manchester). London, 9 February 1829; HPEL-5, Huth & Co. to H. H. Stansfeld (Liverpool). London, 15 January 1830; HPEL-6, Huth & Co. to H. H. Stansfeld (Leeds). London, 13 July 1830.
17 The size of textile manufacturers during the period covered by this book was rather small, so that Huth & Co. permanently requested new suppliers, and when that happened, Stansfeld was praised, as in this case: 'It gives us pleasure to observe that you have secured the connexion of Messrs. Philips Wood & Co.' HPEL-11, Huth & Co. to H. H. Stansfeld (Manchester). London, 4 March 1833.
18 He was, for example, active in getting consignments to markets such as Germany. See HPEL-6. Huth & Co. to H. H. Stansfeld (Leeds). London, 13 July 1830.
19 For example, Huth & Co. would send this sort of request to Stansfeld: 'We shall feel obliged by you making the necessary enquiries and informing us as correctly as possible of the result respecting the credibility of Messrs. Taylor, Weston & Co.' HPEL-5, Huth & Co. to H. H. Stansfeld (Manchester). London, 20 February 1830.
20 For a representative visit of H. H. Stansfeld to a manufacturer sending textiles to South America, see DDX 1156/3, Feilden & Co. to Huth & Co. (London). Blackburn, 29 August 1838.
21 For reports on a visit to Belfast, see HPEL-11, Huth & Co. to H. H. Stansfeld (Manchester). London, 28 January 1833.
22 Frederick Huth and H. H. Stansfeld met regularly in either Liverpool or London. HPEL-3, Huth & Co. to H. H. Stansfeld (Manchester). London, 20 May 1829.
23 HPEL-3, Huth & Co. to H. H. Stansfeld (Leeds). London, 31 March 1829. Another brother of H. H. Stansfeld was James Stansfeld, an attorney based in Halifax.
24 The other three were Frederick Huth, John Frederick Gruning, and Charles Frederick Huth. There were more partners of the company, but they were part of Huth & Co. of Liverpool or Huth Gruning & Co. of the West Coast, rather than Huth & Co. of London.
25 In 1820 Daniel Meinertzhagen was sent by his father to Nantes to work as a clerk, at only 18 years of age. He was subsequently sent to Bordeaux in 1822 on similar terms. In Nantes he made friends with Jules Dufou, who in 1822 was working for Huth & Co. in London, after being sent there by Dufou's father. Meinertzhagen, *A Bremen Family*, pp. 250–252.
26 According to the biographer of Frederick Huth, Daniel arrived in London in 1826. Murray, *Home from the Hill*, pp. ix and 136. Apparently the information was wrongly taken from Meinertzhagen, *A Bremen Family*, p. 252 and Meinertzhagen, *Diary of a Black Sheep*, pp. 8–9. Nonetheless, I gathered evidence of Daniel being employed in Huth & Co. from earlier on, that is, as of July 1823. HPJ-224, p. 316.
27 Freedman, *A London Merchant Banker*, p. 17.
28 See in particular G. J. Milne, *Trade and Traders in Mid-Victorian Liverpool: Mercantile Business and the Making of a World Port* (Liverpool: Liverpool University Press, 2000).
29 Huth & Co. used the services of Robert MacWilliam from at least 1817 until at least 1824. For some examples see HPIL/R/38. Entries in Account Current, 1 August 1817; HPGL-183. Huth & Co. to Robert MacWilliam (Liverpool). London, 22 Feb 1823 and 22 July 1823; HPJ-224.

The Liverpool branch

30 For some examples, see HPEL-5, Huth & Co. to Castellain, Schaezler & Co. (Liverpool). London, 7 January 1830. According to a report produced by Baring Brothers, before joining forces with Adolphus Frederick Schaezler, Alfred Castellain was formerly in partnership with a Mr De Berckern, trading under the firm De Berckern Castellain & Co., which stopped operating in 1819. This firm was 'very much connected with a house in the Netherlands'. It was after that that Castellain formed a new concern in conjunction with Mr Schaezler, who was clerk with a Mr J. J. Romen (a French merchant). Thus, according to the same report, Castellain, Schaezler & Co.'s 'connection in Italy and France are said to be very good'. HC 16/1, Undated, c.1830s. These French and Italian contacts were undoubtedly offered to Huth & Co. after the agency contract was settled.

31 Bibby & Co. started to perform as Huth & Co.'s agents from at least 1830. For some examples see HPEL-6. Huth & Co. to John Bibby & Co. (Liverpool). London, 30 November 1830; HPEL-11. Huth & Co. to John Bibby & Co. (Liverpool). London, 12 and 17 January 1833.

32 For some examples see HPSL-183, Huth & Co. to Robert MacWilliam (Liverpool). London, 22 February & 22 July 1823; HPEL-5, Huth & Co. to Castellain, Schaezler & Co. (Liverpool). London, 7 and 27 January 1830; HPEL-6, Huth & Co. to Castellain, Schaezler & Co. (Liverpool). London, 9 September 1830.

33 HPEL-11, Huth & Co. to Bibby & Co. (Liverpool). London, 12 and 17 January 1833.

34 For instance, Huth & Co. would dispose in London of Bibby's merchandise (e.g. gum Arabic, knife handles, tea and silk) sent from Asia to Bibby & Co. of Liverpool. HPEL-21. Huth & Co. to John Bibby & Co. (Liverpool). London, 11 September 1838.

35 Bibby & Co. frequently asked Huth & Co. to buy cochineal on their behalf and send it to Asia directly from London. HPEL-31. Huth & Co. to John Bibby & Co. (Liverpool). London, 11 January 1841. Clearly London was a more relevant port than Liverpool in the trades with Asia.

36 BT 1/1/2, Circular by Huth & Co. London, 1 January 1839. Castellain and Schaezler started their business in 1819. See HC 16/1, Undated, c.1830s.

37 BT 1/1/2, Circular by Schaezler & Co. Liverpool, 1 January 1834. Later on, one of the members of Brentano's family was made partner in Schaezler's house at Liverpool, which was now styled Schaezler & Brentano.

38 The share of Huth London on Huth Liverpool (50 per cent) was divided between the London partners as followed: Frederick Huth, 40 per cent; J. F. Gruning, 20 per cent; Daniel Meinertzhagen, 20 per cent; and C. F. Huth, 20 per cent. HPJ-230 and HPJ-231.

39 It is interesting to note that as Alfred Castellain and Daniel Meinertzhagen had done before, Augustus Kindermann also married one of Frederick Huth's daughters. Freedman, *A London Merchant Banker*, p. 66. Lacking wealthy members of his own family to take as partners (the usual practice at that time), Frederick Huth's alternative strategy was to marry his daughters to partners from outside his family and business or partners-to-be then working as employees of Huth & Co.

40 BT 1/1/2, Circular by Huth & Co. London, 1 January 1839. Perhaps helping Huth's decision to select Castellain as their agents is the fact that Frederick Huth was known for being risk-averse, while Baring Brothers was of the opinion that after the failure of De Berckern Castellain & Co., Alfred Castellain in particular 'would not involve himself in any risk', something surely known to Frederick Huth after so many years dealing with Castellain, Schaezler & Co. HC 16/1, Undated, c.1830s. At this point it is interesting to note that according to Freedman (*A London Merchant Banker*, p. 66) neither Castellain nor Kindermann held stock in the Liverpool branch, which directly contradicts this circular and the evidence available in the journals. Huth London had a 50 per cent holding in Huth Liverpool, and within the 50% share of Huth Liverpool that did not belong to Huth London, the main partners were Castellain and Kindermann.

98 *The Liverpool branch*

41 Freedman (*A London Merchant Banker*), suggested that the Liverpool branch was opened mainly to promote trade with the United States. Judging from the extant business correspondence, although the Liverpool branch was in charge of this branch of trade (apart from the West Coast and other concerns), the US market was never as important as Huth's dealings with Valparaiso and Callao, for example. If any one trade was most important than others, it was the trade with Chile, Peru and other Latin American quarters.
42 A. H. Kindermann was the main partner of Huth's South American branches after Coit's departure, and therefore Kindermann was their legal representative in Chile and Peru. Indeed, in legal disputes with local merchants in Chile, Kindermann acted as the legal representative of Huth, Gruning & Co. See for example, ANCH, VJP-318-4. Valparaiso, March–April 1831.
43 HPEL-31. Huth & Co. to Huth & Co. (Liverpool). London, 12 January 1841.
44 HPEL-26. Huth & Co. to Huth & Co. (London). Liverpool, 6 June 1839.
45 Wake, *Kleinwort Benson*, p. 48.
46 Roberts, *Schroders*, p. 32; Chapman, *The Rise*, p. 42; Chapman, 'The International Houses', p. 35.
47 HPEL-22, Huth & Co. to Huth & Co. (Liverpool). London, 10 January 1839.
48 Freedman, *A London Merchant Banker*, p. 220.
49 Freedman, *A London Merchant Banker*, pp. 273–274.
50 HPEL-26, Huth & Co. to Huth & Co. (London). Liverpool, 1 April 1839.
51 HPEL-26, Huth & Co. to Huth & Co. (London). Liverpool, 6 April 1839.
52 HPEL-26. H. H. Stansfeld to Huth & Co. (Liverpool). Manchester, 18 April 1839. The unnamed new agent for this product was MacFarlane & Fielding of Manchester. HPEL-23. Huth & Co. to Huth & Co. (Liverpool). London, 8 April 1839.
53 See for example, HPEL-3, Huth & Co. to H. H. Stansfeld (Leeds). London, 11 April 1830. Here Stansfeld was sent the following message: Huth & Co. expected Stansfeld's 'next trip [to Yorkshire] as productive of real business, as the former ones have generally been of promises' only. See also HPEL-6, Huth & Co. to H. H. Stansfeld (Leeds). London, 5 August 1830; HPEL-13, Huth & Co. to H. H. Stansfeld (Leeds). London, 20 January 1834.
54 HPEL-6, Huth & Co. to H. H. Stansfeld (Leeds). London, 29 July 1830. In the same vein, see also HPEL-3, Huth & Co. to H. H. Stansfeld (Leeds). London, 11 April 1829.
55 HPEL-11, Huth & Co. to H. H. Stansfeld (Leeds). London, 31 January 1833.
56 HPEL-11, Huth & Co. to H. H. Stansfeld (Leeds). London, 11 March 1833.
57 HPEL-11, Frederick Huth to H. H. Stansfeld (Leeds). London, 11 March 1833.
58 HPEL-11, Frederick Huth to H. H. Stansfeld (Leeds). London, 27 March 1833.
59 According to Davis (*The Industrial Revolution*, p. 15), cottons accounted for 49 per cent of all British exports (of all British produce, textiles and non-textiles), while the comparable share for woollen goods was only 15 per cent for this period.
60 HPEL-16, Huth & Co. to H. H. Stansfeld (Leeds). London, 3 August 1836.
61 HPEL-17, Frederick Huth to H. H. Stansfeld (Leeds). London, 8 June 1837. Frederick Huth would surely agree with a Barings' agent conclusion that 'an agent unless he is a very clever man and stands high does an injury to any house'. Quoted in Hidy, *The House of Baring*, p. 99.
62 HPEL-31, Huth & Co. to Huth & Co. (Liverpool). London, 27 January 1841.
63 HPEL-31, Frederick Huth to H. H. Stansfeld (Leeds). London, 3 March 1841.
64 Freedman, *A London Merchant Banker*, pp. 64–65.
65 As late as 1835, Huth's outstanding balance due on American accounts was just 3.5 per cent of the total outstanding for the whole business. Freedman, *A London Merchant Banker*, pp. 16–18.
66 See, for example, operations recorded in HPJ-224.

67 B. R. Mitchell, *British Historical Statistics* (Cambridge: Cambridge University Press, 1989), p. 334.
68 It is fair to mention that raw cotton was the main product exported by the USA during this period; it could account for over 50 per cent of the total value of exports. In turn, cotton prices started to increase, as well as the volume of trade, together with the increasing mechanization of cotton weaving in Britain. Freedman 1968, pp. 2–3.
69 For instance, Huth & Co. financed the shipment of railway iron to the Eastern Railroad Company in Boston, an important project at that time. HPEL-23. Huth & Co. to Eastern Railroad Company (Boston). London, 19 April 1839.
70 Freedman, *A London Merchant Banker*.
71 To give an idea of the importance of this correspondent, Goodhue & Co. enjoyed an open credit of £20,000 per month with Huth & Co. HPEL-16. Huth & Co. to Goodhue & Co. (New York). London, 6 May 1836; HPEL-18. Huth & Co. to Goodhue & Co. (New York). London, 14 November 1837; HPEL-22, Huth & Co. to Huth & Co. (Liverpool). London, 10 January 1839. During the early 1840s the importance of Goodhue declined for Huth, but later on, following a deterioration of the relations between Huth and Perit, Goodhue & Co. reclaimed its former significance.
72 Hidy, *The House of Baring*, p. 187. Explaining this connection, it is worth mentioning that Jonathan Goodhue had been a former partner of Thomas Wren Ward, Baring Brothers' famous agent in the US. Freedman, *A London Merchant Banker*, p. 21.
73 Goodhue & Co. was very active in recommending to Huth several firms that could draw against Huth & Co. because they were regarded by Goodhue as trustworthy.
74 Freedman, *A London Merchant Banker*, pp. 34–35.
75 HPEL-21 Huth & Co. to John W. Perit (Philadelphia). London, 19 August and 17 November 1838; HPEL-23. Huth & Co. to John W. Perit (Philadelphia). London, 19 April 1839.
76 In contrast, for instance, Baring Brothers' agent in the US enjoyed an annual minimum allowance of £2,000, apart from his commissions. Hidy 1949, p. 98.
77 HPEL-23, Huth & Co. to John W. Perit (Philadelphia). London, 6 April 1839.
78 According to Freedman, Huth placed too much reliance on Jaudon, 'which proved unfortunate both for their clients and for themselves', given the poor fate of so many American stocks, adventures in which Huth entered upon Jaudon's recommendation. Freedman, *A London Merchant Banker*, p. 370.
79 Adams & Whitall were allowed a 1 per cent commission on mutual business, but were held liable for 50 per cent of any losses arising from these operations. Freedman, *A London Merchant Banker*, p. 84.
80 Before the Bank of the United States (BUS) decided to open an agency in London (led by Samuel Jaudon), it could be stated that Huth & Co. was the 'most favoured English connection' this American bank had in Britain. Huth & Co. and the BUS entered several times in association to dispose of American securities in European soil, as well as to support raw cotton exports from the US to Britain. In turn, the BUS controlled the Merchant Bank of New Orleans, another key correspondent of Huth in the southern states. For some examples, see Freedman, *A London Merchant Banker*, pp. 51, 72–74.
81 This house, for instance, was granted a £5,000 credit to facilitate the purchase and shipment of raw cotton from New Orleans to Liverpool. HPEL-31. Huth & Co. to Clason & Ules (New Orlenas). London, 3 February 1841. According to Freedman (*A London Merchant Banker*, p. 370), Clason & Ules possessed the most active of Huth's American accounts, at least as far as acceptances are concerned.
82 HPEL-16 Huth & Co. to Thomas Russell (New York). London, 22 April 1837.
83 HPEL-22, Huth & Co. to Huth & Co. (Liverpool). London, 4 January 1839; HPEL-23, Huth & Co. to J. W. Perit (Philadelphia). London, 6 April 1839.
84 Hidy, *The House of Baring*, pp. 237–239.
85 Freedman, *A London Merchant Banker*, pp. 115–116.
86 HPEL-22, Huth & Co. to Huth & Co. (Liverpool). London, 10 January 1839.

87 HPEL-27. Huth & Co. to J. & G. Pattison (New York). London, 8 February 1840.
88 W. B. Smith, *Economic Aspects of the Second Bank of the United States* (Cambridge: Harvard University Press, 1953), pp. 260–263.
89 To give an idea of the impact this crisis had on trade, US exports to the world in 1843 were just two-thirds of the value reached in 1840. D. C. North, *The Economic Growth of the United States, 1790-1860* (New Jersey: Prentice Hall, 1961), p. 233.
90 Freedman, *A London Merchant Banker*, p. 165.
91 Freedman, *A London Merchant Banker*, pp. 219, 371.
92 Freedman, *A London Merchant Banker*, p. 207.
93 Freedman, *A London Merchant Banker*, pp. 352–355.
94 Freedman, *A London Merchant Banker*, p. 360.
95 For some examples, see HPEL-54. Huth & Co. to Brune & Son (Baltimore). London, 19 July 1847. It is worth noting that Mr Brune was one of the Directors of the Merchants' Bank; HPEL-54. Huth & Co. to Eslava Murrell & Co. (Mobile). London, 19 July 1847.
96 For instance, Huth & Co. participated in the export of iron rails to the Hudson River Railroad Company.
97 Freedman, *A London Merchant Banker*, p. 222. Around this time, British investors' trust in American securities had not recovered. See for instance HPEL-41. Huth & Co. to J. E. Thayer & Brothers (Boston). London, 3 June 1844.
98 To give an idea of the real extent of this crisis, important Anglo-American houses such as Reid Irving & Co. failed during this period.

5 A global enterprise of trade and lending

The editors of *Business History Review* recently reminded us that 'important subjects are waiting for investigation'. Among them, they highlighted globalization, further adding that 'business historians must make the case that entrepreneurs and firms, not governments or markets, have driven and shaped globalization'.[1] Partly in response to this challenge, this chapter concentrates on the diversification strategies followed by Huth & Co., and compares them to the path followed by other competitors. It is argued here that before 1850 most London merchant bankers were typically cautious and did not diversify the remit of their operations either geographically or in the range of products they traded during this period. Huth & Co. ploughed their own furrow, however, and in the process established an impressive global network of trade and lending.

It has already been mentioned that multinational traders had to make a number of key decision, principally: on whether to go global or to concentrate on one or a few markets only; on whether to focus on a small number of products or as many goods as possible; on whether to trade on commission and/or own account (or joint account); on whether to carry on trading only, or to combine trading with the financing of trade, or just concentrate on financing trade and other financial activities thus abandoning purely mercantile activities; if they were financing international trade, on whether to finance the trade of primary products only (and how many) or to finance trade in manufactures as well; on whether to execute all (or most) or just a few of the most common duties performed by merchant bankers of the time. Finally, they had to consider whether they should deal with a select group of correspondents or with as many businessmen as possible. This chapter examines Huth & Co.'s response to each of these challenges.

Trading *and* financing trade or financing trade only?

Although published 30 years ago, Chapman's *The Rise of Merchant Banking* remains the most authoritative work on this financial activity in Britain. It is clear from the book that merchant banking had purely mercantile origins. In addition, one of Chapman's core propositions is that during the nineteenth century, apart from their financial activities, a majority of merchant bankers 'maintained their roles as general merchants as long as possible'.[2] Therefore, the distinction between international merchant houses and merchant bankers became clear only as of the last quarter of the nineteenth century.[3]

And indeed Huth & Co. conformed to this pattern, as the reader may have anticipated from the preceding chapters. Likewise, Baring Brothers remained general merchants until the late nineteenth century, when the mercantile side of the business was gradually given up.[4] Following Casson, these merchant bankers that remained trading could also be defined as 'hybrid' trading companies.[5] But this is not to say that all merchant bankers followed the same route. The case of Rothschild, for example, proves otherwise. During the 1810s–1820s, Rothschild became much less interested in commodity trade, eventually abandoning trade for finance at an early stage, and even repudiating their early career as merchants.[6] Others who abandoned trade for finance during the 1830s were Wiggin and Morrison, Peabody during the 1830s–1840s[7] and Hambro & Son.[8] Likewise, during the 1830s the House of Brown also decided to concentrate on 'monied business', gradually abandoning trade.[9]

In contrast, although Huth & Co. (like Baring Brothers and many others) performed many financial activities, they never abandoned trade before 1850, and the mercantile side of the business remained a main concern during this period. This is interesting to note because, according to Jones, in the transition from being merchants to being merchant bankers, for most merchant bankers the commission received for accepting bills 'replaced trading as their main income source'.[10] It has also been argued that acceptance of bills came to be regarded as the most important function of the major Anglo-American merchant bankers of the early nineteenth century.[11] But in the case of Huth & Co., pure trading activities were given the same priority as financial transactions. (This is not surprising given that Frederick Huth received his original training as a classic merchant.) Indeed, after settling in London in 1809 and resuming business there as a general commission merchant, that was a role he happily performed for the totality of the period covered by this book. There was no dishonour in doing so, as other aristocratic merchant bankers of the period believed (i.e. thus concentrating on financial matters only and completing neglecting the mercantile side of the business).

Geographical coverage

Another of Chapman's core theses is that during the 1820s–1860s 'almost all the merchant banks focused their activities on one or two countries with which they had a longstanding connection', and that it was only in the latter decades of the nineteenth century that merchant banks were both diversifying geographically and increasing the range of products they traded in (or financed). By 1914, though, many merchant bankers had significantly expanded the remit of their operations, covering wider geographical areas than their original connections in the early decades of the nineteenth century had allowed.[12] This has been accepted by many leading scholars on the subject: Geoff Jones, for example, has also written that the diversification of trading companies was also a late phenomenon, associated with the post 1870 epoch,[13] and this line of argument is in line with the thinking of economic historians who place the start of globalization at c.1870.

A global enterprise of trade and lending 103

But what does the evidence tell us? Merchant bankers that conformed to this pattern of very limited geographical diversification before the 1860s were most famously Rothschild[14] as well as Brandt[15] and Ralli,[16] all of which remained mainly European in their concerns. In the same vein, Gibbs & Sons kept their focus on Spain and South America for the whole of the first half of the nineteenth century,[17] while Brown Shipley,[18] Swire,[19] Cropper & Benson[20] and Rathbone remained concentrated on Anglo-American trade and finance.[21] Before the late 1810s, Frederick Huth conformed to this strategy too for a while. Table 1.1 lists Huth's correspondents for 1812–1813, and it gives us a clear sense of his early geographical concentration in a few countries. Indeed, by 1813 trade with Spain was by far the main strand of the business. Apart from the English connection, which was obviously strong too, Huth had little interest elsewhere.

But as outlined in Chapter 3, this early geographical concentration on Spain changed dramatically after the Napoleonic Wars, when Frederick Huth incorporated a new partner and Huth & Co. started a gradual process of geographical diversification that ended in a truly global enterprise. For example, the German connection soon became very important, as did the connection with other European countries such as France, Norway,[22] Poland and the Netherlands. Likewise, by the early 1820s many new countries in the Americas were also incorporated into Huth & Co.'s trade networks, Mexico, the US, Peru, Chile, Ecuador, Brazil, Haiti, Jamaica, Puerto Rico and St Thomas among them.

Thereafter, during the rest of the 1820s, Huth & Co. was quickly multiplying its network of contacts, and would grow them further in the years to come. The transition from being an international business to a truly global one was well underway, and as part of this process the firm opened its South American branches, as noted earlier. Huth & Co. also decided to appoint confidential agents strategically elsewhere in the world, many of whom performed similar functions to those of a branch house, thus further enhancing and supporting the global character of the firm. Within the Americas, amongst the most important ones were Drusina & Co. in Mexico, Drake & Co. in Cuba, Zimmerman Frazier & Co. at both Buenos Aires and Montevideo, Goodhue & Co. (New York) and John Perit (Philadelphia) in the United States.[23]

But Huth had many other contacts in Latin America too. In Venezuela, merchants in La Guaira and Caracas proved very useful, in particular for the supply of cocoa, tobacco and coffee to Germany and Spain. In La Guaira, among the main suppliers were Sojo-Larralde, Simon Gaspari, Molero Brothers, Gonell Brothers and Esteban Escobar. Many of these houses drew against Huth for cocoa sent to Germany and Spain.[24] In Caracas, Zaldarriaga-Sojo was a long-term connection, while Domenzain was also active in consigning Huth & Co.'s friends in Spain with cocoa, coffee and indigo, while also drawing against Huth & Co. for these cargoes.[25]

Brazil had become important too. Stockmeyer (Rio de Janeiro) consigned sugar and coffee to Huth & Co. in London.[26] Another important connection was Vogeler (Bahia), a house linked to Huth & Co.'s friends in the US. The London firm also funded sugar exports from Brazil to continental Europe: for example, Prevost of

Ghent received sugar from a house in Bahia, which had opened credit with Huth,[27] as did Rupe of Amsterdam.[28] Brazil played a crucial role in intra-regional trade too: Brazilian sugar was regularly sent to Huth & Co.'s houses in Chile and Peru,[29] while hides were dispatched to the US. Finally, in order to supply Mexico and other Latin American quarters, many British textiles were sent to Brazil via Huth & Co.

In continental Europe, Huth & Co. appointed agents in key strategic cities, and perhaps the most important one was De Bruyn & Sons of Amsterdam. De Bruyn was a major sugar trader, and a great deal of the sugar which passed through Huth & Co.'s hands ended up with this merchant. Through Huth & Co., De Bruyn bought sugar from London and Liverpool, or directly from Manila and Havana.[30] Other agents included: Hoffman & Fils (Rotterdam), regularly supplied with iron from Cardiff and Newport in sizeable operations;[31] Hoffmann & Dorrepaal, general merchants receiving a wide range of goods (Amsterdam); Rupe & Son (Amsterdam), another key consumer of sugar;[32] B. R. Scheibler & Co. (Antwerp), an important consumer of cotton forwarded by Huth from Liverpool; Ed. Scheibler & Co. (Antwerp) another important consumer of cotton and sugar;[33] and R. Scheibler & Co. (Ghent), who received sugar from Havana and Brazil via Huth, as well as cotton, also in sizeable volumes.[34] The list goes on – Meier (Bremen), Merck (Hamburg), Mutzenbecher (Hamburg), Ross-Vidal (Hamburg), Dumas of Paris and Tutein of Copenhagen – and other contacts were located in cities as disparate as Wuppertal and St Petersburg. Agents were also appointed in Asia, as we shall see later on.

Huth & Co.'s policy was to link each branch or agency with the others, as well as with the London headquarters and the Liverpool branch, thereby enhancing the trading potential in every locale and creating a multiplying effect in its network of contacts and business opportunities. Indeed, although Table 1.1 and Table 5.1 are illustrative of the company's geographical diversification they do not account for other interesting ramifications. First, Huth & Co.'s dealings with these branches and agencies were not limited to bilateral trades between the countries in which these correspondents resided and Britain. Huth & Co. was very active in promoting trades that never even touched British ports, as we saw in Chapters 2 and 3.

Some other illustrative cases are useful. For example, when Germany was becoming increasingly important for Huth & Co., many merchants there (thanks to the merchant banker's intermediation) cultivated important bilateral trades with Spain, where Huth & Co. was already strong. Later on, Huth & Co. was the essential link between many merchants in Spain, Germany and France with their counterparts in the Americas who were arranging consignments of diverse products in both directions. Likewise, the firm's houses in South America established strong connections with other parts of the world, even beyond Europe. For instance, Chilean copper was sent to the US in exchange for domestics (i.e. a coarse cotton manufacture); Chinese tea and silks were exchanged for silver and copper; and Chilean wheat and flour were sent to Australia. Huth & Co. also supported direct trade between China and the US and between the US and the Caribbean.

A global enterprise of trade and lending 105

Table 5.1 Location of Huth & Co.'s correspondents. A sample for 1846–1848

Country	Number of Correspondents	Share	Country	Number of Correspondents	Share
North America	77	4.2%	United Kingdom	324	17.5%
Mexico	27	1.5%	England	278	15.0%
USA	50	2.7%	Northern Ireland	8	0.4%
			Scotland	26	1.4%
Caribbean	60	3.2%	Wales	12	0.6%
Cuba	44	2.4%			
Haiti	1	0.1%	Europe	1,216	65.7%
Jamaica	2	0.1%	Austria	19	1.0%
Puerto Rico	6	0.3%	Belgium	73	3.9%
Saint Thomas	3	0.2%	Croatia	1	0.1%
Saint Croix	4	0.2%	Czech Republic	6	0.3%
			Denmark	5	0.3%
South America	63	3.4%	Finland	5	0.3%
Argentina	7	0.4%	France	73	3.9%
Bolivia	1	0.1%	Germany	528	28.5%
Brazil	22	1.2%	Gibraltar	1	0.1%
Chile	6	0.3%	Ireland	4	0.2%
Colombia	1	0.1%	Italy	19	1.0%
Guyana	1	0.1%	Latvia	5	0.3%
Peru	10	0.5%	Netherlands	61	3.3%
Uruguay	2	0.1%	Norway	7	0.4%
Venezuela	13	0.7%	Poland	38	2.1%
			Portugal	4	0.2%
Asia	60	3.2%	Russia	11	0.6%
China	12	0.6%	Spain	226	12.2%
India	40	2.2%	Sweden	88	4.8%
Philippines	4	0.2%	Switzerland	40	2.2%
Singapore	1	0.1%	Ukraine	2	0.1%
Sri Lanka	1	0.1%			
Turkey	2	0.1%	No available	39	2.1%
Africa	5	0.3%	Australia	6	0.3%
Sierra Leone	1	0.1%			
South Africa	4	0.2%	Grand Total	1,850	100.0%

Source: HPSL-177; HPSL-178; HPEL-49; HPEL-50; HPGL-122; HPGL-123.

But this complex system was firmly directed from London. Table 5.1 gives an idea of the continuing growth of Huth & Co.'s London global networks during the 1820s–1840s, and contains a sample of nearly 2,000 correspondents for 1846–1848. The number of countries covered – 52 – is truly impressive. England aside, Spain, Germany, France and the Netherlands – not to mention Austria, Belgium, Italy, Sweden, Cuba, Mexico, the US, Brazil, China, India and Australia – had also became key strategic locations for Huth & Co.

Indeed beyond Europe and the Americas, another interesting feature of Huth & Co.'s geographical expansion during the 1830s–1840s was trade with Asia, with

China, the Philippines and India in particular entering its radar. Among the main correspondents in Asia was Edmond Bibby & Co. of Bombay, a contact of John Bibby & Co. of Liverpool (one of Huth & Co.'s agents on the Mersey, analyzed in Chapter 4). Bibby's associated house in Canton, Bibby, Adam & Co., proved another fruitful connection. But Bibby was not Huth & Co.'s sole link in Asia: the American house of Russell Sturgis (Canton and Manila) was another vital associate.[35] (Perit was one of the junior partners of this Asian connection, which explains the good relations established with them.) From as early as 1832, Huth & Co. traded with Russell Sturgis of Canton and Manila. For example, some of Huth & Co.'s friends in Hamburg, such as Merck and Ewald, consigned woollens to the Chinese market.[36] Likewise, Russell Sturgis of Canton regularly supplied silks and tea,[37] while the Manila branch sent sugar and indigo. The Manila connection was not new to Huth & Co. (they had previous contacts with Spanish houses there), but what *was* new was the volume of trade: Manila sugar started to pass through Huth & Co.'s supply chain as never before. In exchange, Huth & Co. became Russell Sturgis' link to the supply of British and German textiles, mainly via Muir & Laurie, Stewart & Wilson and Stewart and McAulay & Co. (all of Glasgow), Stocks & Sons of Manchester and Merck of Hamburg.[38]

In China, Huth & Co. added new important connections during the 1840s such as Nye Parking & Co. (strong in teas and silk),[39] Nye Gideon & Co. and F. S. Hathaway. Another new addition in Canton was Kennedy McGregor, which consigned vast cargoes of tea to Huth. Within Asia, correspondence with India also increased substantially from the early 1840s. In Calcutta, for instance, Lackersteen & Brothers became very important, consigning raw silk (from Bengal and China), hides, castor oil, indigo, turmeric, corahs (i.e. Indian silks) and many other products.[40]

We can only but conclude, judging from the available studies on other merchant bankers of the period, that Huth & Co.'s reach and expertise at this time was unique. Houses such as Rothschild, Brandt and Swire retained a very narrow geographical focus, and the House of Brown had branches or agencies in Britain and the United States only.[41] Likewise, Ralli, with headquarters in London and a branch in Manchester, opened a branch outside Britain (in India) only during the second half of the century,[42] while Schroder of London just had one branch in Hamburg and another in Liverpool before 1850. One competitor, Gibbs, did open branches in Chile and Peru, but before 1850 they remained firmly focussed on Britain, South America and Spain. Given the poor state of transport and communications during *c.*1810–1850 (when information flows were slow, unreliable and expensive), going global was a laborious and risky option for any merchant banker, but Huth & Co. embraced it.

That said, it is true that, as far as geographical diversification is concerned, Baring Brothers came close to Huth & Co. before 1850 and were not as restrained about this issue as Rothschild *et al*. The Barings' principal focus until the late 1840s was in North America, some quarters of Latin America and the Far East, though,[43] and although Barings could be considered an international house, only Huth should be taken as a truly global one before 1850, despite Austin's claims that 'Barings' operations had terrific geographical spread'.[44] While this statement is true if compared to the likes of Rothschild & Sons, it is not the case for Huth & Co. according to the evidence provided by Austin (who did not have Huth & Co.'s data to hand). Chapman himself believed that both Rothschild and Baring retained 'diversified financial and commodity business, within a specific geographical area'.[45]

Product trading coverage

Huth & Co.'s geographical diversification was impressive and greater than that of most other merchant bankers of their generation before 1850, but so was the range of products in which they participated. The company was expertly and regularly dealing with an impressive variety of different goods (mostly on commission), including commodities traded extensively worldwide such as wheat, sugar (both raw and refined), tobacco (and cigars), rum, coffee, tea, cocoa, indigo, cochineal, timber, pepper, cinnamon, pimento, jerked beef, wine, silver, quicksilver, gold, copper, cottons, woollens, silks, pig iron, iron railways, earthenware, tin plates, lead, firewood, hides, tallow, raw silk, cotton and wool. I have discussed some of these trades in earlier chapters.

But the company also traded rice, logwood, butter, herring, hats, Chinese ink, toys, nutmeg, Brazilian wood, Nicaraguan wood, furniture, flax, saltpetre, indigo, salt armoniac, ponies, flutes, pianos (and piano covers), candles and paper, as well as exotic goods such as gum Arabic, ebony, horse hair, castor oil, salt volatile, mahogany, feathers, annatto, gum anime, boric acid, oxalic acid, sarsaparilla, tortoise shell, pongees, knife handles, deer and buffalo horns, elephant teeth, billiard balls, walnuts, 'natural curiosities' (e.g. insects) and chinchilla skins. Huth & Co. eventually specialized in many of these products, both in sourcing supplies and arranging their final destinations. Again, in this way it was unique among its peers during the 1810s–1840s, when it was much more usual for multinational merchants and merchant bankers to concentrate on just a small range of commodities – and sometimes on one alone.[46] For example, Baring Brothers and Rothschild & Sons 'focused on two or three sectors of world trade in which they had come to specialise'.[47] In a similar vein, during the first half of the nineteenth century Schroders' main areas of trade were grain, cotton and sugar,[48] while Ralli specialized in textiles and grains.[49] Finally, Brown focussed most of their energies on the cotton trade.

Huth & Co.'s product diversification process was fast. As shown in Chapter 1, during his first years in London Frederick Huth consigned to Spain a wide range of British products, such as cottons, woollens, silks, cutlery, pottery and wheat, while he also re-exported non-British products such as tallow, hides, cinnamon, pepper, tobacco, Indian cottons, rum and sugar. He also engaged in British imports of wool and wine. Of these products, wool shipments became Huth's first important area of expertise in international trade, but many other products would also become significant for his company: by the early 1820s, for instance, in addition to wool Huth & Co. was strong in British imports of sugar and tobacco,[50] hides and tallow, coffee and cocoa, timber, grains and, increasingly, silver. Huth

& Co. was a prime mover too in the re-export side of British trade and dispatched colonial produce to Europe and the Americas, gaining greater expertise in products such as pepper and cinnamon in the process. As the firm eventually expanded into China, it added tea and silk to their main branches of trade and expertise. From Canton, for example, Bibby and Russell Sturgis regularly consigned large amounts of silks and tea to Huth & Co. in London or Liverpool.[51]

Perhaps more interestingly, Huth & Co. also took the difficult decision to combine trade in primary products with trade in manufactures. This was challenging, because to deal in manufactures merchants needed to have an in-depth knowledge of the demands of an item in its final destination, given the heterogeneity of manufactured goods and the uniqueness of local demands. Other merchants, such as Brown and Ralli, were engaged in trades of primary products and manufactures too, but the narrow geographical scope of their business meant it was relatively easy to master the few demands they faced. The task facing Huth & Co. was evidently much larger and thus the role played by the company's confidential agents and branches was crucial, since they provided detailed information on the sort of products needed in their respective markets. As we learned in Chapter 4, for instance, Huth & Co. became active in the textile trade. The company had also begun trading in earthenware and iron products. All of these British manufactures were exported to a wide range of international correspondents, where local demands were very specific (e.g. a product widely consumed in Mexico might not be popular in China). Having branches in Latin America and many confidential agents elsewhere meant that Huth & Co. gained a profound knowledge of several markets and their detailed local demand for British manufactures. Huth, Gruning & Co., for instance, specialized in the import of textiles, becoming one of the main traders on the West Coast of South America. In Mexico, Drusina & Co., who were supplied mainly by Huth & Co., also became expert textile traders, as did many other merchants linked to Huth in other parts of Latin American, Europe and Asia.

The connection to Drusina & Co. is a good illustration of Huth & Co.'s product diversification philosophy. Huth & Co. sent them a wide range of products, including widely traded goods such as quicksilver, woollens and silks, but also pianos, flutes and telescopes. Textiles were the most popular import, though, with a sizeable number of British manufacturers consigning to Drusina, many of which drew against Huth & Co. This represented effectively an extension of credit not only to these manufacturers but also to Drusina.[52] The Drusinas remitted mainly with silver,[53] and were also happy to obtain consignments for Huth & Co.'s connections in Europe (e.g. logwood for Antwerp).[54]

The nature of products whose trade was financed

Apart from trading, another key function performed by most merchant bankers was that of advancing. Indeed, although Huth & Co. continued trading goods for the totality of the period covered by this article, by the 1830s its transition from merchant to merchant banker was over. What did that transition comprise of? In broad strokes, Huth & Co. was very active in advancing to a wide range of merchants in a number of markets and products. If, according to Chapman, London merchant bankers 'preferred to allow credit to agents permanently resident in Britain' because they thought that the legal process of recovering debts abroad was too expensive,[55] then the geographical dispersion of Huth & Co.'s advances also seems to have been unique.

For example, Huth & Co. provided liberal advances to British textile manufacturers consigning to Chile, Peru, Mexico, North America, Europe, Asia and elsewhere, well before goods were sold. But the company also gave advances to merchants in virtually any country consigning to Britain or any other market linked to its connections. Huth & Co. issued letters of credit to a wide range of merchants in all continents, by means of which these merchants could draw against it from anywhere for consignments to Huth & Co. itself or to its friends elsewhere. By 1850 the capital of the firm had increased to £500,000, and thus it certainly had the expanded means by which to provide advances, and in any case, if the bills did not mature, no cash was disbursed.

At this point it is interesting to note that, in marked contrast to Huth & Co., most merchant bankers of the period advanced monies for a handful of goods only. In particular, for these financiers 'the heart of the business was the finance of international trade in raw materials', rather than manufactures.[56] For Schroder of London, for example, Roberts found that in the acceptances book of the company, 'there is hardly any mention of shipments of manufactured goods'.[57] Likewise, the House of Brown, the leading banking house in Anglo-American trade during the period covered by this book, during the 1810s–1820s were in the habit of advancing for both British exports to America and for American exports to Britain. However, during the mid-1830s the Browns decided to reduce and eventually eliminate their participation in the consignments of British manufactures, since the business was considered too risky on account of slow sales in the United States, but in particular because advances were usually involved.[58] Thus, the Browns concentrated their advances on the consignment of cotton from the US to Britain. In the same vein, Rathbone concentrated their advances on raw cotton up to the 1840s.[59] In contrast, Baring Brothers extended advances in most commodities traded between the US and Britain,[60] coming close to Huth & Co. in this respect.

According to Chapman, the earliest development of British merchant banking, as far as acceptances is concerned, was in connection with US trade, to the extent that by 1837 it is believed that something like half of all British acceptances were for Anglo-American trade, and for a long time the United States remained the principal recipient of British commercial credits.[61] This may have been the situation for most players, but again Huth & Co. did not follow the general trend followed by most merchant bankers of the period. Its acceptances for trade before 1835 were negligible,[62] and moreover its merchant banking activities did not emerge out of bilateral trade with the United States. Instead, as discussed, the firm's acceptances for trades linked to Latin America, Spain and Germany were far more important from its early days, and they were therefore linked to a wider range of products.

Furthermore, and more importantly, one of the main implications of Huth & Co.'s impressive global networks and the diversity of products in which it was involved is that, although we knew that many merchant bankers in London financed British foreign trade,[63] Huth & Co.'s interests went beyond financing British imports, re-exports and exports. As we have noted above, perhaps more crucially Huth & Co. was not only financing many trades which never touched on British ports and which reached an impressive array of different locations on all continents, but also issuing credit for a wider range of products than any other contemporary merchant banker.

The impressive diversification that Huth & Co. displayed in its approach to credit helped to finance world trade and complemented its geographical and product diversification processes. For example, many houses in Venezuela drew against the company for produce sent to Germany and Spain from South America. In Caracas, to mention one typical case, Domenzain was active in consigning cocoa, coffee and indigo to Huth & Co.'s friends in Spain, while also drawing against Huth & Co. for these cargoes, as so many merchants in the Americas did. Indeed, the London firm also financed sugar exports from Brazil to continental Europe. For example, Prevost of Ghent received sugar from a house in Bahia, which had opened credit with the London firm, as did Rupe of Amsterdam. In the same vein, Zimmerman Frazier shipped hides to Bremen from the River Plate, and drew against Huth & Co. Finally, Chinese tea exports to South America and North America also received advances from Huth & Co. This is quite different to the picture provided by Chapman, who – drawing on evidence obtained from Anglo-American houses such as Baring Brothers and Brown Shipley – concluded that merchant bankers specialized 'in the finance of particular branches of trade' only.[64]

The number of correspondents kept by merchant bankers

Regarding the number of correspondents merchant bankers cultivated, according to the extant evidence on other merchant bankers for the period $c.1810–1850$, Huth & Co. was again unique; it had as many correspondents as trust and reputation allowed, regardless of these correspondents' capital or lineage. In sharp contrast, other merchant bankers of the period preferred to focus on a portfolio of select correspondents only. According to Chapman, 'both Barings and Rothschilds conducted a highly restrained, highly selective kind of business, an elitism that appeared to be supported by their aristocratic lifestyles and aloofness from lesser families', adding that they preferred to keep simplicity and safety combined with a large turnover.[65] Indeed, before 1850, Baring Brothers 'granted credits almost exclusively to established, wealthy merchants whose accounts were little trouble to administer'.[66] In turn, Barings asked their correspondents for exclusivity in their dealings, a policy which doubtless constrained the number of people who wanted to deal with them.[67]

Having arisen from humble origins of its founder, Huth & Co., by contrast, was very friendly to men from these 'lesser' families if they were men of trust. By

1850 Huth & Co. had around 2,000 correspondents all over the world (Table 5.1), and it was not alone in this strategy. The House of Brown's policy was also that of opening numerous small credits for men of 'ability and integrity',[68] and neither Brown nor Huth & Co. asked any of their correspondents for exclusivity. An important consequence of having a large number of correspondents was that some of the dealings with Huth & Co.'s friends related to very important issues involving considerable sums of money, while others were minor in comparison. Indeed, the varying size of Huth & Co.'s operations is remarkable: it would participate in operations worth £100,000 but also in trifling operations involving only a few pounds. Similarly, the face value of the bills of exchange accepted for the company could be as little as £2 or £4 only, and this during the 1820s, 1830s and even the 1840s.[69]

In 1856 one of Huth & Co.'s partners confirmed that the firm's transactions 'are frequently of the magnitude of entering into the sale of a floating cargo, and some times so minute as to dealing with a small quantity of sugar or indigo',[70] adding that 'it is not the greater or smaller profits that matter as much as the safety and regularity with which the concern is conducted'.[71] This last phrase encapsulates the London company's business philosophy. One drawback to this, however, was the very high level of associated administrative costs; thousands of contracts had to be monitored and enforced. Likewise, the considerable amount of information received from such a vast network of associates and correspondents in so many languages had to be processed in a meaningful way. To undertake this task Huth & Co. employed bright clerks, who were specialists in the markets and products they were dealing with. It is true that it reduced transaction costs for its associates but increased its own costs. That said, these costs were compensated for by the certainty of having a wider variety of regular income streams of income and also greater risk diversification.

The range of other activities performed by merchant bankers

Trading and financing international trade aside, merchant bankers performed many other activities. These included the issue of loans, trading in securities, and active participation in the insurance and exchange markets. Rothschild & Sons, Hambro & Son, Schroder and other important bankers of the time participated actively in the market for issuing sovereign debt on behalf of states.[72] Such was also the case of Baring Brothers, who became extensively involved in British and French government public debt, in particular during the Napoleonic Wars.[73] However, Huth & Co. did not share its peers' interest in this matter, and eschewed that market, just as did Rathbones.[74] In fact, it kept a low profile within British politics, and this would explain in part the firm's lack of involvement in the issuing of public debt.

But Huth & Co.'s refusal to enter the sovereign debt business was probably an exception to the rule. As we know, the company had actively diversified its range of activities and it had been extremely active in the floating of US securities on the European market during the first half of the nineteenth century (what we would now call the secondary market), at a time when not even Baring Brothers or Rothschild & Sons were doing so.[75] Another merchant banker to follow Huth & Co.'s path was George Peabody, Baring Brothers' principal rival in transatlantic finance in the 1830s–1840s, and who in time would also become a major dealer in US securities.

For Huth & Co. in particular, as discussed in Chapter 4, by the late 1830s the financial connection with the US had become significant, not just because of the financing of trade, but also the trading of American securities in the European markets. Huth & Co. was successful in mobilizing capital from the US into Europe under terms that favoured both the European buyers and the issuing American states. Their main connections in the US for these businesses were Goodhue and Perit. They both enjoyed open credit to buy securities in the US if the selling price locally was lower than that available in London or continental Europe. In fact Huth & Co. was ready to make available credit for sums of around £100,000 if good opportunities arose.[76] For instance, it traded New Orleans city stocks, New York State stocks, Morris Canal & Banking Company bonds and New York Life Insurance & Trust bonds.[77] To give an idea of the scale of these transactions, in 1837 Huth & Co. received on consignment shares of the Bank of the United States valued at £100,000,[78] while in 1839 it received consignments of Arkansas bonds for US$300,000.[79]

Huth & Co. also used its founder's business connections in Europe beyond Spain to sell US and British securities. The Netherlands, for example, was an important consumer of American financial products.[80] Likewise, many correspondents in Germany entrusted the company with the purchase of both US and British securities in London, including Anderson Hober (Hamburg).[81] By this time, Huth & Co. was also active in the London securities market. Often the company traded on the bonds of the 1825 British loan to Mexico, or on the 1818 British loan to Prussia.[82] Likewise, it also traded extensively on British consols.

Huth & Co. was also very active in the market for bills of exchange, negotiating on behalf of other merchants. Among the firm's main correspondents were now the Bank of Manchester, the Bank of Liverpool and the Banco Español de San Fernando (Madrid), to name just a few. The company became an important broker of bills of exchange between continental Europe and Britain, and to that end received a wide range of bills from locations as diverse as Madrid, Genoa, Trieste, Hamburg and Vienna, negotiating these drafts and receiving acceptances. It did the same for British merchants and British bankers, all over Europe: it was not easy for an institution such as the Bank of Liverpool to negotiate a bill payable in Antwerp, Madrid or Hamburg where they had no agency, but this task could be accomplished on its behalf by Huth & Co., thanks to its strong connections across the Continent. For these services it charged a bill brokerage, a commission and postage expenses.[83] Although most merchant bankers of the time were also involved in the exchange market, because of Huth & Co.'s greater geographical diversification and greater number of correspondents, it dealt in a greater variety of bills of exchange. Indeed, the same services offered in bills to European correspondents were offered to friends elsewhere. For example, Huth & Co. acted as financial agents of the River Plate house of Zimmerman Frazier in London, in the process receiving regularly many bills of exchange for numerous London merchants on Zimmerman's credit, negotiating them and securing acceptance. Zimmerman Frazier also drew against Huth & Co. to clear its accounts with many other British merchants.

Furthermore, as previously noted, ever since Frederick Huth's early days in London, his company was very active in the marine insurance market. It also acted as an insurance broker, even if it had no interest whatsoever in the cargoes. London was by this time the world's principal marine insurance centre, and although marine insurance had developed into a specialized form of business, many countries lacked a local equivalent: this was certainly the case in Chile, Peru, as well as in the River Plate provinces. But even merchants resident in developed countries with their own insurance industries often asked Huth & Co. to effect marine insurance on their behalf since it was more easily or cheaply done in London. For example, a merchant in Canton would ask the London firm to insure a cargo of tea from China to New York, a service which Huth & Co. was glad to provide.

Finally, any discussion of Huth & Co.'s extensive range of services must include a special mention of the connection with Lucas Alaman of Mexico. Among the many political positions held in his career, Alaman was Foreign Minister and Home Secretary. More interestingly, he was the administrator of the estates belonging to the descendants of the famous Spanish conqueror Hernan Cortes.[84] Cortes' heirs, the duke of Terranova and Monteleone, lived in Palermo, Sicily, and were entitled to receive rent from these Mexican holdings. Alaman channelled sizeable funds from Mexico to Palermo via Huth & Co., usually making use of drafts on the directors of the Compañía Unida de Minas of London, Alaman being president of the Mexican Board.[85] It is doubtful that Huth & Co. got much in the way of revenue from these complex operations, but it was a service they were happy to provide to any friend anywhere in the world.

Notes

1 Friedman and Jones, 'Business History', pp. 3 and 5–6.
2 Chapman, *The Rise*, p. 127.
3 Lisle-Williams, 'Beyond the Market', p. 268.
4 Austin, *Baring Brothers*, p. 6; Chapman, *The Rise*, pp. 17, 25–26.
5 Casson, 'The Economic Analysis'.
6 Chapman, *The Rise*, pp. 17–18 and 25; Ferguson, *The House of Rothschild*, pp. 35–59. Perhaps mercury was the only commodity in which they had an interest between the Napoleonic Wars and the 1870s (Chapter 2). It was only at the end of the 1870s when 'the third generation of the family was inclined towards a change of tack in their business strategy', thus participating in the trade of several products, in particular non-ferrous metals. López Morell and O'Kean, 'Rothschilds' Strategies', p. 722.
7 Kynaston, *The City of London*, p. 117; Chapman, *The Rise*, pp. 126–127.
8 Their banking business became by far their predominant activity, this being a house for which in the past 'there was scarcely any merchandise in demand in which they did not trade'. Bramsen & Wain, *The Hambros*, pp. 157–158, 189. Hambro & Son was opened in London in 1840, after moving from Copenhagen to Britain. This year

114 *A global enterprise of trade and lending*

Joseph Hambro took all his capital from Copenhagen, liquidated his business there, and moved to London. Yet, strictly speaking, the first Hambro arrived in London in 1832, when Carl Joachim Hambro asked his father Joseph Hambro (Copenhagen) to open a branch office in London, a proposal that was accepted. The branch was opened, and soon after Carl Joachim married an English woman in 1833 and things went going well. However, Carl Joachim was psychologically unstable, and moved to Denmark between 1834 and 1838. This latter year he moved back again to London, but psychiatric problems forced him to spend almost a year in a clinic. This accelerated his father's permanent move to London. It was only in 1842 that Carl Joachim returned to business, and even then, he did so slowly. In the meanwhile, his father Joseph had made London his permanent residence and was in charge of the whole business until his death in 1848, when Carl Joachim eventually took charge of the whole business and the house was styled C. J. Hambro & Son.

9 Perkins, *Financing Anglo-American Trade*, p. 92; Chapman, *The Rise*, p. 126.
10 Jones, *Merchants to Multinationals*, p. 23.
11 Jones, *International Business*, p. 110.
12 Chapman, *The Rise*, pp. 38, 59–60, 105.
13 Jones, 'Multinational Trading Companies', p. 6.
14 Chapman, *The Rise*, p. 18.
15 Chapman, *The Rise*, p. 122.
16 They specialized in trade between Britain, the eastern Mediterranean and Russia during the first half of the nineteenth century. Jones, *Merchants to Multinationals*, pp. 24–25; Roberts, *Schroders*, p. 53.
17 It was only during the last quarter of the nineteenth century that they reached other markets beyond Europe and South America. Jones, *International Business*, p. 34; Chapman, *The Rise*, p. 130; Jones, *Merchants to Multinationals*, p. 29.
18 Perkins, *Financing Anglo-American Trade*, pp. 17 and 112–113; J. R. Killick, 'Risk, Specialisation and Profit in the Mercantile Sector of the Nineteenth Century Cotton Trade: Alexander Brown and Sons, 1820-80', *Business History*, 16 (1974), pp. 1–2; Chapman, *Merchant Enterprise in Britain*, p. 152.
19 The business did not expand until the second half of the century. S. Marriner, and F. E. Hyde, *The Senior John Samuel Swire, 1825–1898* (Liverpool: Liverpool University Press, 1967); Jones, *Merchants to Multinationals*, p. 37; Jones, *International Business*, pp. 145–146.
20 Although Cropper & Benson had some dealings with Cuba, Russia and China, the core of their business was Anglo-American trade and finance. Wake, *Kleinwort Benson*, pp. 39–40, 42–45.
21 During the second half of the century they expanded geographically. S. Marriner, *Rathbones of Liverpool, 1845–1874* (Liverpool: Liverpool University Press, 1961), pp. 5-10; Jones, *Merchants to Multinationals*, p. 36.
22 Helping to foster the connection with Norway, it is worth mentioning that their main contact there was Andreas Gruning & Co. (Christiania). Huth & Co. and this company had extensive dealings in wool. In exchange Huth sent them sundries (i.e. all sort of goods, including ink, hardware, iron chain, coffee, lead, soap, sugar and tin plates). HPJ-224, HPJ-225.
23 HPEL-21. Huth & Co. to J. W. Perit (Philadelphia). London, 19 August and 17 November 1838.
24 HPSL-179. Huth & Co. to Lopez Doriga (Santander). London, 29 January 1849; HPSL-181. Huth & Co. to Lopez Doriga (Santander). London, 18 January 1851; Huth & Co. to Agustín Basabe (Bilbao). London, 5 and 22 January 1849.
25 HPSL-175. Huth & Co. to Pedro Domenzain (La Guaira). London, 1 February and 15 March 1843.
26 HPEL-17. Huth & Co. to Stockmeyer & Co. (Rio de Janeiro). London 4 and 19 January 1837.

A global enterprise of trade and lending 115

27 HPEL-45. Huth & Co. to Provost (Ghent). London, 3 and 5 January 1845.
28 HPEL-23. Huth & Co. to Rupe & Zoon (Amsterdam). London, 19 April 1839.
29 HPEL-26. Huth & Co. to Huth & Co. (London). Liverpool, 16 January 1839; HPEL-31. Huth & Co. to J. W. Perit (Philadelphia). London, 3 March 1841.
30 HPEL-23. Huth & Co. to De Bruyn & Sons (Amsterdam). London, 2 and 12 April 1839.
31 HPEL-6. Huth & Co. to Hoffmann & Fils (Roterdam). London, 7 and 20 July 1830; HPEL-11. Huth & Co. to Hoffmann & Fils (Rotterdam). London, 4 and 8 January 1833.
32 HPEL-23. Huth & Co. to Rupe & Zoon (Amsterdam). London, 19 and 26 April 1839.
33 HPEL-21. Huth & Co. to B. R. Scheibler (Antwerp). London, 1 and 14 September 1838; HPEL-26. Huth & Co. to Huth & Co. (London). Liverpool, 26 and 27 February 1839.
34 HPEL-21. Huth & Co. to P. Scheibler (Ghent). London, 3 and 7 September 1838.
35 This house was also well connected to Baring Brothers. Chapman, *The Rise*, p. 27.
36 HPEL-9. Huth & Co. to Russell (Canton). London, 19 April 1832.
37 HPEL-23. Huth & Co. to Russell Sturgis (Canton). London, 13 and 30 April 1839.
38 UGSC. MS Gen 531/14. Stewart & Wilson to Huth & Co. (London). Glasgow, 25 April and 4 November 1836; HPIL/S/SCOT/18. Stewart & Wilson to Huth & Co. (London). Glasgow, 16 December 1836; HPEL-17. Huth & Co. to Russell Sturgis (Canton). London, 19 January and 1 May 1837; HPEL-21. Huth & Co. to Russell Sturgis (Canton). London, 24 November 1838.
39 HPEL-45. Huth & Co. to Nye Parking (Canton). London, 7 and 18 January 1845. This house had an open credit of £30,000. HPEL-59. Huth & Co. to Nye Parking (Canton). London, 24 February 1849.
40 HPEL-45. Huth & Co. to Lackersteen & Brothers (Calcutta). London, 2 and 7 January 1845.
41 Perkins, *Financing Anglo-American Trade*, p. 56; Chapman, *The Rise*, p. 42.
42 Jones, *Merchants to Multinationals*, pp. 24–25; Roberts, *Schroders*, p. 53.
43 Austin, *Baring Brothers*, pp. 65–67; Chapman, *The Rise*, pp. 26–27. It was only during the 1870s that Barings focussed their attention on other quarters beyond the US and the Far East.
44 Austin, *Baring Brothers*, p. 6.
45 Chapman, *The Rise*, pp. 35–36.
46 Chapman, *The Rise*, p. 8.
47 Chapman, *The Rise*, pp. 35–36.
48 Roberts, *Schroders*, chapter 1.
49 Jones, *Merchants to Multinationals*, pp. 24–25.
50 During the 1810s–1840s, Huth wrote to over 130 correspondents in Cuba alone.
51 HPEL-17. Huth & Co. to Bibby & Co. (Canton). London, 1 and 14 March 1837; HPEL-23. Huth & Co. to Russell Sturgis (Canton). London, 13 and 30 April 1839.
52 For example, Kessler of Manchester usually drew against Huth for cottons sent to Drusina. HPEL-45. Huth & Co. to Petersen Huth & Co. (Hamburg). London, 21 January 1845.
53 HPEL-8. Huth & Co. to Drusina & Co. (Mexico). London, 6 and 21 July 1831; HPEL-31. Huth & Co. to Drusina & Co. (Mexico). London, 4 January 1841.
54 HPEL-45. Huth & Co. to Drusina & Co. (Veracruz). London, 1 January 1845.
55 Chapman, *Merchant Enterprise in Britain*, p. 135.
56 Jones, *International Business*, p. 63.
57 Roberts, *Schroders*, p. 51.
58 Perkins, *Financing Anglo-American Trade*, p. 92.
59 Marriner, *Rathbones of Liverpool*, p. 5.
60 Chapman, *The Rise*, pp. 25–26.
61 Chapman, *The Rise*, p. 105.

62 Freedman, *A London Merchant Banker*, p. 1.
63 Chapman, *The Rise*, pp. 8–9.
64 Chapman, *The Rise*, pp. 11, 14–15
65 Chapman, *The Rise*, pp. 18 and 35. Rothschild & Sons in particular retained just a handful of correspondents, focussing on safety, simplicity and large turnover.
66 Chapman, *The Rise*, p. 42; Perkins, *Financing Anglo-American Trade*, p. 119.
67 Perkins, *Financing Anglo-American Trade*, p. 119; Hidy, *The House of Baring*, p. 227. It is fair to mention that Baring Brothers expanded later on, to the extent that by the mid-1850s they had 1,200 correspondents. Yet from Table 5.1 it is clear that the experience of Huth & Co. was far more impressive.
68 Chapman, *The Rise*, p. 42.
69 See for example HPBP for 1820, 1822, 1836 and even 1846.
70 BPP, 'Report from the Select Committee of the House of Lords, on the Mercantile Law Amendment Bill', 294 (1856).
71 Quoted in Wake, *Kleinwort Benson*, p. 114.
72 Roberts, *Schroders*, pp. 47, 58–60; Bramsen & Wain, *The Hambros*, pp. 166, 172.
73 Austin, *Baring Brothers*, pp. 11–13.
74 Marriner, *Rathbones of Liverpool*, p. 219.
75 Chapman, *The Rise*, p. 92. It is worth mentioning that during the 1810s–1820s there were relatively few capital movements between the US and Europe. It was only from the 1830s that American securities started to flood Europe. Freedman, *A London Merchant Banker*, p. 3.
76 HPEL-16. Huth & Co. to J. W. Perit (Philadelphia). London, 7 May 1836.
77 HPEL-16. Huth & Co. to Goodhue & Co. (New York). London, 14 November 1836; HPEL-17. London, 6 and 21. January 1837; Huth & Co. to Perit (Philadelphia). London, 21 and 30 January 1837.
78 HPEL-18. Huth & Co. to J. W. Perit (Philadelphia). London, 8 and 22 July 1837.
79 HPEL-23. Huth & Co. to Murray (New York). London, 29 May 1839; HPEL-24. Huth & Co. to Goodhue & Co. (New York). London, 31 August 1839.
80 HPEL-21. Huth & Co. to J. W. Perit (Philapdelphia). London, 13 December 1838.
81 HPEL-45. Huth & Co. to Anderson Hober (Hamburg). London, 7 January and 14 February 1845.
82 HPEL-8. Huth & Co. to Menet & Cazenove (London). London, 10 July and 2 November 1831.
83 HPEL-59. Huth & Co. to Bank of Liverpool (Liverpool). London, 2, 5 and 12 January 1849.
84 J. Bazant, 'Los Bienes de la Familia de Hernán Cortés y su Venta por Lucas Alamán', *Historia Mexicana*, 19 (1969).
85 HPEL-6. Huth & Co. to Lucas Alaman (Mexico). London, 19 August and 20 November 1830.

6 Risk-management credit strategies

Non-banking institutions played a pivotal role in supporting the expansion of international trade before the so-called first globalization *c*.1870–1913, and before the existence of modern deposit banks. Amongst these institutions there were certainly some British-based merchant bankers. As has been noted in the preceding chapters, the leading merchant bankers of the first half of the nineteenth century provided a crucial financial service by advancing monies to consignors of products from all over the world, and indeed the provision of credit was an intrinsic part of the activities of any international merchant during this period. Such was the importance of advances that the acceptance business became the most important way of financing world trade for most of the nineteenth century.[1] Indeed, a leading merchant banker in this pre-1870 period would have had hundreds, if not thousands, of clients whose trade it supported.[2]

Without this form of credit most international trade operations could not have taken place, in particular those related to long-distance trade, not only in developing regions lacking capital but also in the main western economies as late as the first half of the nineteenth century. It was the merchant bankers' credit system which provided the international mercantile community with a permanent source of loanable funds with which to facilitate the expansion of international trade. We must remember that even in Britain, the first industrial nation and premier economic power of the nineteenth century, the size of manufacturing enterprises (including exporters) remained relatively small,[3] and these units of production were, therefore, very often short of working capital. They had, necessarily, to resort to credit to fund the regular course of their operations. In the words of Chapman, the authority on merchant banking: 'the numerous small family firms that conducted most of the British industry were seldom able to assume the financial burden of marketing abroad.'[4]

In turn, regardless of their size, manufacturers and producers of primary products all over the world were not usually in direct contact with the final consumer, and therefore, given the high transaction costs common in this period, both trading and financial intermediaries were often needed.[5] Likewise, during the 1820s–1850s British merchant bankers not only dealt with credit associated with the movement of goods but also with that linked to the international movement of capital, in particular linked to the financing of US industrialization and railroad construction. This is not surprising given that Britain remained the largest capital exporter in the world during these decades.[6]

Despite the important extant literature on merchant bankers, our knowledge regarding the peculiarities behind the extension of credit to fund international trade and capital movements remains incomplete. This is particularly the case with regard to the means by which merchant bankers protected themselves from the risks arising from these operations, at a time when international enforcement was still weak and information asymmetries prevailed. This is most important in Huth & Co.'s case given the truly global extension of credit established by this merchant banker from one locale (in this case, London) to nearly everywhere in the world.

In addition, and as has been shown extensively, Huth & Co. financed trade operations (of goods and securities) between Britain and the rest of the world, but also many trades which had no contact with British ports. As Chapman has already argued, merchant bankers' patronage 'was by no means limited to British exporters or British trade',[7] but it is still worth noting that a single merchant banker (i.e. Huth & Co.) could finance many trades in many different products all over the world and at a comparatively early period. Transport was poor and precarious communications facilities constrained both the scale and the geographic spread of merchants' activities. There were no law courts with international jurisdiction, and therefore lenders had either to rely on foreign courts to enforce potential unpaid debts or seek to protect themselves effectively so as not to be obliged to overseas institutions.[8]

Aiming to fill these gaps in the literature, this chapter explores in more detail the credit activities of Huth & Co. The previous chapters have shown that Huth & Co. was no ordinary merchant banker. Although most of its London peers remained cautious and did not diversify the remit of their operations before 1850, Huth & Co. took a completely different path by establishing a unique and impressive global network of trade and lending. Of special relevance for this chapter is the fact that many of the company's correspondents benefited significantly from its credit, and it would be useful therefore to explore the risk-management strategies it adopted. Given its global credit network, Huth & Co. needed to protect itself against the risk arising from lending to a wide variety of people in many locations and in such a number of different trades at a time when international contracts were not always enforced, and when information about clients' honesty and financial health was difficult to gather and even more complicated to assess. Indeed, Huth & Co.'s credit networks were seemingly beyond the limits a single credit network could support before 1850, when face-to-face contacts were unusual. Finally, the chapter will also contribute to a better understanding of under-explored commercial practices during this period, such as the use of letters of credit, advances on consignments and the various arrangements needed to succeed in multilateral trades involving complex transactions.

The nature of Huth & Co.'s credit activities

Huth & Co. extended a great deal of credit to finance international trade, but there are some clear dividing lines as far as Huth's involvement in these trades is concerned. Although Huth & Co. operated occasionally on its own account and via joint accounts, most of its dealings were on commission, and in turn most of the credit advanced by it to other merchants was for commission-based business.[9] As we know, Huth of London received a great number of consignments from many quarters of the world. Most of these exporters outside Britain lacked capital, and therefore asked Huth for advances, and very often these were granted. This was common to all merchant bankers of the period, but because of Huth & Co.'s unique diversification, the bills accepted by the firm originated from a wider geographic area than those of any other merchant banker of this time, and in turn these drafts also reflected the wider diversity of goods handled by Huth & Co. than its competitors. A sampling exercise of the bills accepted by the company shows that for 1846 alone, it accepted over 5,000 bills from more than 250 different cities worldwide.[10]

Similarly Huth & Co. also obtained consignments in Britain of diverse products to be sent to their branch houses in Chile and Peru, and to agents and 'friends' elsewhere in the world. For example, suppliers of cottons in Manchester would consign to Huth & Co.'s establishments in South America, but also to the company's contacts in Mexico, the River Plate and many other places. Many of these British industrialists, although based in a region rich in capital, often requested advances from Huth & Co. too. In the same vein, French and German merchants consigning to its establishments in South America or contacts in Spain and Asia would also request advances, which were frequently granted.

Finally, Huth & Co. also advanced funds to many merchants even if they were not consigning to either Huth in London (or Liverpool) or to the firm's branches or agencies elsewhere in the world. For instance, Huth & Co. made credit available to Thayer Brothers of Boston for US trades with China, Brazil and the West Indies, although Thayer was not the company's agent in the United States.[11] This confirms Chapman's judgement that merchant bankers based in London 'were free to recognize and patronize innovating enterprise from whatsoever corner of the globe it came'.[12] But more importantly, by financing trades that never docked in Britain (e.g. accepting bills from issuers who did not belong to Huth & Co.'s jurisdiction) or in places where Huth & Co. had a branch or a confidential agent, Huth & Co. was expanding its most 'obvious' lending network beyond its normal limits.

So far we have only mentioned Huth & Co.'s credit and advances. But what exactly was an 'advance'? An advance was a flexible form of credit, which varied between merchant bankers. In Huth & Co.'s case, it took the form of funds supplied to consignors as a proportion of the invoiced cost of cargoes. The most usual practice was that the consignor was permitted to draw on the consignee (e.g. Huth & Co.) or on another merchant backing the consignee for a proportion of the value of the consignment, most usually at three to six month's sight but also for six to twelve months' sight too, well before remittances for these consignments were received. In other words, Huth & Co.'s advances were used for short-, medium- and long-term finance. After agreeing terms, the merchant banker would accept the bill, but only after charging 0.5 per cent–1 per cent as acceptance commission (in exceptional cases, this commission could be as high as 2.5 per cent).[13] The drafts could be cashed at maturity or discounted immediately by the consignor after acceptance (thus receiving the face value of the bill minus a discount rate).

As is clear, advances were funds provided by merchant bankers before sales had taken place or before remittances had been received, usually at an interest rate of 5–6 per cent per annum. This was applied from the time the bill expired to the actual payment of the funds by the consignor, which was financed by the remittances associated with the consignment. Naturally Huth & Co. was not willing to wait for too long to be paid, as its capital was not unlimited. Its usual policy was as follows: 'if any goods should remain on hands at the expiration of twelve months from their first landing, the advance therein is to be entirely repaid to us.'[14] Note too that if the drafts were cashed by the consignor after acceptance (or by anyone to whom the bill was endorsed), the usual discount rate (given Huth & Co.'s high reputation in the London market) was very close to that of the Bank of England,[15] a practice which did not bother the company: 'it may be quite indifferent to us through whom they discount their bills.'[16] Once Huth & Co. had accepted the draft, all they cared about was paying it upon maturity and subsequently recovering the funds as soon as possible.

Advances were given because of the considerable time that used to elapse between the delivery of goods and the receipt of the related remittances,[17] in particular before the transport and communications revolutions of the second half of the nineteenth century (e.g. the expansion of railroads all over the world, the launching of steam-packet companies, and the introduction of the telegraph and submarine cabling). For example, British textile exporters to South America might have to wait for around 18 months before they received the final payment for their exports. Yet during that time manufacturers nonetheless needed to buy the raw materials required to continue production. If it was not the manufacturer who exported but an intermediary merchant, the latter had to buy new manufactured goods to continue shipping. Producers of raw materials consigning to Europe were under similar constraints and needed cash to continue operations. Therefore, to avoid liquidity problems the consigner from the emerging market often had no option but to borrow money from a merchant banker in London by drawing upon it.

Despite its apparent simplicity, advancing was a very complex and varied system, about which it is difficult to generalize. The bills accepted by Huth & Co. did not amount to a homogenous financial instrument; the agreed terms depended on many variables such as the standing of the issuer and the nature of the goods whose trade was financed. It all depended on diverse factors such as the saleability of the goods being shipped, the availability of credit in the market, the economic situation in the destination market and the trustworthiness of the consigner. For instance, Huth & Co. tolerated a great deal of flexibility over the rate of advances rather than standardizing them at, say, half the invoice value of cargoes. Furthermore, the same rate of advance was not always extended to a given supplier. With Rawson & Saltmarshe (experienced textile suppliers), Huth & Co. had not one but several accounts for exports to South America or Europe, for some of which Huth advanced one-fifth of the invoice value of cargoes; for others, the company advanced as much as four-fifths. Similarly once his partnership with Edward Rawson was dissolved, Huth & Co. advanced Arthur Saltmarshe between one-fifth and three-quarters of the invoice value.

There was, of course, an upper limit to the proportion of advances given. For Huth & Co. this was around three-quarters of the invoice value of cargoes – already an exceptional rate. The reasons for establishing a limit were clear. On the one hand a consignor needing 80–100 per cent of the value of the consignments would be considered as a man of little property or with a proclivity to speculation. On the other hand, Huth & Co. wanted to lend but needed the associated export operation to be fully covered to avoid over-advancing: the risks of adverse selection were always present. Issuers might be tempted to inflate the expected value of the return sales of their goods.

Only in very exceptional cases would Huth & Co. advance 100 per cent of an invoice's bona fide value. This would happen for example for commodities such as tea, about which the company's expertise became outstanding, as was its prediction of future prices.[18] It could also happen when there was too much competition for a particular product and if advances right up to the full invoice cost were not given, other competitors would take the whole business. This commonly happened with exports of raw cotton from the United States to the UK, when Huth & Co. often had no option but to advance the entire amount of the invoice.[19] Another exception was Stock & Sons, the only English manufacturer that received advances for the whole value of their invoices because their goods were considered as 'articles of the first importance'[20] for British exports. A high rate of advance might also be justified due to a succession of profitable deals that rendered a particular trade or merchant very safe.

In contrast, if Huth & Co. was not conversant with a trade, advances were rarely offered for those products. It is important to note that for British-based consigners (i.e. residents in the same jurisdiction as Huth & Co.) the rate of advance was usually higher than for those located elsewhere, since it was easier to recover unpaid debts if the receiver of the advances resided in the same country as the merchant advancing monies, given the institutions in place in Britain at that time to protect private property, including loans. Experience had taught London merchant bankers that the legal process of recovering debts abroad was extremely expensive,[21] and at times impossible.

Apart from all these differences with regard to rates and upper limits of advances, there were other variations. With some suppliers, advances were given only against a bill of lading, which was called a 'documentary credit'. The bill of lading was taken as collateral security for ultimate reimbursement. For example, one of Huth & Co.'s agents in Glasgow (Guthrie & Co.) could draw against the company on account of advances for textiles shipped to the Americas only after Huth & Co. had received the corresponding bill of lading through which legal title of the goods remained with it.[22] A similar situation occurred with Clason & Ules' drafts for raw cotton shipments from New Orleans to Liverpool. For others – usually those who were new to the business or who had proved less reliable – loans were made only when the goods had arrived at the final destination, as happened when Rawson, a woollen supplier of Halifax, started to consign to Huth & Co.[23] In extreme cases, the arrival of goods at their destination was a necessary, but nonetheless insufficient condition on which to make an advance. In addition, the goods needed to have been sold (usually on credit). That is, advances were given against an account credit sale.[24] It is safe to summarize that Huth & Co. clearly classified correspondents according to their standing in relation to the London firm's perceived risks in dealing with them.

Therefore, the nature of the collaterals requested by Huth & Co. was bound up with the borrower's reputation, and varied according to the type of correspondents thus classified by the firm. This differential treatment of clients was also practised by other merchant bankers of the period, such as Baring Brothers. For example, in their Anglo-American trade, Barings classified their customers in the United States as follows: men of unquestioned means and trust; men of slightly more modest account and reputation; and safe respectable businesses on a smaller scale. To the first group of reliable contacts, advances were liberally extended and no invoices, bills of lading or insurances were requested (for those who made the list no physical collateral was required), but when dealing with the third group Barings asked for full shipping documents (including insurances) to be sent to London.[25]

When advances involved the consignment not of British manufactures going abroad but of primary products sent from many quarters to Britain or continental Europe, then the most usual requirement from Huth & Co. was for the consignor to send the drafts with the bill of lading (and order for insurance), a practice that would ensure that the drafts 'will be duly honoured on presentation'.[26] For example, Merle and Frey, cotton consigners of New Orleans, were authorized to draw against Huth & Co. for up to two-thirds of the value of the consigned cotton, but only after sending the bill of lading.[27] Likewise, Nye Parkin & Co. of Canton regularly sent Huth in London consignments of tea and raw silk, but received advances only if the drafts were sent with the corresponding bill of lading.

In relation to Huth & Co.'s practices, limits were not only imposed on the upper rate of the advance, but also on the total amount of loans made. That is, a consigner could not continue to ship cargoes at the agreed rate of advances (e.g. 50 per cent) if he exceeded the limit on money borrowed in absolute terms (e.g. £5,000). That is, Huth & Co. wanted to control not only the size of individual credits related to specific operations but also the total volume of credits. For instance, when the rate of advance for Rawson was set at two-thirds, Huth & Co. also established that 'we should at the same time limit the extent of our acceptancy to ten thousand pounds at the utmost'.[28] However, in the same way that on occasion the limit on the rate of advance was relaxed, so also was the limit on the total amount lent to exporters.

Why was this the case? There was always a temptation to boost revenues, as well as to treat some customers better than others. Yet this relaxation of terms had a clear limit. No matter how trustworthy a merchant was, Huth & Co. never went above £20,000 as an overall acceptance limit. The risk of default was always there, regardless of the client, in particular during a period of financial crisis. For example, when in 1830 Guthrie & Co. of Glasgow failed, according to one of Huth & Co.'s agents there were rumours circulating in the market that they owed

£30,000 to the company in advances, gossip it was quick to correct: 'it is not likely that we shall ever run into such an advance with any house how much so ever superior in credit to the one above mentioned.'[29] And even if a consignor had an overall acceptance limit of, say, £15,000, limits were often also established on individual transactions or expeditions, in our example, say £5,000.[30] Risks associated with moral hazard could materialize at any moment, as Huth & Co. well knew, and thus for all bills it accepted in 1820, 1822, 1831 and 1836, the highest value was £3,000, £3,000, £5,000 and £10,000, respectively.[31] And indeed, taking a closer look for a particular year, between October 1845 and September 1846, the individual value of Huth & Co.'s acceptances was highly concentrated in values below £2,500, as can be seen in Figure 6.1. There was just a handful of bills over £7,000.

It is important to note that Huth & Co. was often only an intermediary in the whole credit chain. For example, a textile manufacturer consigning to a house in Mexico via Huth & Co. would draw against the firm because no one in Manchester would take a draft from a house in Mexico. On maturity, however, the draft had to be covered by the Mexican house if it actually wanted to receive the consignments. For this kind of service, which was offered only to very close friends or agents, Huth & Co. charged 1 per cent upon the value of the draft,[32] but if the draft was not covered at maturity, then the commission would increase to 2.5 per cent. To their branch houses in South America or confidential agents elsewhere, Huth & Co. offered a similar service whereby return remittances were sent with a bill of exchange drawn on Huth London (instead of using local produce or bullion/

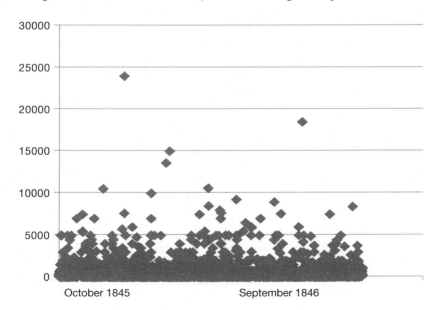

Figure 6.1 Value (£) of bills accepted by Huth & Co. between October 1845 and September 1846 (5,011 bills in total)
Source: HPBL-199.

specie). For example, imagine a manufacturer in Britain was sending goods on consignment to Huth & Co.'s houses in South America, receiving remittances on a bill of exchange at several months' sight on Huth London and waiting for 'the usual remittance to cover it' (e.g. silver). In this case, the consigner could either discount the bill with any merchant or with Huth & Co. of London themselves, a service the firm was happy to provide: 'If you have no objection, we should much prefer to pay this bill under discount at 4 per cent per annum',[33] which was certainly a preferential rate.

Apart from the advances system above described, another form of credit used by Huth & Co. was the letter of credit. Letters of credit were similar to bills of exchange, but were not endorsable (i.e. they could be used by a designated merchant only) and were generally used by Huth & Co. for trades between two locations at considerable distance from Britain. The letter of credit was thus an instrument that depended to a great extent on geography, and it is also worth mentioning that the volume of Huth & Co.'s credit associated with this instrument in particular was far lower than that associated with bills of exchange. But how did the company's letters of credit work?

Huth & Co. of London would grant a business 'letter' (serving as a means of introduction) for a close connection (buyer of goods) directed to another connection (seller of goods) allowing the bearer of the letter (buyer) to buy in a third location goods to a maximum amount (e.g. £5,000) from the seller. Huth & Co. of London in turn promised to pay the seller at a given time, usually with a draft, after receiving the shipping documents associated with the operation. In this way, the letter was a direct promise to the seller of goods; it was an instrument based on trust since the seller unquestionably trusted Huth & Co. as a guarantor Indeed, for the period covered by this article, letters of credit were 'confined to those cases where there was constant dealing between two or more mercantile houses that normally traded on an open account or credit basis'.[34] That is, they were employed for regular trades involving merchants known to each other: Huth & Co. had to trust the buyer and the seller trusted Huth & Co. It was only the London company's international reputation that allowed its close friends to buy goods internationally under this system, often in places where the legal framework did not cover protests. This is a clear example of a case where different credit instruments needed different collateral. In this case, more reputation was needed than would have been necessary for ordinary bills of exchange, in particular because – as noted above – Huth & Co.'s letters of credit were generally used in locations where the legal framework was not geared to recovering debts.

For the purposes of our study, letters of credit were used between Huth & Co. and their branches, agents or good friends lacking capital to buy goods in distant markets. They were not granted to anyone else. For example, to Russell of New York (one of the company's US contacts), Huth & Co. granted letters of credit to purchase sugar in Cuba or Brazil from Huth & Co.'s agents or usual correspondents there (or to other merchants who could be trusted and were willing to trust the London firm) for the consignment of Huth's houses in either Chile or Peru.[35] The sellers would then draw against Huth London on account of these shipments from, say, Cuba. Likewise, to Kennedy McGregor & Co. of Canton, Huth & Co. granted letters of credit to procure tea in China and send it to Huth in London for up to £20,000,[36] while Nye Parkin & Co. of the same city was granted a letter of credit for £30,000 for the same purposes.[37] In all of these cases Huth & Co. did not run major risks since the produce bought was eventually consigned to headquarters or one of its branches.

And yet in other cases, Huth & Co. *did* take risks. For example, in 1839 it provided Maneglier (an agent for the Société de Commerce of Antwerp), letters of credit to purchase produce in Manila from Russell Sturgis for the consignment of the Société de Commerce in Belgium.[38] Likewise, when the Royal Prussian Maritime Company of Berlin dispatched a ship to the west coast of America from whence she was intended to proceed to Manila in order to take in a return cargo for Germany, Huth & Co. granted a letter of credit to the captain of the said ship to purchase produce in Manila from Russell Sturgis for up to £8,000,[39] a significant amount at that time. In these cases Huth did not have a 'physical' collateral to cover their accepted drafts, only the intangible reputation of the buyers and sellers.

Additional credit risk-management strategies

Huth & Co.'s predisposition to extend advances did not translate into a frantic search to lend. Some basic precautions taken by the company to protect against the risks associated with lending were outlined above. Merchant houses in Britain lent to those they thought could repay, to individuals whose collateral and/or likelihood of repayment inspired trust. Or, in the words of Chapman, 'credit required trust, and trust could only be accorded to customers whose means and probity were assured'.[40] To ensure clients' means and integrity, Huth & Co. endeavoured to obtain as much detail as possible about the borrower's financial health. Crucial to this task was the information the company collected periodically on all established or potential clients. This included the reports sent by its branches, confidential agents and business friends on particular clients, which contained critical and confidential information. Take, for instance, a confidential report sent by Huth Liverpool after Huth London sent them a special information request about two potential new borrowers:

> Both the houses about which you enquire enjoy a very good credit here. The former is a cotton broker & dealer said to be very rich and trustworthy. The latter has not long been established, his business is confined exclusively to cotton imports & purchases of the same article for his friends at Havre and we believe he is strongly backed by one of the leading houses there.[41]

But even old clients were regularly monitored, in particular when there was a significant change in the market situation, as seen in this example: 'Can you ascertain how far Messrs Aschen & Co. of your city, with whom we have a similar transaction to a small extent, have been affected by the late events?'[42]

Indeed, when advancing, other merchant bankers such as Baring Brothers concentrated overwhelmingly on ensuring the credit worthiness of the lender:

'Barings frequently issued unsecured credits and counted totally upon their selectiveness in choosing reliable customers to reduce their risk',[43] and to have few accounts with little trouble to administer.[44] In contrast to Barings, apart from ensuring the borrower's reliability and credit record, Huth & Co.'s advances were given mostly to those who could ship saleable products. More often than not, when extending credit, for Huth & Co. the quality of goods shipped was more important than the exporter's standing. Furthermore, Huth & Co. did not restrict the number of clients they had in their credit portfolio, even if they had to administer many hundreds of accounts, as the company explained to one of its Glasgow agents.[45]

Huth & Co.'s wider than usual portfolio was undoubtedly difficult to monitor. And although it is true that its advances never exceeded the estimated value of the consignments upon which the advance was extended, it is also the case that Huth & Co. was very aware of the fact that often some connections sent consignments simply 'for the sake of advances'.[46] The threat of moral hazard or adverse selection could always arise, despite the adoption of some basic precautions such as those described in the previous section. In truth advancing could be a risky operation during the first half of the nineteenth century if the lender did not take additional provisions. Indeed, often merchants intentionally consigned goods which were not fully suitable for the destination market, and as a consequence the final price on arrival could be far lower than expected – and sometimes the goods were not sold at all. For example, in 1839 a German firm wanted to draw against Huth & Co. on account of advances for goods which had remained on hand for longer than expected, and Huth & Co.'s belief at that time was that 'it seems to us that Messrs. Eisenstuck & Co., seeing that they are unsaleable, wish to saddle us with them in this way'.[47]

Therefore, to protect against these kinds of risks, as a general rule Huth & Co.'s advances were given only if they had a good knowledge of both the product being traded and the foreign market to which goods were exported. This close monitoring was crucial for heterogeneous goods such as textiles, since demand for these products was specific to each market. For example, as far as exports to South America are concerned, Huth & Co. advanced only to those producing manufactures specially designed for the local markets, following clear advice from its local branches or agents. If consignors did not follow those instructions, then a warning was given. In 1830, for instance, Huth & Co. expressed some concerns about advances given to some of the Glasgow connections of one of their agents there, since some of the cargoes associated with these consignments were of poor quality, which rendered the business too risky.[48]

Although the risks associated with unsaleability mainly affected heterogeneous goods such as textiles, it was also the case that more standardized products (e.g. sugar, cotton and wool) suffered on many occasions. For example, as we have learned, one of Huth & Co.'s most important trades was imports of raw wool from many quarters. Yet despite the company's expertise in this area, it was saddled with poor quality primary products several times, such as when William Rhodes of Buenos Aires was authorized to draw against Huth & Co. for wool consignments.

The first of these cargoes was of very poor quality. After acknowledging receipt of the items in question, 'which have been landed in a good condition', Huth & Co. reported in rather sarcastic terms that 'on examination we find, however, to our sincere regret, the quality of these wools so greatly inferior to the description you gave us of them, that we can hardly help thinking some mistake or other must have occurred in regard to this shipment on your side'.[49]

All in all, advances were to be given for saleable goods only, regardless of their nature. And indeed, for those trades or products falling within Huth & Co.'s expertise, the rate of advance was always higher than for other products about which it did not feel particularly comfortable, even for advances given to the same merchant. For example, to Nye Parkin & Co. of Canton, Huth & Co. was happy to advance as much as 75 per cent of the value of tea or raw silk consignments, but for any other product consigned from China to London never more than 50 per cent.[50] Likewise, to Adams Whitall of New Orleans, Huth was happy to advance up to 75 per cent for raw cotton shipments, but only 67 per cent for tobacco cargoes.[51] This difference was on account of Huth & Co.'s greater expertise in tea and cotton, trades they came to dominate from the 1830s.

Another related risk for the merchant advancing was that even if the goods consigned were saleable, they could be invoiced at an unrealistic (higher than market) value, and therefore the advance given could be even higher than the eventual sale. According to Huth & Co., more often than not there was a 'general system of overcharging the invoices' among unscrupulous merchants.[52] Furthermore, even if the consignor had no intention of overcharging an invoice, it could happen because market conditions usually changed, in particular in long-distance trades where a considerable period elapsed between the time the goods left the exporting warehouses and the arrival time at the final destination.[53] That was one of the main reasons why limits were established upon the rate of advance given. To protect against this risk the merchant-consignee advancing monies had to be a genuine expert in the product being traded, so as to anticipate future realistic prices. For example, when a textile supplier in Britain receiving advances from Huth & Co. for exports to South America tried to invoice at higher values than those which the London firm thought were realistically in the destination, it was quick to reply, pointedly, that: 'the proceeds will not cover the invoice, and if the invoice prices are the real cost, we could not encourage further shipments unless a change takes place either here or in the sale prices... we would not upon any account induce you to embark again in a losing concern.'[54]

In addition, to ensure the repayment of advances, most of the time Huth & Co.'s advances were closely linked to consignments it controlled, where the consigned merchandise was regarded as collateral. In this case we are talking about consignments sent directly to Huth & Co. in London and Liverpool, or to branch houses, agents or very close friends elsewhere in the world. In this way, Huth & Co. (or its allies) would have access to the potential income for selling the merchandise under consignment, which was the only effective way of ensuring repayment against all events. Even when the consignments receiving advances were not sent directly to Huth & Co., it often requested that the bill of lading and invoices went under its name, as occurred when sugar cargoes were dispatched from Havana to St Petersburg.[55] It is true that collateral could suffer from moral hazard issues, and that the merchandise associated with it could not be repossessed, but Huth & Co.'s main aim was to shoulder most risks for other merchants while retaining control of the trade. For example, when an American merchant asked Huth & Co. of Liverpool for credit to be placed at the disposal of Rhodes of Buenos Aires for shipments of hides to continental Europe or eventually to the United States, to parties which were not sufficiently close to Huth & Co., the firm answered that 'it would be contrary to the principles of a Liverpool house to grant a simple banking credit for shipments not coming under its own control'.[56]

Another risk was that of the goods being damaged or lost, usually at sea or because of fire. During the 1810s–1850s, seawater damage was a recurrent issue in long-distance international trade. As outlined in Chapter 3, all kinds of products were damaged, from textiles, to sugar, cinnamon, hides, tobacco and jerked beef. To protect against this risk, Huth & Co. customarily effected marine insurances and fire insurances by themselves to protect those goods in which its advances were involved, as the company felt that that those risks 'must in these cases be always covered through us'.[57] In turn, the insurance policy would state that in case of any loss, payment had to be made to Huth & Co. by the underwriters, thus further protecting the business. Indeed, when a consigner receiving advances wanted to insure his goods himself, Huth & Co. replied as follows: 'If we have to make advances, we must of course make ourselves the insurance.'[58] Huth & Co. was protecting itself against both exogenous risks to their commercial activity (which depended on variables such as transport quality and weather conditions, for example) and endogenous risks to the firm's activities (which depended mainly on the quality of Huth's network).

In the case of open credit (either through bills or letters of credit), in instances in which Huth & Co. did not have exact knowledge of when the merchandise associated with its advances left the port of origin, open insurance policies were always put in place beforehand to further protect its credit, as seen in this letter: 'We shall take care to open policies of insurance to the amount of £45,000 intended specially to cover all shipments made in virtue of this letter of credit.'[59] Likewise, given the recurrent seawater damage suffered by products traded internationally during the period dealt with in this monograph, Huth & Co. gave clear indications about how to pack the goods upon which advances were given. For example, the firm enthusiastically advised consignors receiving advances to use tarpaulin, oil cloth or tin cases to better protect the goods being shipped. When safe packing was not possible, for example for bulk cargoes of jerked beef from Buenos Aires to Havana, then Huth & Co. would very often be reluctant to advance for this kind of consignment.[60]

Regarding insurance charges, it is worth noting that when Huth & Co. dealt with the insurance on behalf of other merchants, they were actually advancing the cost of the premium to consigners at an annual rate of 5–6 per cent until return remittances had been received.[61] That is, by dealing with insurance on behalf of others, Huth were actually deploying their own capital to make premium payments on behalf of their correspondents as well as spending a great deal of time managing the whole process. As a result, in addition to the interest payments it requested, Huth & Co. also charged a commission of roughly 0.5 per cent to cover the complexities inherent in securing insurance for such a wide range of cargoes of so many different products to a vast number of destinations.

A different risk emerged when Huth & Co.'s advances involved consignments which never docked at either British ports or the foreign ports in which Huth & Co. had branch houses or agencies. (In other words, cases in which Huth & Co. acted as a mere financial intermediary but did not fully control the property shipped under its credit.) We are talking here about a merchant in, say, Puerto Rico or Venezuela drawing against Huth & Co. on account of shipments to several markets in continental Europe in which the firm had no official agents. In such scenarios Huth & Co. would credit the account of the overseas merchant and debit the consignees' accounts. For example, Bermudez of Caracas was in the habit of consigning cocoa to Porrua Egusquiza & Co. of Santander,[62] this latter not being an agent of Huth & Co., just a good 'friend' or business partner in terms already defined. For these shipments Bermudez drew against Huth & Co. on the understanding that Porrua Egusquiza had to cover the drafts at maturity. That is, Bermudez's draft was credited to him but debited into Porrua Egusquiza's account. The main risk here was that Porrua Egusquiza would not cover the draft and Huth & Co. had no control of the consignment which would enable him to recover the advance.[63] Huth & Co. could ask for the bill of lading to be in its name, but since it did not have agents in the port in which the goods were finally landed, this additional provision would not erase all the risks being taken because the merchandise arrived in a different jurisdiction. It was all a matter of faith: Huth & Co. fully trusted Porrua Egusquiza, having maintained good relations with him for many years. For Huth & Co., many merchants 'afford no other security but their honesty',[64] which was not always a hindrance to trade.

Likewise, for example, Elzaburu & Co. of Puerto Rico had an open credit to draw against Huth & Co. for sugar shipments from San Juan to Queheille & Sons of San Sebastian. Elzaburu's debts to the London company had to be covered by Queheille upon maturity of the drafts, with either a bill or produce.[65] Again, in this case Huth & Co. and Queheille were correspondents for over 30 years and the risks of embezzlement were very small, or so the former gauged.[66] Indeed, such open credits were extended by Huth & Co. only when a sufficient number of successful previous dealings demonstrated that the borrower was reliable. These are instances of what Huth & Co. used to call 'uncovered credits', which were governed purely by trust and the reputation of those involved; there was no other collateral here. Alternatively we could say that in these cases reputation acted as a substitute for physical collateral.[67]

When Huth & Co. acted as financial intermediaries, it usually charged 1 per cent commission to accept the drafts, although 1.5 per cent was also applied in cases of men of 'lower standing or repute'. Often too, if the merchant enjoying an open 'confirmed' credit with Huth & Co. did not use it, a commission of 0.5 per cent could be charged anyway, and if subsequently the credit was used, then the other 0.5 per cent was charged. The reason for charging a small commission even for unused credit was logical: Huth & Co. had a limited number of confirmed open credits it could offer worldwide, and if a merchant left to lie fallow, Huth & Co. missed out on the opportunity to give it to another merchant who would pay the full 1 per cent or 1.5 per cent commission.[68] That is, Huth & Co. would waste the potential earnings of the capital reserved for a merchant who failed to use its credit.[69]

Uncovered credits applied not only to consignments of primary products from the periphery of the world economy to Europe, but also to consignments of European manufactures to South America and many other quarters. For example, Bencke of Hamburg had an open credit with Huth & Co. for £6,000 which allowed the German merchant to draw against the London broker for textile shipments to Buenos Aires.[70] But in many other similar trades, in which Huth & Co. advanced for consignments that never involved British ports, Huth & Co. requested that the return remittances be sent directly to Huth London. For example, when the Hamburg house of Clarson, which had a branch house in New Orleans, asked Huth London for advances for consignments from Hamburg to New Orleans, Huth & Co. agreed, on condition that the returns from New Orleans to Clarson were sent directly to the London headquarters.[71] In other cases Huth & Co.'s tactics were less explicit, but it had other collateral on hand. For example, Mainer of Montevideo would draw against Huth & Co. for jerked beef shipments to Menendez Mendive of Havana, which had to be covered by Menendez.[72] Huth & Co. was at the same time in the habit of receiving Menendez Mendive's consignments of sugar from Havana. Thus although it was not made explicit, should Menendez fail to cover Mainer's drafts at maturity, Huth & Co. could probably secure repayment by taking possession of Menendez's sugar.

Finally, it goes without saying that the extent to which merchants advanced credit at a particular moment was predicated by the trade cycle in which they were immersed. For example, if Huth & Co. needed to accumulate cash to meet bills previously drawn on the company, then it would probably be reluctant to carry on advancing monies on a sizeable scale. Similarly if Huth & Co. heard rumours that one of its debtors was in difficulties, then the firm would probably be inclined to stop advancing to other suppliers until that situation had been clarified. In addition, merchant bankers themselves borrowed from banks,[73] and during periods of financial crisis they found their own credit facilities curtailed, which made it very difficult for them to advance monies even if they wanted to. Indeed, during financial crises advances were rarely extended by merchant bankers such as Huth & Co., who survived all the panics that broke out during our period of study.

In the crisis of 1837–1839, for example, Huth London made it clear to its Liverpool branch that 'we have as you are well aware of for time past declined making advances on any consignment whatever and the state of our money market does not in any case tempt us to break this rule'.[74] In the 1847–1848 crisis something similar happened. Huth & Co. systematically refused to extend advances, even for shipments of British textiles to the United States, despite its familiarity with textiles and the US textile market.[75] There were sound reasons to be cautious, though: as we have learned, even the reputable houses of the 'Three Ws' (George Wildes & Co., Thomas Wilson & Co. and Timothy Wiggins & Co.) and Reid Irving & Co. failed during the 1837 and 1847 crisis, respectively. In all, in Huth & Co.'s case there was a substantial reduction of its credit proportional to the whole network it had, as well as a complete denial of credit to the riskiest correspondents in times of turmoil.

Financing the trade of securities

So far we have talked about the role of Huth & Co.'s credit in financing international trade. Nonetheless, although such trade formed a less important branch of its activities, the company also financed capital flows across borders, in particular from the United States into Britain, and within Europe thereafter. Thus, as we have seen in previous chapters, Huth & Co. also became intermediaries in international capital flows, procuring funds from investors in one country to invest them in other countries. What is interesting to highlight here is that very often these operations were made possible not only due to the firm's intermediation, but also thanks to its extension of credit.

As part of this process, many well-connected US businessmen consigned American securities to Huth & Co. as if they were consigning potatoes.[76] These merchants would in turn draw against Huth & Co. on account of these consignments (waiting for the securities to be sold within an agreed time), and it had the securities as collateral. The exact nature of the contract was very flexible – and at times complex – as protracted negotiations often took place before agreement could be reached.[77] The most important terms of the contracts, which had to be drawn up fresh for each deal, included the commission to be charged, which in turn depended on the selling price of the securities (e.g. a limit of 95 per cent the nominal value), on the existence of advances to fund the floating and the time it took to dispose of the lot (e.g. no more than 60 days).[78] Furthermore, on occasion Huth & Co. entered into joint-account operations with some of these merchants, in particular with Goodhue & Co. of New York,[79] and less frequently bought US securities on own account.[80] In any case, most of these atypical own-account operations were followed by a quick resale of the securities. On occasion, Huth & Co. received securities not to sell them in London but as collateral for advances on the consignment of merchandise. For example, the firm would advance a British merchant exporting railway iron to the Unites States, and in exchange the US consignee would provide American securities as collateral until return remittances had been received by Huth in London for the sale of the railway iron upon arrival.[81] Alternatively, a US merchant, such as S. & F. Dorr & Co., might be permitted to draw up to £12,000 against the deposit of an equivalent sum in bonds held by Huth & Co. as collateral security.[82] Complicating things further, take for instance this case: in 1841 Huth & Co. was happy to extend advances to Mitchell Cayley & Co. (St Petersburg) on account of Russian bale-rope exports to the US (specifically to W. H. Robertson of Philadelphia). In this case the bill of lading was to be sent to John Perit (Huth & Co's's agent in Philadelphia), who in turn was to receive some stocks as collateral. Only on receipt of Robertson's remittances would Perit release the bill of lading and the securities held as collateral.[83]

Although the consignment of American securities operated in a similar fashion to that of commodities, Huth & Co. offered a far lower rate of advance for them: never more than 50 per cent of the expected market value of the securities, and usually as little as 20 per cent[84] or even 15 per cent.[85] According to Huth & Co., this measure was justified because although securities were in general safe collateral, very often they could not be realized on the market and funds could be locked up during an uncertain period. Or if sold, securities could reach far lower prices than those originally envisaged.[86] Indeed, security prices were more volatile than those of staple commodities, and more importantly, if there were panic or loss of confidence in certain US states, then the securities associated with these states could either plummet in value or become altogether unsaleable in London. Therefore, in any of these cases the collateral upon which the advances rested would evaporate, and fairly quickly, as happened with some Arkansas stocks in 1840 which eventually had to be returned to the US by Huth.[87] We should also bear in mind that if an issuing US state defaulted on its debt, which sometimes happened, Huth & Co. was not conversant with the local law pertaining to the recovery of unpaid interests or the principal, and neither did it have an in-country branch to assist them on these technicalities at a time when, as discussed above, international enforcement was still weak.

Finally, Huth & Co. received US securities on consignment and while it usually liquidated them on British soil, it also did so in continental Europe, in particular in Spain, Germany and the Netherlands. At this point, it is worth noting that in the same way that Huth was skilled in adapting textiles to the taste of their clients all over the world, they were also quick to adapt financial goods to specific European demands. For example, the Dutch purchased large amounts of US securities via London.[88] In order to penetrate the Dutch market, Huth adapted securities to the wants of local clients, as this extract shows: 'We have lately had some negotiations in Holland respecting American securities ... we have seen that we could sometimes dispose of large sums there, if the stock is in a shape corresponding to the views of the Dutch capitalists.'[89] In these cases advances were also considered.

Notes

1 Jones, *Merchants to Multinationals*, p. 23.
2 Chapman, *The Rise*, p. 115.
3 Jones, *Merchants to Multinationals*, p. 22; Chapman, *Merchant Enterprise in Britain*, p. 181; S. D. Chapman, 'The Commercial Sector', in M. B. Rose (ed.), *The Lancashire Cotton Industry: A History Since 1700* (Preston: Lancashire County Books, 1996), p. 92.
4 Chapman, *The Rise*, p. 15.
5 Chapman, 'British Marketing Enterprise', p. 205; Jones, 'Multinational Trading Companies', Casson, 'The Economic Analysis'.
6 Jones, *Merchants to Multinationals*, p. 20; Jones, 'Multinational Trading Companies'.
7 Chapman, *Merchant Enterprise in Britain*, p. 232.

8 On this, although for the eighteenth century, but equally applicable here, see V. A. Santarosa, 'Financing Long-Distance Trade without Banks: The Joint Liability Rule and Bills of Exchange in 18th-century France', Working Paper (Michigan: University of Michigan, 2012).
9 That is, Huth were intermediaries in international trade, linking buyers and sellers. For a theoretical discussion of this point see Casson, 'The Economic Analysis', pp. 24–25.
10 HPBP-199.
11 HPEL-44. Huth & Co. to J. E. Thayer & Brothers (Boston). London, 3 October and 3 December 1844.
12 Chapman, *Merchant Enterprise in Britain*, p. 232.
13 It is worth noting that the most usual acceptance commission was 1 per cent. Nonetheless, when the drafts were not covered before maturity, then this 1 per cent commission was increased to 2.5 per cent. The commission charge varied according to Huth's evaluation of their correspondents' standing and the length of the drafts, amongst other factors. On this, see HPEL-5. Huth & Co. to F. Frey & Co. (New Orleans). London 21 May 1836. At the lower end, a 0.5 per cent commission was rare, applied to very sure European trades only or to imports of raw cotton from the US when it was not possible to get consignments otherwise. For instance, Huth & Co. was happy to lower its acceptance commission for bills drawn by Clason & Ules for shipments of cotton to Liverpool. HPEL-62. Huth & Co. to Clason & Ules (New Orleans). London, 10 November 1849.
14 HPEL-45, Huth & Co. to Rawson (Halifax). London, 16 January 1845.
15 HPIL-S/SCOT/4. Finlay Neilson to Huth & Co. (London). Glasgow, 13 May 1833.
16 HPEL-6, Huth & Co. to H. H. Stansfeld (Leeds). London, 18 August 1830.
17 S. D. Chapman, 'Financial Restraints on the Growth of Firms in the Cotton Industry, 1790–1850', *Economic History Review*, 33 (1979), p. 55.
18 For example Kennedy McGregor of Canton drew against Huth for up to £20,000 for advances on tea consigned to London at a rate of 75 per cent of the value of the cargoes, and for up to £5,000 at a rate of 100 per cent of the value of the invoice if strictly necessary. HPEL-59. Huth & Co. to Kennedy McGregor & Co. (Canton). London, 24 February 1849.
19 For some examples, see HPEL-20. Huth & Co. to J. W. Perit (Philadelphia). London, 5 May 1838; HPIL. Adams & Whitall to Huth & Co. (Liverpool). New Orleans, 24 March 1839.
20 HPEL-14, Huth & Co. to H. H. Stansfeld (Leeds). London, 17 July 1835.
21 Chapman, *Merchant Enterprise in Britain*, p. 135.
22 UGSC, MS Gen 533/2, Guthrie & Co. to Huth & Co. (London). Glasgow, 9 April 1832.
23 HPEL-37, Huth & Co. to Huth & Co. (Liverpool). London, 24 February 1843.
24 HPEL-13, Huth & Co. to Stewart & Wilson (Glasgow). London, 13 January 1834.
25 Austin, *Baring Brothers*, p. 46.
26 HPEL-45. Huth & Co. to Nye Parkin & Co. (Canton). London, 7 January 1845.
27 HPEL-22, Huth & Co. to Huth & Co. (Liverpool). London, 10 January 1839. The House of Brown requested the same before advancing for consignments from the USA to Britain. Perkins, *Financing Anglo-American Trade*, p. 21.
28 HPEL-37, Huth & Co. to Huth & Co. (Liverpool). London, 24 February 1843.
29 HPEL-6, Huth & Co. to H. H. Stansfeld (Leeds). London, 9 November 1830.
30 HPEL-23, Huth & Co. to Henry Ward (Baltimore). London, 16 May 1839.
31 HPBL, for 1820, 1822, 1831 and 1836.
32 HPEL-59, Huth & Co. to Drusina & Co. (Vera Cruz). London, 1 January 1849.
33 HPEL-58, Huth & Co. to Smith & Co. (Dundee). London, 28 November 1848.
34 B. Kozolchyk, 'The Legal Nature of the Irrevocable Commercial Letter of Credit', *American Journal of Comparative Law*, 14 (1965), p. 398. See also Roberts, *Schroders*, p. 27.

35 HPEL-17, Huth & Co. to Russell (New York). London, 30 January 1837.
36 HPEL-59, Huth & Co. to Kennedy McGregor & Co. (Canton). London, 1 January 1849.
37 HPEL-59, Huth & Co. to Nye Parkin & Co. (Canton). London, 24 February 1849.
38 HPEL-23, Huth & Co. to Russell Sturgis (Manila). London, 2 April 1839.
39 HPEL-16, Huth & Co. to Russell Sturgis (Manila). London, 18 October 1836.
40 Chapman, *Merchant Enterprise in Britain*, p. 46.
41 HPEL-26, Huth & Co. to Huth & Co. (London). Liverpool, 6 June 1839. Before opening the branch in Liverpool, Castellain, Schaezler & Co. were the main source of intelligence, as is seen in this example, amongst many: 'Messrs. Penny Brothers as well as Watson Brothers are in the Mexican trade and enjoy a fair credit, though they are not supposed to have any large property.' HPIL, Castellain, Schaezler & Co. to Huth & Co. (London). Liverpool, 24 August 1831.
42 HPSL-178. Huth & Co. to Gil Kennedy & Co. (Paris). London, 13 April 1848.
43 E. J. Perkins, 'Financing Antebellum Importers: the Role of Brown Bros. & Co. in Baltimore', *Business History Review*, 45 (1971), p. 431.
44 Chapman, *The Rise*, p. 42.
45 HPEL-13, Huth & Co. to Stewart Wilson (Glasgow). London, 13 January 1834.
46 HPEL-11, Huth & Co. to Finlay Neilson (Glasgow). London, 11 January 1833.
47 HPEL-23, Huth & Co. to Huth & Co. (Liverpool). London, 24 April 1839.
48 HPEL-6, Huth & Co. to Laurie Hamilton (Glasgow). London, 26 August 1830.
49 HPEL-35, Huth & Co. to T. Gowland & Co. (Buenos Aires). London, 6 Jul 1842.
50 HPEL-45, Huth & Co. to Nye Parkin & Co. (Canton). London, 7 January 1845.
51 HPEL-22, Huth & Co. to Adam & Whitall (New Orleans). London, 26 January 1839.
52 HPEL-6, Huth & Co. to Laurie Hamilton & Co. (Glasgow). London, 26 August 1830.
53 This happened often, even for standardized commodities such as cotton. See for example Perkins, *Financing Anglo-American Trade*, pp. 35–36.
54 HPEL-14, Huth & Co. to John Halliday (Sanquhar). London, 22 July 1835.
55 HPEL-45, Huth & Co. to Drake Brothers (Havana). London, 15 February 1845.
56 HPEL-31, Huth & Co. to Pope & Aspinwall (Philadelphia). London, 3 March 1841.
57 HPEL-13, Huth & Co. to Stewart Wilson (Glasgow). London, 13 January 1834. A similar practice was enforced by the House of Brown. See Perkins, *Financing Anglo-American Trade*, p. 21.
58 HPEL-3, Huth & Co. to H. H. Stansfeld (Manchester). London, 20 April 1829.
59 HPEL-45, Huth & Co. to Nye Parkin & Co. (Canton). London, 7 January 1845.
60 HPSL-181, Huth & Co. to Adolfo Van Praet (Buenos Aires). London, 8 May 1851.
61 HPSL-170, Huth & Co. to Bermudez (Caracas). London, 15 February 1838.
62 Porrúa Egusquiza & Co. were prominent merchants of Santander during the first half of the nineteenth century. On Santander's merchant elites during this period, see A. Hoyo, *Todo Mudó de Repente. El Horizonte Económico de la Burguesía Mercantil en Santander, 1820–1874* (Santander: Universidad de Cantabria, 1993).
63 HPSL-170, Huth & Co. to Faustino Bermudez (Caracas). London, 15 February 1838.
64 HPEL-6, Huth & Co. to Webster (Morley). London, 9 November 1830.
65 HLSL-177, Huth & Co. to Pedro Queheille & Sons (San Sebastian). London, 8 and 13 January 1847. Pedro Queheille had French origins. The founder of the firm arrived in the Basque Country in 1780. Soon after, it ranked amongst the top merchant houses of San Sebastian during our period of study. Rubio 1997, p. 31; C. Larrinaga, 'Los Comerciantes Banqueros y la Industrialización Guipuzcoana a Mediados del siglo XIX', *Historia Contemporánea*, 27 (2003), p. 842.
66 This is a very different situation to the embezzlement described by Greif when discussing other long-distance trades in the medieval era. This phenomenon belonged more to pre-modern trades than to those dealt with in this book. A. Greif, *Institutions and the Path to the Modern Economy: Lessons from Medieval Trade* (Cambridge: Cambridge University Press, 2008)

Risk-management credit strategies 135

67 Other merchant bankers of the period did the same, in particular in Anglo-American trades. According to Freedman (*A London Merchant Banker*, pp. 5–6), British houses became overconfident of American reliability for some of their correspondents and stopped requesting bills of lading of invoices for these clients.
68 HPEL-5, Huth & Co. to F. W. Brune & Son (Baltimore). London, 15 April 1836.
69 Not all merchants charged this 0.5 per cent commission for unused credit. For example, the Rathbones did not, much to their regret. Marriner, *Rathbones of Liverpool*, pp. 207–208. Brown Shipley, like Huth, also forced potential borrowers to pay at least 0.5 per cent of any unused credit on account of the opportunity cost of unused capital. Perkins, 'Financing Antebellum Importers', p. 429.
70 HPEL-59, Huth & Co. to Zimmerman Frazier & Co. (Buenos Aires). London, 4 January 1849.
71 HPEL-26, Huth & Co. to Huth & Co. (London). Liverpool, 21 January 1839.
72 HPSL-172, Huth & Co. to Francisco Mainer & Co. (Montevideo). London, 2 December 1840.
73 Huth bankers were Glyn, Mills, Hallifax & Co. of London.
74 HPEL-25, Huth & Co. to Huth & Co. (Liverpool). London, 28 November 1839. A similar position was taken by the House of Brown during this crisis. Perkins, *Financing Anglo-American Trade*, pp. 100–101.
75 HPEL-53, Huth & Co. to Cranby Wheeler (Philadelphia). London, 19 April 1847.
76 Many of these consignments of securities were accepted by Huth & Co. on the expectation of also receiving consignments of raw cotton.
77 For example, if the securities were bonds, rather than shares, Huth often had to guarantee potential investors the payment of the first year's interest, which added further complexity to these consignments. Dividends could be sent from the US in cash, in commodities such as raw cotton or even in securities themselves. Likewise, a minimum selling price was often set by the consignee, who also set a maximum time to hold the securities before liquidating them on the market.
78 For some examples see HPEL-20. Huth & Co. to J. W. Perit (Philadelphia). London, 14 June and 4 July 1838; HPEL-21. Huth & Co. to J. W. Perit (Philadelphia). London, 19 September 1838.
79 HPEL-15, Huth & Co. to Goodhue & Co. (New York). London, 6 May and 6 September 1836.
80 Such was the case, for example, in 1835, when Huth bought some stocks issued by the state of Florida for £4,500, or when in 1837 Huth bought on its own account a few bonds of the Morris Canal. HPEL-29, Huth & Co. to Goodhue & Co. (New York). London, 3 July 1840.
81 This happened for example when Huth & Co. financed the export of railway iron to build the Eastern Railroad in 1839. In this case Massachusetts state stocks were pledged as security against Huth's advances. See HPEL-23. Huth & Co. to Eastern Railroad Company (Boston). London, 23 August and 31 December 1839. Eventually, securities held as collateral could be taken as direct payment if agreed by the parties involved.
82 HPEL-17, Huth & Co. to S. and F. Dorr & Co. (New York). London, 22 April 1837.
83 This is well explained in HPEL-40. Huth & Co. to A. J. Burnley. London, 10 November 1843.
84 HPEL-17, Huth & Co. to Goodhue & Co. (New York). London, 14 March 1837.
85 HPEL-16, Huth & Co. to Goodhue & Co. (New York). London, 26 December 1836.
86 HPEL-16, Huth & Co. to Goodhue & Co. (New York). London, 14 October 1836.
87 HPEL-29, Huth & Co. to North American Trust & Banking Company (New York). London, 24 July 1840.
88 McGrane, *Foreign Bondholders*, p. 10.
89 HPEL-21, Huth & Co. to John Perit (Philadelphia). London, 13 December 1838.

7 Conclusions

The 1810s–1840s provided a new world of opportunities for London merchant bankers and allowed them to expand worldwide. Amongst these we should mention in particular the following:

- the Spanish American Empire collapsed during the 1810s–1820s and Brazil was opened up to international trade in 1808;
- peace came to Europe after the Napoleonic Wars, promoting intra-European trades, long-distance trades and capital flows;
- British manufacturing was further expanding in the wake of the Industrial Revolution and dramatic export price reductions were occurring, just as the demand for imported raw materials rose;
- industrialization was also taking place in continental Europe and the United States, and with that the introduction of railroads accelerated in these regions, in part funded by British capital;
- India and China were opened up to private merchants, after the end of the regulated trade systems (i.e. private business networks became more important than before);
- the internationalization of several branches of the insurance industry accelerated.

As key actors in international businesses during this period, London merchant bankers were quick to react and make the most of these new commercial avenues. But there were many different ways to operate on this new international stage and therefore key decisions had to be taken, many of which profoundly shaped the character of these firms. One of these decisions was whether or not to diversify the sphere of their activities. Most London merchant bankers in the first half of the nineteenth century remained cautious and did not diversify the remit of their operations either geographically or in the products they traded (or trade they financed) during this period. In this sense we could conclude that they behaved unadventurously.

As we have learned, Huth & Co. took a completely different path; it decided to 'go global' well before any other competitor, while it remained engaged in the trade of – and financing of trade in – a wide range of both manufactures and primary products. By adopting such an international approach so early, Huth & Co. defied the conventional wisdom of that era. Before the 1840s, transport facilities and communications in the world were very poor. Trade between Britain and Chile, for instance, was conducted in small sailing vessels; it took between 120 and 150 days for such vessels to reach Valparaiso from the Mersey, conveying goods but also essential correspondence, at a time when steam-packet companies were just emerging. There were, therefore, profound information asymmetries in international trade. Consequently, cross-border transaction costs were high, as were agency costs for those who ventured to open branches or appoint agents beyond their headquarters. Despite these evident barriers to long-distance trades, the number and geographical dispersal of Huth & Co.'s correspondents by 1850 is extraordinarily impressive for a London merchant banker, all the more so given Frederick Huth's humble origins.

To give an idea of the scale and intensity of operations, Huth & Co. of London wrote between 25 and 60 business letters a day, so roughly 7,000–15,000 per annum (excluding letters from Liverpool or from agencies on Huth & Co.'s behalf) to thousands of individuals or firms. If social capital refers to connections between individuals, 'to social networks and the norms of reciprocity and trustworthiness that arise from them',[1] whose value is the direct result of the time and effort invested in nurturing and expanding those connections',[2] then Huth & Co.'s social capital stock was surely well above that of any contemporary competitor. The company had a comparative advantage in this respect, and indeed, social capital is only a metaphor about advantage: 'people who do better are somehow better connected.'[3]

Compared to most peers, Huth & Co. adopted less personalized ways of engaging in long-distance trade and the movement of securities at the end of the 'age of sail'. Indeed, if the whole period covered by this monograph is considered, Huth & Co. of London sustained correspondence with over 6,000 people in over 70 countries (using modern geographical borders) and over 600 cities/towns (see Table 7.1). This vast number of correspondents is explained by the fact that Huth & Co. was incredibly active in promoting British imports, exports and re-exports, but also a wide range of different trades which never touched Britain. Indeed, from London, Huth & Co. provided an increasing boost to the multilateralization of international trade taking place during this period. In many cases the firm was truly a market-maker for several branches of many countries' foreign trade before 1850.

This is a clear example of the value generated by a social network when 'individuals join together and invest resources in the formation of ongoing and structured relationships with each other', thus generating collective and individual benefits; in other words, social capital again.[4] Thanks to Huth & Co.'s connections and reputation, many members of this social network could broker connections between otherwise unconnected elements. In London, Huth & Co. was able to bring these contacts together.[5] It also had the advantage of possessing a very robust network, and indeed many of its connections stayed close to the company for the whole period covered by this study. All in all, the firm's success seems to confirm Pearson and Richardson's judgement that those prepared to engage with

Table 7.1 Location of Huth & Co.'s correspondents. A sample for *c.*1812–1850

Americas			Rest of Europe			Asia		
Argentina	50	0.8%	Austria	57	0.9%	China	26	0.4%
Belize	2	0.03%	Belgium	222	3.5%	India	76	1.2%
Bolivia	2	0.03%	Croatia	1	0.0%	Philippines	12	0.2%
Brazil	75	1.2%	Czech Republic	37	0.6%	Singapore	3	0.05%
Canada	3	0.05%	Denmark	14	0.2%	Sri Lanka	3	0.05%
Chile	15	0.2%	Finland	6	0.1%	Turkey	5	0.1%
Colombia	5	0.1%	France	364	5.8%	*Asia*	*125*	*2.0%*
Costa Rica	1	0.02%	Germany	1,440	23.0%			
Cuba	132	2.1%	Gibraltar	15	0.2%		*Africa*	
Curazao	3	0.05%	Greece	2	0.03%	Madeira	1	0.02%
Ecuador	11	0.2%	Guernsey	3	0.05%	Libya	1	0.02%
Guyana	3	0.05%	Hungary	1	0.02%	Mauritius	4	0.1%
Haiti	5	0.1%	Ireland	20	0.3%	Sierra Leone	1	0.02%
Jamaica	13	0.2%	Italy	94	1.5%	South Africa	9	0.1%
Mexico	143	2.3%	Latvia	24	0.4%	Tunisia	2	0.0%
Nicaragua	1	0.02%	Lichtenstein	1	0.02%	*Africa*	*18*	*0.3%*
Panama	5	0.1%	Lithuania	1	0.02%			
Peru	70	1.1%	Luxembourg	2	0.03%		*Australia*	
Puerto Rico	22	0.4%	Malta	5	0.1%	Australia	24	0.4%
Uruguay	10	0.2%	Netherlands	168	2.7%			
USA	197	3.1%	Norway	31	0.5%			
Venezuela	29	0.5%	Poland	124	2.0%	*Not available*	*202*	*3.2%*
Virgin Islands	17	0.3%	Portugal	27	0.4%			
Americas	*814*	*13.0%*	Russia	32	0.5%			
	United Kingdom		Spain	870	13.9%	*Grand Total*	*6,274*	*100%*
England	1,115	17.8%	Sweden	124	2.0%			
Northern Ireland	28	0.4%	Switzerland	88	1.4%			
Scotland	152	2.4%	Ukraine	5	0.1%			
Wales	18	0.3%	*Rest of Europe*	*3,778*	*60.2%*			
UK	*1,313*	*20.9%*						

Source: HPSL, HPEL, HPGL, several volumes.

less personalized business networks could provide a considerable competitive advantage over competitors.[6]

Furthermore, although many of these branches of trade saw no British port, they were made possible thanks to Huth & Co.'s credit network. The lack of working capital (not only social capital) was a fundamental barrier to many exporters and importers worldwide during this period and yet Huth & Co. was ready to provide it from London to many of their connections. By the late 1840s Huth & Co. was accepting over 5,000 bills every year from a wide range of different countries, amounting to the staggering figure of between £2 million to £3 million per annum.[7]

Overall, it is quite remarkable that a business started in London in 1809 by a German immigrant without family business connections, backed by a handful of Spanish friends and with a meagre capital of less than £700 and no more than 100 correspondents (mainly concentrated in Europe), ended up as a global enterprise with a capital of around £500,000 million by 1850,[8] and with some 2,000 active correspondents worldwide (Table 5.1) by the mid-nineteenth century. There is also little doubt that Huth & Co. made the most of the retirement or bankruptcy of many important traders of the previous generation and of the new opportunities emerging for multinational traders during the 1810–1840s.

These correspondents were located in North America, Central America and the Caribbean, South America, and throughout Britain, continental Europe, Africa, Asia and Australia. They consigned many products to Huth & Co. and its friends; they received many other goods also on consignment, from either Huth & Co. or

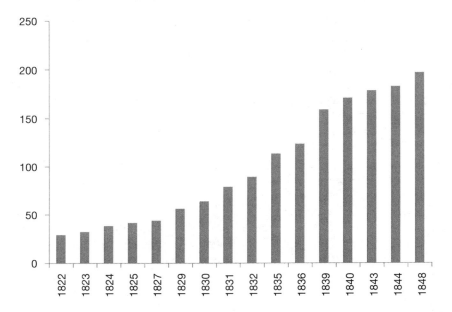

Figure 7.1 Huth & Co.'s capital, thousand of £ each year, 1809–1850 (includes the capital of the London partners only)
Source: HPJ, several volumes.

from its connections; traded on securities (buying and selling); and borrowed extensively from Huth London. The diversity of the company's contacts was striking, and they facilitated hitherto unimagined new business leads. If, as Jones has argued, knowledge about products and regions was the trading companies' main asset during the period covered by this monograph,[9] then Huth & Co.'s 'invisible' capital was truly remarkable. Indeed, its diversification of business, both geographically and across so many products, gave the firm an advantage in that it could survive any fluctuations in trade with a particular country or in a given commodity. If things went wrong in one quarter it could switch more energies to another, and the same could be done if trading in a particular product became particularly difficult. Another reason why the firm survived so many financial crises was that it mainly traded on commission rather than on own account (except for a handful of products, and rather sporadically), a strategy that, although it generated lower profits, was certainly less risky. And indeed, Figure 7.1 shows how Huth & Co.'s London capital increased steadily during the 1820s–1840s.

It has been said many times that 'the flows of people, trade, and capital created a "global economy" for the first time in history' during the last quarter of the nineteenth century.[10] I do not want to enter here into a debate about when globalization started (we could end up in the Neolithic revolution), or to apply one merchant's experience to other contemporary businesses, but it seems clear to me that, as far as the flow of goods, securities, bills of exchanges and credit is concerned, by 1850 Huth & Co. managed to build a real global network of trade, exchange and lending, well before the worldwide diffusion of the railroad, the steamships and the telegraph of the second half of the nineteenth century. Perhaps more importantly, Huth & Co.'s vast global network was driven by a conscious process led by a merchant and banker who wanted to expand his business. It was down to clever and persistent entrepreneurship, to friends who could be trusted and the cultivation of friendships, to fruitful business trips, to patience, to caution and perseverance; to possessing a substantial social capital. It was not down to the actions of governments or markets, otherwise others would have followed Frederick Huth's path before 1850. Not many were tempted.

Thus, making use of untapped primary sources, in particular the Huth papers at UCL, this monograph sheds new light on international business during the first half of the nineteenth century. Apart from contributing to the general literature on the emergence of a global economy during that time, it is expected that it will also be of interest to colleagues working on specific markets and trades. For instance, it may be useful to those researching the process of insertion of the new Latin American republics into the world economy after severance from Spain, in particular for the Chilean and Peruvian cases. Chapter 2 in particular shows how Huth & Co.'s branches in South America could profit so easily from the wider business's global networks, and its physical and social capital. For example, they gained direct access to 'new' markets, as well as to services supporting the international trade of the new republics (in particular insurance, shipping and credit), which were scarce in these countries. The chapter also shows how effective

Huth & Co. was in building commercial bridges between otherwise unconnected parts of many markets.

In the same vein, for those interested in Anglo-Spanish economic relations and Spain's foreign trade more generally, Chapter 3 improves our understanding of Spanish international trade, financial services and insurance during the first half of the nineteenth century. In particular, the chapter answers a key question which is applicable not only to Spain but to many other markets in which Huth & Co. had strong connections (e.g. Germany): why did Spanish traders and investors need the services of a London-based merchant banker? Why could they not use the services of Spanish institutions instead? Indeed, the answers provided to these questions are equally applicable to Chile, Peru, Mexico, the River Plate, China and many other markets in which Huth & Co. operated either with branches or via agents.

For the particular case of Spain, Huth & Co.'s experience shows in detail how London merchant bankers were able to provide lower transaction costs to Spanish clients than those available in Spain. Huth & Co. was part of a select group of essential intermediaries in Spain's international trade and finance at a time when trading and moving capital internationally was very risky and plagued with uncertainties. Huth & Co. effectively linked Spanish sellers and buyers with traders in the wider world who would have otherwise lacked direct contact with sellers and buyers beyond Spain, making possible a larger and more secure transaction of goods and securities for their Spanish clients and on better terms than could be procured using Spanish institutions only. Thus, to those belonging to their network, Huth & Co. effectively reduced transaction costs, as well as the risks and uncertainties inherent in Spain's international trade and capital flows due to the lack of information and trust, and the existence of language and cultural barriers. Huth & Co. possessed invaluable information about so many different markets, products and cultures that few merchants could easily match them in Spain. We also know that information circulates more within than between groups,[11] so those Spanish clients that belonged to Huth & Co.'s social network were at an advantage if compared to most other competitors. Belonging to a social network promotes trust,[12] and Huth & Co.'s network was immense. The poor state of both transport and communications during the first half of the nineteenth century made the intermediation of this firm (and that of other London merchant bankers' of the period) crucial in reducing the risks associated with trading, providing services and moving capital across borders.

Huth & Co.'s early and increasing knowledge of the Spanish, the South American, the Cuban, the Mexican, and many other markets became a major asset for the firm, with little incremental cost, and it was used repeatedly for the benefit of all of its correspondents who wanted to trade with Spain, former and current Spanish colonies or any other place in which they had trustworthy agents. In the same vein, Huth & Co.'s impressive knowledge of so many products and regions could also be used at little cost by its correspondents anywhere in the world lacking first-hand knowledge of the foreign markets of interest to them, at times when the usual pattern for multinational merchants and merchant bankers was to specialize in one or a few commodities only.[13] That is, by gaining expertise in so many products and markets Huth & Co. was able to generate efficiency gains, thus 'selling' information about a market/product to a multiplicity of correspondents and spreading the information costs across a large number of clients. Indeed, the company's several thousand business acquaintances worldwide effectively used its information and contacts at lower costs than they could procure if acting individually without the London firm's intermediation. But Huth & Co.'s friends could also use its 'invisible' assets because of the high level of trust existing between it and a select group of agents and friends. In the words of Burt, Huth & Co. could be defined as a firm adding value by effectively brokering connections between others.[14]

Likewise, it is worth noting that another interesting contrast between Huth & Co. and other prominent British merchant bankers of the period is that most of its main competitors that emerged during the 1810s and 1820s did so thanks to strong family support: 'merchant banking houses of the nineteenth century usually grew out of the existing web of cosmopolitan family connexions.'[15] Such was the case of the English Rothschild & Sons, the London Schroders, Brown Shipley & Co., Bolton Ogden and Ralli. For instance, if Frederick Huth arrived in London with just £700 in his pocket, Nathan Rothschild had over £4,000 when he did the same just over a decade prior,[16] while Carl Joachim Hambro inherited £300,000 from his father when he started C. J. Hambro & Son of London.[17]

Although it is true that Frederick Huth built on the continental European connections he left behind before moving to Britain, it is also the case that he did not have his father's or uncle's fortune to back him up: Huth & Co. relied heavily on personal ties of friendship rather than family relationships on social capital consolidated over time. Huth & Co. achieved far more than might have been predicted for a London merchant during the first decades of the nineteenth century, given its founder's capital and networks. This is crucial, because as a historian of Schroders has recognized, in a statement which is applicable to many merchant bankers of the period, for Schroder of London 'membership of the Schroder international house was vitally important to its success and to the pattern of the development of its business'.[18] In contrast, when Frederick Huth moved to London, he was not joining an already operative Huth international house; he had to build it himself during the 1820s–1840s.

What is also remarkable is the financial strength of the company and the cementing of Huth & Co.'s strong position in London as a recognized merchant banker in such a short period of time. Indeed, the company survived not only the severe 1825 financial panic, but also the much more severe crises of 1837 and 1847, which saw so many British and America merchants fail. This is not surprising given Huth & Co.'s permanent reluctance to take unnecessary risks. In a letter to one of its agents in that dreadful year of 1837, this is made quite clear:

> Money matters still look very gloomy here, and it is difficult to say how and when this state of things will end. In the meantime, great prudence and caution should be observed in all transactions, and for our own part we think it right to keep our funds together as much as possible. We therefore request

you will not encourage for the present any shipments on which advances [credit] are required.[19]

No wonder that, in a secret report produced by one of Baring Brothers' agents, Frederick Huth is classified as 'a more prudent circumspect man and thought high of'.[20]

Nowhere is this prudence more evident than in the credit policy followed by the company during the 1820s–1840s (Chapter 6). We knew that merchant bankers were the main means of financing world trade during a period characterized by the lack of modern deposit banks, information asymmetries and the persistence of weak international enforcement, but we were not aware that a single firm could finance the trade of so many commodities, in so many different regions and connecting such a wide range of locations even for trades that never docked in Britain. We were, therefore, at a loss to understand how a truly global merchant banker such as Huth could protect against the risks which arose from lending to such a number of clients trading in a wide variety of products and across so many locations.

Within this context, the key credit-related risk protection strategies followed by Huth & Co. were:

- to be flexible enough to adapt to clients' (i.e. borrowers') needs, but always to set a maximum amount of credit given, both in relation to the particular operation being financed and the total amount borrowed by the client;
- to trade mainly on commission and usually in goods and markets it knew well;
- to request collateral for the advances given, always trying to keep control of the merchandise upon which credit was extended;
- to trade with honest, trustworthy men when collateral could not be procured and whose sound reputation, therefore, acted as a good substitute for collateral;
- to cultivate friendships and business regularity with all interested parties, while also closely monitoring clients (in particular their financial soundness);
- to collect as much intelligence as possible about all the parties with whom they engaged, as well as on the changing market situation in order to diminish the threat of adverse selection;
- to curtail credit facilities during periods of financial crisis; and to insure against all risks all cargoes in which Huth & Co.'s credit was compromised.

The ultimate idea was for Huth & Co. to transfer as much risk as possible to other parties, even if this meant seeing its profit margins slimmed.[21] Even from mighty London, it was very difficult during the first half of the nineteenth century to form any real appraisal of the true standing of a house thousands of miles away, as many of Huth & Co.'s creditors were. Judging from the success of the company, though, there is no doubt that, as far as credit risk management is concerned, this business philosophy proved to be bullet-proof against bad debts, even when lending at a substantial geographical distance. To be content with modest rewards but at the same time to be protected from avoidable risks was the house's principal credit credo. But this credit-risk management strategy was not confined to lending only: in fact it was applied to all areas of the business. Indeed, the firm survived all the panics of the 1820s–1840s (and there were many), while their capital increased steadily (without interruption) during this whole period of early globalization. No one could question the soundness of its approach.

Notes

1. R. Putnam, *Bowling Alone: the Collapse and Revival of American Community* (New York: Simon & Schuster, 2000). Quoted in Lamikiz, 'Social Capital, Networks', p. 19.
2. Lamikiz, 'Social Capital, Networks', p. 19.
3. R. S. Burt, 'Structural Holes versus Network Closure as Social Capital', in N. Lin, K. Cook, and R. S. Burt (eds), *Social Capital: Theory and Research* (New York: Aldine, 2001), p. 1.
4. S. Aslanian, *From the Indian Ocean to the Mediterranean* (Berkeley: University of Californian Press, 2011), p. 170.
5. For a theoretical discussion on this, see Burt, 'Structural Holes', pp. 1–6.
6. Pearson and Richardson, 'Social Capital', p. 766.
7. HPBP, several volumes for the 1840s.
8. This figure comes from Murray, *Home from the Hill*, which apparently includes the capital of the London partners (Figure 7.1), but also that of the partners in the Liverpool and South American houses.
9. Jones, 'Multinational Trading Companies', p. 19.
10. Jones, *Merchants to Multinationals*, p. 45.
11. Burt, 'Structural Holes', p. 4.
12. Pearson and Richardson, 'Social Capital', p. 765.
13. Chapman, *The Rise*, p. 8.
14. Burt, 'Structural Holes', p. 6.
15. Jones, *International Business*, p. 99.
16. Freedman, *A London Merchant Banker*, p. 12.
17. Bramsen & Wain, *The Hambros*, p. 237.
18. Roberts, *Schroders*, p. 24.
19. HPEL-17. Huth & Co. to H. H. Stansfeld (Leeds). London, 13 March 1837.
20. HC 16/1.
21. Indeed, it is worth noting at this time that often many parties requesting credit from Huth & Co. decided not to approve its proposals on account of its requested collateral. That is, these potential clients looked for credit elsewhere, borrowing from merchant bankers who were more eager to take risks than Huth & Co. was.

Bibliography

Primary sources

Archives

Guildhall Library, London, UK, Huth Papers (GLHP).
ING, London, UK, Baring Brothers papers (HC 16).
Lancashire Record Office, Feilden & Co. Letters (DDX).
National Archives, Chile, Valparaiso Judicial Papers (ANCH-VJP).
National Archives, London, UK, State Papers Domestic (SP).
New South Wales State Library (Australia). Ward papers (NSWST-WP).
Nottingham University Library, Records of William Brandt (BT).
Plymouth & West Devon Record Office, Olver-Huth Correspondence (OHC).
Rothschild Archives, London, UK, Benjamin Davidson Papers (BDP); Huth Papers (RHL).
Smith College, Northampton, Massachusetts, USA, Hiram Putnam Papers (HCP).
UCL Special Collections, London, UK, Huth papers: Spanish Letters (HPSL); Incoming Letters (HPIL); English Letters (HPEL); German Letters (HPGL); Journals (HPJ); Bills Payable (HPBP); Bills Receivable (HPBR); Insurance Ledgers (HPINL).
University of Glasgow, Special Collections (UGSC).
University of Leeds, Brotherton Library, John Anderton papers (JAP).

Contemporary printed sources

Chile, *Estadística Comercial de Chile* (Santiago, 1850–1854).
House of Commons Parliamentary Papers, henceforth BPP, *Journals of the House of Commons*, From January the 21st, 1808, in the Forty-eighth Year of the Reign of King George the Third, to January the 16th, 1809, in the Forty-ninth Year of the Reign of King George the Third (1808).
BPP, *Journal of the House of Lords*, George III, year 59, 18 June 1819 (1819).
BPP, 'Report from the Select Committee of the House of Lords, on the Mercantile Law Amendment Bill', 294 (1856).
Campbell, J. L., *The Lives of the Lord Chancellors and keepers of the Great Seal of England* (London: John Murray, 1847).
Hodgson, J., *Textiles Manufacture, and Other Industries in Keighley* (Keighley: A. Hey, 1879).
Labrada, J. L. *Descripción económica del Reino de Galicia* (Ferrol: Editorial Galaxia, 1804).

Vedia y Goosens, D. *Historia y Descripción de la Ciudad de Coruña* (Ferrol: D. Puga, 1845).

Secondary sources

Alvarez, L. A., *Comercio Colonial y Crisis del Antiguo Régimen en Galicia, 1778–1818* (Santiago de Compostela: Xunta de Galicia, 1986).

Amunátegui, D., 'Origen del Comercio Inglés en Chile', *Revista Chilena de Historia y Geografía*, 103 (1943), pp. 83–95.

Angulo-Morales, A., 'Bilbao, Madrid, Londres. Ganaderos, Comerciantes y Cambistas Vascos en los Mercados Financieros y Laneros del Atlántico', in J. A. Ocampo (ed.), *Empresas y Empresarios del Norte de España a Fines del Antiguo R*égimen (Madrid: Marcial Pons, 2011), pp. 184–210.

Anonymous, 'Las Harinas Chilenas en Australia', *Revista Chilena de Historia y Geografía*, 120 (1952), pp. 223–227.

Apeseg, *100 años en la Historia del Seguro* (Lima: Asociación Peruana de Empresas de Seguros, 2004).

Aragón, A., 'La Guerra de la Convención, la Separación de Guipúzcoa y los Comerciantes Vasco-Franceses y Bearneses', *Pedralbes* 31 (2011), pp.167–229.

Aragón, A. and Angulo-Morales, A., 'The Spanish Basque Country in Global Trade Networks in the Eighteenth Century', *International Journal of Maritime History*, 25 (2013), pp. 149–172.

Aslanian, S. *From the Indian Ocean to the Mediterranean* (Berkeley: University of Californian Press, 2011).

Asdrúbal, H., 'Hamburgo y el Río de la Plata: Vinculaciones Económicas a Fines de la Epoca Colonial, *Jahrbuch für Geschichte Lateinamerikas*, 21 (1984), pp. 189–209.

Austin, P. E., *Baring Brothers and the Birth of Modern Finance* (London: Pickering & Chatto, 2007).

Bader, T., 'Before the Gold Fleets: Trade and Relations between Chile and Australia, 1830–1848', *Journal of Latin American Studies*, 6 (1974), pp. 35–58.

Barbier, J. A., 'Peninsular Finance and Colonial Trade: the Dilemma of Charles IV's Spain', *Journal of Latin American Studies*, 12 (1980), pp. 21–37.

Barbier, J. A., 'Comercio Neutral in Bolivarian America', in R. Liehr (ed), *América Latina en la Epoca de Simón Bolívar* (Berlin: Colloquium Verlag, 1989), pp. 363–377.

Bazant, J., 'Los Bienes de la Familia de Hernán Cortés y su Venta por Lucas Alamán', *Historia Mexicana*, 19 (1969), pp. 228–247.

Ben-Porath, Y., 'The F-connection: Families, Friends, and Firms and the Organization of Exchange', *Population and Development Review*, 6 (1980), pp. 1–30.

Bértola, L., and Williamson, J. G., 'Globalization in Latin America before 1940', in V. Bulmer-Thomas, J. Coatsworth, and R. Cortés-Conde (eds), *Cambridge Economic History of Latin America* (Cambridge: Cambridge University Press, 2006), pp. 9–56.

Blancpain, J. P., *Les Allemands au Chili, 1816–1945* (Colonia and Vienne: Böhlau Verlag, 1974).

Bramsen, B. and Wain, K., *The Hambros, 1779–1979* (London: Michael Joseph, 1979).

Bulmer-Thomas, V., *The Economic History of Latin America Since Independence* (Cambridge: Cambridge University Press, 2003).

Burt, R. S., 'Structural Holes versus Network Closure as Social Capital', in N. Lin, K. Cook, and R. S. Burt (eds), *Social Capital: Theory and Research* (New York: Aldine, 2001).

Bibliography 147

Butrón, G., 'Elite Local, Poder y Cambio Político en Cádiz, del Antiguo Regimen al Liberalismo, 1823–1835', in D. Caro (ed), *El Primer Liberalismo en Andalucía, 1808–1868: Política, Economía y Sociabilidad* (Cádiz: Universidad de Cádiz, 2005), pp. 63–88.

Carmona-Badía, X., *El Atraso Industrial de Galicia: Auge y Liquidación de las Manufacturas Textiles* (Barcelona: Ariel, 1990).

Cavieres, E., *Comercio Chileno y Comerciantes Ingleses* (Santiago de Chile: Editorial Universitaria, 1999).

Casson, M., 'The Economic Analysis of Multinational Trading Companies', in G. Jones (ed.), *The Multinational Traders* (London: Routledge, 1998), pp. 22–47.

Centner, C. W., *Great Britain and Chile, 1810–1914: a Chapter in the Expansion of Europe*, PhD Thesis (Illinois: University of Chicago, 1941).

Centner, C. W., 'Relaciones Comerciales de Gran Bretaña con Chile, 1810–1830', *Revista Chilena de Historia y Geografía*, 103 (1942), pp. 96–107.

Centner, C. W., 'Great Britain and Chilean Mining, 1830–1914', *Economic History Review*, 12 (1943), pp. 76–82.

Cervantes-Rodriguez, M., *International Migration in Cuba: Accumulation, Imperial Designs, and Transnational Social Fields* (Pennsylvania: The Pennsylvania State University Press, 2010).

Chapman, S. D., 'The International Houses: The Continental Contribution to British Commerce, 1800–1860', *Journal of European Economic History*, 6 (1977), pp. 5–48.

Chapman, S. D., 'British Marketing Enterprise: the Changing Roles of Merchants, Manufacturers, and Financers, 1700–1860'. *Business History Review*, 53 (1979), pp. 205–234.

Chapman, S. D., 'Financial Restraints on the Growth of Firms in the Cotton Industry, 1790–1850', *Economic History Review*, 33 (1979), pp. 50–69.

Chapman, S. D., *The Rise of Merchant Banking* (London: George Allen & Unwin, 1984).

Chapman, S. D., *Merchant Enterprise in Britain. From the Industrial Revolution to World War I* (Cambridge: Cambridge University Press, 1992).

Chapman, S. D., 'The Commercial Sector', in M. B. Rose (ed.), *The Lancashire Cotton Industry: A History Since 1700* (Preston: Lancashire County Books, 1996), pp. 63–93.

Contreras, C., 'El Legado Económico de la Independencia en el Perú', *Documento de Trabajo* No. 301 (Lima: Departamento de Economía. Pontificia Universidad Católica del Perú, 2010).

Couyoumdjian, J. R., 'Portales y las Transformaciones Económicas de Chile en su Epoca: una Aproximación', in B. L. Bravo (ed.), *Portales, el Hombre y su Obra* (Santiago: Editorial Jurídica de Chile, 1989), pp. 243–280.

Couyoumdjian, J. R., 'El Alto Comercio de Valparaíso y las Grandes Casas Extranjeras: 1880–1930. Una aproximación', *Historia*, 33 (2000), pp. 63–99.

Cross, R. F., *Sailor in the Whitehouse: The Seafaring Life of FDR* (Annapolis: Naval Institute Press, 2003).

Cuenca-Estevan, J., 'Statistics of Spain's Colonial Trade, 1792–1820', *Hispanic American Historical Review*, 61 (1981), pp. 381–428.

Cuenca-Esteban, J., 'British "Ghost" Exports, American Middlemen, and the Trade to Spanish America, 1790–1819: A Speculative Reconstruction', *William and Mary Quarterly*, 71 (2014), pp. 63–98.

Curry-Machado, J., 'Running from Albion: Migration to Cuba from the British Isles in the 19th Century', *International Journal of Cuban Studies*, 2 (2009), pp. 1–13.

148 Bibliography

Curry-Machado, J., 'Rich Flames and Hired Tears: Sugar, Sub-Imperial Agents and the Cuban Phoenix of Empire', *Journal of Global History*, 4 (2009), pp. 33–56.

Davis, R., *The Industrial Revolution and British Overseas Trade* (Leicester: Leicester University Press, 1979).

Dawson, F. G., *The First Latin American Debt Crisis: the City of London and the 1822–25 Loan Bubble* (New Haven, Yale University Press, 1990).

De Fiore, E. and De Fiore, O., *The British Presence in Brazil, 1808–1914* (Sao Paulo: Editora Paubrasil, 1987).

Deustua, J., *La Minería Peruana y la Iniciación de la República, 1820–1840* (Lima: IEP, 1986).

Díaz Morlán, P., *Los Ybarra. Una Dinastía de Empresarios, 1801–2001* (Madrid: Marcial Pons, 2002).

Dopico, F., 'Felicidad Pública y Libre Mercado. El Surgimiento de Valores Liberales en la Ilustración Gallega', *Revista Galega de Economía*, 16 (2007), pp. 1–19.

Ely, R. T., 'The Old Cuba Trade: Highlights and Case Studies of Cuban–American Interdependence during the Nineteenth Century', *Business History Review*, 38 (1964), pp. 456–478.

Evans, C. and Saunders, O. 'A World of Copper: Globalizing the Industrial Revolution, 1830–1870', *Journal of Global History*, 10 (2015), pp. 3–26.

Ferguson, N., *The House of Rothschild. Volume 1* (London: Penguin, 1999).

Fernández, M A., 'Merchants and Bankers: British Direct and Portfolio Investment in Chile During the Nineteenth Century', *Ibero–Amerikanisches Archiv*, 9 (1983), pp. 343–379.

Fontana-Lazaro, J., 'Colapso y Transformaciones del Comercio Exterior Español entre 1792 y 1827. Un Aspecto de la Economía del Antiguo Régimen en España', *Moneda y Crédito*, 115 (1970), pp. 3–23.

Freedman, J. R., *A London Merchant Banker Anglo-American Trade and Finance, 1835–1850*. PhD Thesis (London: University of London, 1968).

Friedman, W. A. and Jones, G., 'Business History: Time for Debate', *Business History Review*, 85 (2011), pp. 1–8.

Gibbs & Sons, A., *Merchants and Bankers, 1808–1958* (London: The Firm, 1958).

Gilman, W. C., *A Memoir of Daniel Wadsworth Coit of Norwich, Connecticut, 1787–1876* (Cambridge: Cambridge University Press, 1909).

Goebel, D. B., 'British–American Rivalry in the Chilean Trade, 1817–1820', *Journal of Economic History*, 2 (1942), pp. 190–202.

Greenberg, M., *British Trade and the Opening of China, 1800–42* (Cambridge: Cambridge University Press, 1969).

Greif, A., *Institutions and the Path to the Modern Economy: Lessons from Medieval Trade* (Cambridge: Cambridge University Press, 2008).

Guenther, L. H., *British Merchants in Nineteenth–Century Brazil: Business, Culture, and Identity in Bahia, 1808–1850* (Oxford: Oxford University Press, 2004).

Harley, C. K., 'International Competitiveness of the Antebellum American Cotton Textile Industry', *Journal of Economic History*, 52 (1992), pp. 559–584.

Hidy, R. W., *The House of Baring in American Trade and Finance* (Cambridge: Harvard University Press, 1949).

Hoyo, A., *Todo Mudó de Repente. El Horizonte Económico de la Burguesía Mercantil en Santander, 1820–1874* (Santander: Universidad de Cantabria, 1993).

Hudson, P., *The West Riding Wool Textile Industry: a Catalogue of Business Records from the Sixteenth to the Twenty Century* (Edington: Pasold Research Fund Ltd., 1975).

Jenks, L. H., *The Migration of British Capital to 1875* (London: Nelson & Sons, 1963).
Jones, G., 'Multinational Trading Companies in History and Theory', in G. Jones (ed.), *The Multinational Traders* (London: Routledge, 1998), pp. 1–21.
Jones, G., *Merchants to Multinationals: British Trading Companies in the Nineteenth and Twentieth Centuries* (Oxford: Oxford University Press, 2000).
Jones, G. and M. B. Rose, 'Family Capitalism', *Business History*, 35 (1993), pp. 1–16.
Jones, C., *International Business in the Nineteenth Century* (Brighton: Wheatsheaf, 1987).
Jones, C., 'Huth, Frederick Andrew (1777–1864)', *Oxford Dictionary of National Biography* (Oxford: Oxford University Press, 2004).
Killick, J. R., 'Risk, Specialisation and Profit in the Mercantile Sector of the Nineteenth Century Cotton Trade: Alexander Brown and Sons, 1820–80', *Business History*, 16 (1974), pp. 1–16.
Kinsbruner, J., 'The Political Influence of the British Merchants Resident in Chile during the O'Higgins Administration, 1817–1823', *The Americas*, 27 (1970), pp. 26–39.
Kozolchyk, B., 'The Legal Nature of the Irrevocable Commercial Letter of Credit', *American Journal of Comparative Law*, 14 (1965), pp. 395–421.
Kynaston, D., *The City of London. Volume 1: a World on its Own 1815–1890* (London: Chatto & Windus, 1995).
Lambert, A., 'Cochrane, Thomas, Tenth earl of Dundonald (1775–1860), Naval Officer'. (Oxford: Oxford Dictionary of National Biography, 2004).
Lamikiz, X., *Trade and Trust in the Eighteenth-Century Atlantic World* (London: Boydell & Breaver Press, 2010).
Lamikiz, X., 'Social Capital, Networks and Trust in Early Modern Long-Distance Trade: A Critical Appraisal', in M. Herrero and K. Kapps (eds), *Merchants and Trade Networks in the Atlantic and the Mediterranean, 1550-1800: Connectors of Commercial Maritime Systems* (London: Pickering & Chatto, 2016).
Larrinaga, C., 'Los Comerciantes Banqueros y la Industrialización Guipuzcoana a Mediados del siglo XIX', *Historia Contemporánea*, 27 (2003), pp. 831–854.
Liedtke, R., 'Modern Communication: the Information Network of N. M. Rothschild & Sons in the Nineteenth-Century Europe', in Feldman, G. D. and Hertner, P. (eds), *Finance and Modernization, a Transnational and Transcontinental Perspective for the Nineteenth and Twentieth Centuries* (Surrey: Ashgate, 2008), pp. 155–164.
Lisle-Williams, M., 'Merchant Banking Dynasties in the English Class Structure', *British Journal of Sociology*, 35 (1984), pp. 333–362.
Lisle-Williams, M., 'Coordinators and Controllers of Capital: the Social and Economic Significance of the British Merchant Banks', *Social Science Information*, 23 (1984), pp. 95–128.
Lisle-Williams, M., 'Beyond the Market: The Survival of Family Capitalism in the English Merchant Banks', *British Journal of Sociology*, 35 (1984), pp. 241–271.
Llorca-Jaña, M., 'Knowing the Shape of Demand: Britain's Exports of Ponchos to the Southern Cone, c.1810s–1870s', *Business History*, 51 (2009), pp. 602–621.
Llorca-Jaña, M., 'The Marine Insurance Market for British Textile Exports to the River Plate and Chile, c.1810–1850', in R. Pearson (ed), *The Development of International Insurance* (London: Pickering & Chatto, 2010), pp. 25–35.
Llorca-Jaña, M., 'The Organization of British Textile Exports to the River Plate and Chile: Merchant Houses in Operation, c.1810–1859', *Business History*, 53 (2011), pp. 820–865.
Llorca-Jaña, M., *La Historia del Seguro en Chile, 1810–2010* (Madrid: Fundación Mapfre, 2011).

150 Bibliography

Llorca-Jaña, M., 'To be Waterproof or to be Soaked: Importance of Packing in British Textile Exports to Distant Markets. The Cases of Chile and the River Plate, *c*.1810–1859', *Revista de Historia Económica / Journal of Iberian and Latin American Economic History*, 29 (2011), pp.11–37.

Llorca-Jaña, M., 'The Economic Activities of a Global Merchant-Banker in Chile: Huth & Co. of London, 1820s–1850s', *Historia*, 45 (2012), pp. 399–432.

Llorca-Jaña, M., *The British Textile Trade in South America in the Nineteenth Century* (New York: Cambridge University Press, 2012).

Llorca-Jaña, M., 'Connections and Networks in Spain of a London Merchant-Banker, 1800–1850', *Revista de Historia Económica / Journal of Iberian and Latin American Economic History*, 31 (2013), pp. 423–458.

Llorca-Jaña, M., 'Shaping Globalization: London's Merchant Bankers in the Early Nineteenth Century', *Business History Review*, 88 (2014), pp. 469–495.

Llorca-Jaña, M., 'British Merchants in New Markets: the Case of Wylie and Hancock in Brazil and the River Plate, *c*.1808–1820', *Journal of Imperial and Commonwealth History*, 44 (2014), pp. 215–238.

López-Morell, M. A., *La Casa Rothschild en España* (Madrid: Marcial Pons, 2005).

López-Morell, M. A. and O'Kean, J., 'Rothschilds' Strategies in International Non-Ferrous Metals Markets, 1830–1940', *Economic History Review*, 67 (2014), pp. 720–749.

Lynch, J., *The Spanish American Revolutions, 1808–1826* (London: W. W. Norton & Company, 1986).

Manchester, A. K., *British Pre-Eminence in Brazil: its Rise and Decline* (New York: Octagon Books, 1964).

Marzagalli, S., 'Establishing Transatlantic Trade Networks in Time of War: Bordeaux and the United States, 1793–1815', *Business History Review*, 79 (2005), pp. 811–844.

Marriner, S., *Rathbones of Liverpool, 1845–1874* (Liverpool: Liverpool University Press, 1961).

Marriner, S. and Hyde, F. E., *The Senior John Samuel Swire, 1825–1898* (Liverpool: Liverpool University Press, 1967).

Mathew, W. M., 'The First Anglo-Peruvian Debt and its Settlement, 1822–1849', *Journal of Latin American Studies*, 2 (1970), pp. 81–98.

Mathew, W. M., 'Peru and the British Guano Market', *Economic History Review*, 23 (1970), pp. 112–128.

Mayo, J., 'Before the Nitrate Era: British Commission Houses and the Chilean Economy, 1851–80', *Journal of Latin American Studies*, 11 (1979), pp. 283–302.

Mayo, J., 'Britain and Chile 1851–1886. Anatomy of a Relationship', *Journal of Inter-American Studies and World Affairs*, 23 (1981), pp. 95–120.

Mayo, J., *British Merchants and Chilean Development* (Boulder: Westview Press, 1987).

Mayo, J., 'British Merchants in Chile and Mexico's West Coast in the Mid-Century: the Age of Isolation', *Historia*, 26 (1991), pp. 141–171.

McGrane, R. C., *Foreign Bondholders and American States Debt* (New York: MacMillan, 1935).

Meinertzhagen, G., *A Bremen Family* (London: Longmans, 1912).

Meinertzhagen, R., *Diary of a Black Sheep* (London: Oliver and Boyd, 1964).

Méndez, L. M., *El Comercio entre Chile y el Puerto de Filadelfia en los Estados Unidos de Norteamérica: Estudio Comparado Binacional* (Valparaíso: Universidad de Playa Ancha, 2001).

Miller, R., *Britain and Latin America in the Nineteenth and Twentieth Centuries* (Essex: Longman, 1993).

Milne, G. J., *Trade and Traders in Mid-Victorian Liverpool: Mercantile Business and the Making of a World Port* (Liverpool: Liverpool University Press, 2000).
Mitchell, B. R., *British Historical Statistics* (Cambridge: Cambridge University Press, 1989).
Moraes, M. I. and Stalla, N., 'Antes y Después de 1810: Escenarios en la Historia de las Exportaciones Rioplatenses de Cueros desde 1760 hasta 1860', *Documentos de Trabajo* 11, Sociedad Española de Historia Agraria (2011).
Murray, A., *Home from the Hill* (London: Hamish Hamilton, 1970).
North, D. C., *The Economic Growth of the United States, 1790–1860* (New Jersey: Prentice Hall, 1961).
Ortiz de la Tabla, J., *Comercio Exterior de Veracruz, 1778–1821* (Sevilla: Escuela de Estudios Hispano-Americanos, 1978).
Pearce, A., *British Trade with Spanish America, 1763–1808* (Liverpool: Liverpool University Press, 2007).
Pearce, A., 'Huancavelica 1563–1824: History and Historiography', *Colonial Latin American Review*, 22 (2013), pp. 422–440.
Pearson, R. and Richardson, D., 'Social Capital, Institutional Innovation and Atlantic Trade before 1800', *Business History*, 50 (2008), pp. 765–780.
Pereira, E., *La Actuación de los Oficiales Navales Norteamericanos en Nuestras Costas* (Santiago: Universidad de Chile, 1935).
Pereira, E., 'Las Primeras Relaciones Comerciales entre Chile y el Oriente', *Boletín de la Academia Chilena de la Historia*, 39 (1948), pp. 1–19.
Pereira, E., 'Las Primeras Relaciones Comerciales entre Chile y Australia', *Boletín de la Academia Chilena de la Historia*, 53 (1955), pp. 5–36.
Pereira, E., *Los Primeros Contactos entre Chile y Los Estados Unidos, 1778–1809* (Santiago: Editorial Andrés Bello, 1971).
Perkins, E. J., 'Financing Antebellum Importers: the Role of Brown Bros. & Co. in Baltimore', *Business History Review*, 45 (1971), pp. 421–451.
Perkins, E. J., *Financing Anglo-American Trade: the House of Brown, 1800–1880* (Cambridge: Harvard University Press, 1975).
Platt, T., 'Spanish Quicksilver: A Preliminary Note: The London Market, Global Trade and the Rothschild Monopoly (1820–50)', *The Rothschild Archive Review of the Year*, 2011, pp. 38–48.
Platt, T., 'Container Transport: from Skin Bags to Iron Flasks. Changing Technologies of Quicksilver Packaging between Almadén and America, 1788–1848', *Past & Present*, 214 (2012), pp. 205–253.
Platt, T., 'Espacios Económicos y Suministro de Azogues en los Andes: Transportes, Remesas, Contratos. El Conflicto entre Bolivia y Rothschild, 1835–1853', Paper presented in honour of Carlos Sempat Assadourian in CLADHE 3, Bariloche, Argentina (2012).
Pons-Pons, J., 'Spain: International Influence on the Domestic Insurance Market', in P. Borscheid and N. V. Haueter (eds), *World Insurance: the Evolution of a Global Risk Network* (Oxford: Oxford University Press, 2012), pp. 189–212.
Prados de la Escosura, L., *Comercio Exterior y Crecimiento Económico en España, 1826–1913* (Madrid: Banco de España, 1982).
Prados de la Escosura, L., 'Comercio Exterior y Cambio Económico en España, 1792–1849', in J. Fontana (ed.), *La Economía Española al Final del Antiguo Regimen, Volumen III, Comercio y Colonias* (Madrid: Alianza Editorial, 1982), pp. 171–249.

Bibliography

Prados de la Escosura, L. and Tortella G., 'Tendencias a Largo Plazo del Comercio Exterior Español, 1714–1913', *Revista de Historia Económica*, 1 (1983), pp. 353–367.

Prados de la Escosura, L., 'El Comercio Hispano–Británico en los Siglos XVIII y XIX. I. Reconstruccion', *Revista de Historia Económica*, 2 (1984), pp. 113–162.

Prados de la Escosura, L., 'Las Relaciones Reales de Intercambio entre España y Gran Bretaña Durante los Siglos XVIII y XIX', in P. Martin Aceña and L. Prados de la Escosura (eds.), *La Nueva Historia Económica en España* (Madrid: Tecnos, 1985).

Prados de la Escosura, L., 'Una Serie Anual de Comercio Exterior Español, 1821–1913', *Revista de Historia Económica*, 4 (1986), pp. 103–150.

Prados de la Escosura, L., 'La Pérdida del Imperio y sus Consecuencias Económicas en España', in L. Prados de la Escosura, and S. Amaral. (eds.), *La Independencia Americana, Consecuencias Económicas* (Madrid: Alianza Editorial, 1993), pp. 253–300.

Putnam, R., *Bowling Alone: the Collapse and Revival of American Community* (New York: Simon & Schuster, 2000).

Ramírez, H., *Historia del Imperialismo en Chile* (Santiago: Empresa Editora Austral Limitada, 1960).

Reber, V. B., *British Mercantile Houses in Buenos Aires* (Cambridge: Harvard University Press, 1979).

Rector, J., *Merchants, Trade and Commercial Policy in Chile, 1810–1840*. PhD Thesis (Indiana University, 1976).

Rector, J. L., 'El Impacto Económico de la Independencia en América Latina: el Caso de Chile', *Historia*, 20 (1985), pp. 295–318.

Rippy, F. J., 'Latin America and the British investment "Boom" of the 1820's', *Journal of Modern History*, 19 (1947), pp. 122–129.

Roberts, R., *Schroders: Merchants and Bankers* (London: Macmillan, 1992).

Rubinstein, W. D., *Men of Property: The Very Wealthy in Britain Since the Industrial Revolution* (Surrey: Croom Helm, 1981).

Rubio, C., *Fueros y Constitución: la Lucha por el Control del Poder, País Vasco, 1808–1868* (Bilbao: Servicio Editorial Universidad del País Vasco, 1997).

Salazar, G., 'Dialéctica de la Modernización Mercantil: Intercambio Desigual, Coacción, Claudicación (Chile Como *West Coast*, 1817–1843)', *Cuadernos de Historia*, 14 (1994), pp. 21–80.

Santarosa, V. A., 'Financing Long-Distance Trade without Banks: The Joint Liability Rule and Bills of Exchange in 18th-century France', Working Paper (Michigan: University of Michigan, 2012).

Sierra, M., *La Familia Ybarra, Empresarios y Políticos* (Sevilla: Muñoz Moya Editores, 1992).

Smith, W. B., *Economic Aspects of the Second Bank of the United States* (Cambridge: Harvard University Press, 1953).

Stein, B. and Stein S. *Edge of Crisis: War and Trade in the Spanish Atlantic, 1789–1808* (Baltimore: Johns Hopkins University Press, 2009).

Train, G. F., *My Life in Many States and Foreign Lands. Dictated on my Seventy Four Fear* (New York: Library of Alexandria, 1902).

Valenzuela, L., 'The Chilean Copper Smelting Industry in the Mid-Nineteenth Century: Phases of Expansion and Stagnation, 1834–58', *Journal of Latin American Studies*, 24 (1992), pp. 507–550.

Véliz, C., 'Egaña, Lambert, and the Chilean Mining Associations of 1825', *Hispanic American Historical Review*, 55 (1975), pp. 637–663.

Wake, J., *Kleinwort Benson: the History of Two Families in Banking* (Oxford: Oxford University Press, 1997).

Weber, K., 'The Atlantic Coast of German Trade: German Rural Industry and Trade in the Atlantic, 1680–1840', *Itinerario*, 26 (2002), pp. 99–119.

Wilkins, M., *The History of Foreign Investment in the United States* (Cambridge, Massachusetts: Harvard University Press, 1989).

Wu, C., *Generals and Diplomats: Great Britain and Peru, 1820–1840* (Cambridge: Center for Latin American Studies, 1991).

Young, G. K., *Merchant Banking, Practice and Prospects* (London: Weidenfeld and Nicholson, 1971).

Index

Adalid, M.F. de 14, 16, 64
Adams & Whitall 91–2, 127
advances 1, 23, 36–7, 39–41, 43; agents 82, 87; credit strategies 117–32; opportunities 143; Spanish connections 57–8, 66–7, 72; US connections 108–10
adverse selection 121, 126, 143
Africa 21, 139
Age of Commerce 3
agents 21, 38–9, 59, 61–2, 69, 79–94, 108, 119, 123, 125
Alabama 61
Alaman, L. 113
Alava, M. 61
Alliance Assurance Co 72
Alliance Marine Insurance Co 71
Almadén 42, 44
Almadenejos 42
alpaca 35
Alsina, J. 17
American Houses 91–2, 106
American Wars of Independence 4
Americas 7, 12, 20–3, 44–6, 84; credit strategies 121, 125, 128; global enterprise 103–4, 108, 110; Spanish connections 64, 67, 70
Amsterdam 11–12, 19, 64, 68, 104, 110
Anderson Hober 112
Anderton, J. 7, 81
Andes 33
Anglo-American War 4

annatto 107
Antwerp 12, 67–8, 104, 108, 112, 125
Arica 33
Arkansas 61–2, 112, 132
arms 31
Aschen & Co 125
Asia 21–2, 37–8, 46, 64, 80–1, 84–5, 104–6, 108–9, 119, 139
Aspinwall Brothers 31
Athens 63
Atlantic 11, 14, 33, 80
Atlas Insurance Co 72
Austin, P. 106–7
Australia 7, 38, 40–1, 46, 86, 104–5, 139
Austria 19, 105

Baguer y Rivas, F. 63
Bahia 41, 103–4, 110
Balbiani & Co 68
bale-rope 131
Baltimore 90–1
Banco de Cadiz 69
Banco de Isabel II 69
Banco de San Carlos 69
Banco Español de San Fernando 69, 112
Banco Nacional de San Carlos 14
Bank of Liverpool 112
Bank of Manchester 112
Bank of Spain 69
Bank of the United States (BUS) 60–3, 91–2, 112

bankruptcy 4, 39, 139
banks 3, 14, 43, 60–3, 69–70, 85, 91–2, 101, 112, 130, 143
Barbier, J.A. 12
Barcelona 55, 65, 69
Baring Brothers 4, 7, 21, 61, 68–9, 91, 102, 106–7, 109–12, 122, 125–6, 143
Barrié, J.F. 13–14, 70
barriers to entry 4, 66, 137
Basque Country 7, 11–13, 65
Bastian, J.W. 73
Bayonne 11
beef 20, 40, 67, 107, 128, 130
Belfast 82
Belgium 37–8, 68, 105
Belman, E.L. 63
Bencke & Co 130
Bengal 106
Bengoechea & Co 65, 68
Berlin 38, 73, 125
Bermudez, F. 67, 129
Bevan & Humphreys 41, 92
Bibby & Co 38, 84–6, 106, 108
Bibby, A. 106
Bibby, E. 106
Bibby, J. 106
Bilbao 16, 18, 57, 64–6
billiard balls 107
bills of exchange 1, 39, 67, 69, 85, 109, 111–3, 123–4, 140
bills of lading 121–2, 127, 129, 131–2
Birley Hornby Kirk 81
Birmingham 21
Bivanco, J. de 63
black boxes 65
Blanc, Dupont & Co 37
Blanco & Co 41
Blanco, P. 41
Bobo e Hijos 65
Bohemia 19, 37, 64
Bolivia 42–5
Bolton Ogden 142
Bombay 106
bonds 61–3, 70, 112, 131

Bordeaux 11, 19, 37, 84
boric acid 107
Boricua 68
Boston 91, 93, 119
Boxer 32
Bradford 81
branches 79–95
Brandt Sons & Co 21, 103, 106
Brandt, W. 7
Brazil 5, 20, 22, 37, 41, 82, 103–5, 110, 119, 124, 136
Bremen 18–19, 72–3, 84, 104, 110
Brentano Bovara & Urbieta 12, 73
Brentano Urbieta & Co 11–12, 14–15, 17–19, 85
Bristol 16, 21, 80, 82
Britain 4–7, 13, 15–17, 21–3, 29–36; agents 79–94; beyond bilateral trades 64–5; credit strategies 117–22, 124–5, 129–32; expansion 39–40; financial services 66–7, 69–70; German connections 55, 72–3; global enterprise 101, 104, 106–11, 113; insurance brokers 71–2; opportunities 136–7, 139, 142–3; quicksilver trade 45–6; Spanish connections 56–61; US connections 90–3
British Empire 11
British Overseas Bank 3
brokers 1, 22, 58, 71–2, 80, 112–13, 137, 142
Brown & Co 91, 102, 106–9, 111
Brown Shipley & Co 4, 21, 86, 103, 110, 142
Brown, W.J. 91
Brune & Son 90
Buchanan & Young 82
Buenos Aires 6, 11–12, 17, 20, 33, 41, 64–7, 82, 103, 126, 128, 130
buffalo horns 107
bullion 1, 40, 42, 123
Burt & Sons 82
Burt, R.S. 142
Burton & Sons 81

business 1–3, 5, 7, 13–14, 16; agents 79–80, 86–9, 91–3; credit strategies 124, 128–9; early activities 18–20, 22; expansion 34, 38–9; global enterprise 101, 111–12; insurance brokers 71; opportunities 136, 139–40, 142–3; schools 11; Spanish connections 55, 70; US connections 93
Business History Review 101
butter 107

Cabanyes, J.B. 22, 69
Cabello e Hijos 65
Cadiz 11–12, 14, 16, 21, 43, 55, 67
Calcutta 106
California 44–6, 94
Callao 12–13, 30, 32–3, 35, 38, 40, 42, 45, 65, 82, 87
candles 107
Canton 40, 106, 108, 113, 122, 125, 127
Cape Horn 33
Capetillo & Co 68
capital movement 1, 4, 57, 68–9, 92, 109, 112, 117–19, 131, 136, 139–41
capitalism 2, 5
Caracas 67, 70, 103, 110, 129
Cardenas Railroad 68
Cardiff 104
Caribbean 12, 22, 37, 68, 104, 139
Carlist Wars 60
cartels 44–5
Casas, A.F. 16
Casson, M. 102
Castellain, A. 21, 62, 85–6, 93
Castellain, Schaezler & Co 84–6
Castillo, M. 63
castor oil 106–7
Catalonia 69
Cavieres, E. 30, 42
Central America 11, 16, 41, 139
Cervantes-Rodriguez, M. 6
Chañarcillo 42

Chapeaurouge & Co 18, 73
Chapman, S.D. 5, 56–7, 65, 101–2, 107, 109–10, 117–19, 125
chartered trading companies 5
cheese 64
Child, G. 22
Chile 6–7, 13, 20, 29–30, 32–4; agents 81–2, 85–7; beyond bilateral trades 65; credit strategies 119, 124; establishing operations 30–4; financial services 67; global enterprise 103–4, 106, 109, 113; National Archives 7; operations (1820s-1840s) 34–41; opportunities 137, 140–1; quicksilver trade 41–6
China 29, 37–8, 40, 89, 104–6; credit strategies 119, 125, 127; global enterprise 108, 110, 113; opportunities 136, 141
chinchilla skins 107
Church of England 21
cigars 107
cinnamon 16, 107–8, 128
Clarson & Co 130
Clason & Ules 64, 92, 121
clerks 12–13, 22, 31, 34, 43, 66, 69, 84, 111
Cleveland & Lewis 92
coal 59
cochineal 11, 16, 107
Cochrane, Lord 32
cocoa 22, 32, 67–8, 103, 107, 110, 129
cod 16
coffee 11, 22, 68, 103, 107, 110
Coit, D.W. 31–6, 39, 41, 82
collateral 121–2, 124–5, 127–32, 143
Colom & Co 69
colonies 11, 16–17, 22, 33, 55–7, 59, 64, 67, 72, 80, 108, 141
commissions 1–2, 14–16, 18, 22, 31–3; agents 79–80, 82, 85, 89; credit strategies 119, 123, 129–31; expansion 37, 39–40, 43; global enterprise 101–2, 107, 112;

insurance brokers 71; opportunities 140, 143; Spanish connections 58–9, 62, 66, 69; US connections 91
Compañia Unida de Minas 113
compensation 89
competitive advantage 42
confidential agents 21, 38–9, 59, 61–2, 69, 79–94, 108, 119, 123, 125
consignors 80, 117, 119–23, 126–8
contracts 1, 36, 79, 111, 118, 131
Copenhagen 104
Copiapó 36, 43
copper 7, 35–40, 86, 104, 107
Coquimbo 36
Cora & Polo 65
corahs 106
corn 65
Corral y Puente, P. del 43
correspondents 1–3, 7, 13, 15–16, 18–21; credit strategies 118, 122, 124, 129, 131; expansion 30, 37; global enterprise 101, 103–6, 108, 110–12; opportunities 139; role 137, 139, 141–2; Spanish connections 63–6, 69, 71–3; US connections 79–83, 89–93
Corrientes, M. 63
corruption 60
Cortes, H. 113
Corunna 7, 11–18, 31, 55, 64–5, 67, 72
cottons 16–17, 21, 36, 39, 66; credit strategies 119, 121, 125–7; global enterprise 104, 107, 109; US connections 82, 85–7, 89–92, 94
credit strategies 8, 36, 38, 41, 57–8; agents 91–2; global enterprise 104, 108–10, 112; opportunities 139–40, 143–4; risk management 117–32; Spanish connections 62, 64, 66, 68; US connections 93–4
Cropper & Benson 21, 103
cross-border trade 1–2, 4, 13, 137
Cruz, J.A. 16

Cuba 6, 18, 20, 29, 41; credit strategies 124; global enterprise 103, 105; opportunities 141; Spanish connections 57, 64, 67–8, 70; US connections 85
Cullingworth 81
currency 43
Curry-Machado, J. 6
cutlery 16, 107

Darthez Brothers 57
Davis, R. 80
Day & Phillips 80
De Bruyn & Sons 104
debt 1, 31, 56, 62, 70; credit strategies 118, 121, 124, 129–30, 132; global enterprise 109, 111; opportunities 143; US connections 89, 93
deer horns 107
Demblans, M.F. 16
Denmark 63
Detmering, H.L. 37
discount 39, 66–7, 120, 124
documentary credits 121
Domenzain & Co 103, 110
Doriga, L. 16, 18
Dorr & Co 131
Dorr, F. 131
Dorr, S. 131
Downes & Rogers 92
drafts 40, 66–8, 86, 112–13, 119–25, 129–30
Drake & Co 67, 103
Drake & Pert 67
Drake Brothers & Co 68
Drake, J. 67–8
Drusina & Co 37, 44, 103, 108
Drusina, W. de 37, 44
Du Fay & Co 81
Dublin 21
Dubois, E. 35
Dubois, J. 35
Dufou, J. 84
Dugdale & Brother 81
Dumas & Co 104

Dunlap, T. 63
duties 32, 70

earthenware 21, 107–8
ebony 107
Echarte & Co 72
economists 2, 102
Ecuador 20, 32, 103
Edinburgh 30
Edwards & Co 22, 80
Edwards, G. 22, 80
Egusquiza, P. 67, 129
Eisenstuck & Co 126
elephant teeth 107
elites 4, 57, 68, 110
Elseneur 63
Elzaburo & Co 129
embezzlement 39
Embil & Co 67
Embil, M. de 67
England 5, 11, 14–15, 17, 21; credit strategies 121; expansion 30, 32; global enterprise 103, 105; opportunities 142; Spanish connections 70; US connections 80, 82, 84, 86
English language 6, 14, 19, 66
entrepreneurs 3, 101, 140
Escobar, E. 103
ethics 88
ethnicity 19, 31
Europe 1–2, 4–5, 11–12, 14–15, 17–19; agents 80–2, 84, 90; beyond bilateral trades 64; credit strategies 120, 122, 128–32; early activities 21–3; expansion 32–3, 35–8, 40, 46; financial services 67–8; global enterprise 103–4, 108–12; opportunities 136, 139, 142; Spanish connections 57–8, 60–2, 73; US connections 94
Ewald & Co 106
exchange rates 1, 69
exogenous shocks 92–3
Ezquiaga & Nephews 68, 70

Fagoaga, J. de 69
Falmouth 22, 80, 82
Far East 106
feathers 107
fees 39, 43, 80
Fehrman & Co 91
Ferdinand VII, King of Spain 59–60, 70
Ferguson, J.S. 82
financial crises 60, 69, 84, 91–4, 122, 130–1, 140, 142–4
financial sector 2, 30, 42, 55–7, 66–71; credit strategies 117–32; global enterprise 101–2, 108–10, 112–13; opportunities 141, 143
Finlay & Co 86
firewood 107
flax 64–5, 68, 72, 107
Florez-Mendez, M. de 14
Florida 93
flour 40, 70, 86, 94, 104
flutes 107–8
Forbes & Co 44
Fox & Co 22, 80
Fox, G.C. 80
Fox, R.W. 80
France 11–14, 17, 19–20, 22, 29–30; credit strategies 119; expansion 32, 35–7; global enterprise 103–5, 111; Spanish connections 58, 68, 70, 73
Frankfurt 73
Frazier, W.W. 92
Freedman, J.R. 6, 89–90
freelance operatives 85
Frege & Co 73
French language 6, 14, 66
Frey & Co 91, 122
Friedman, W.A. 3
Frige, C. 16
Fruhling & Goschen 4
Funez y Carrillo 60–1, 63
furniture 107
furs 3
further research 57–8

Gaedechens & Co 67, 103
Galceran, N. 70
Galicia 12–14, 17, 23, 64–8
Galup, A. 17
Galup, J. 17
Garcia & Co 16, 65, 68
Garcia-Fernandez 65
Gaviria, M. de 60–1, 69–70
Genoa 112
geographical diversification 19, 102–7, 112
German language 6, 14, 66
Germany 3, 5, 7, 11, 13; agents 79–80, 83–4, 91; beyond bilateral trades 64; credit strategies 119, 125–6, 130, 132; early activities 15, 17–22; expansion 29, 31, 35, 37–8; financial services 68; global enterprise 103–6, 109–10, 112; opportunities 139, 141; trade connections (1820s-1840s) 55, 72–3
Ghent 104, 110
Gibbs & Sons 29, 44–5, 103, 106
Gibbs, A. 29
Gibraltar 32–3
Giroud, M. 17
Glasgow 30, 81–3, 106, 121–2, 126
Glasgow University Archives 7
glasses 17–18, 64
global lending enterprise 101–13, 118–19, 121–2, 125–6, 139–40, 143–4
globalization 1, 3–4, 29–30, 101–2, 117, 136, 140, 144
glue 85
Godeffroy, J.C. 18–19, 73
gold 17, 34–5, 41–2, 94, 107
Gonell Brothers 103
Gonzalez, A. 16
Goodhue & Co 38–9, 61–2, 91–3, 103, 112, 131
Goodhue, J. 91
Gower & Co 57
grains 22, 107

Greaves & Son 16
Grinnell Minturn & Co 39–40
Groning & Co 18, 64, 73
Gruning, J.F. 14, 19, 21, 30–4, 72, 84
guano 29
Guayaquil 32
Guildhall Library 6, 40
gum anime 107
gum Arabic 107
Guthrie & Co 81–2, 121–2

Hague, The 64
Haiti 20, 68, 103
Halifax 81, 83, 122
Hambro & Son 4, 12, 102, 111, 142
Hambro, J. 12, 142
Hamburg 7, 11–16, 18–19, 35, 37, 63–4, 67, 72–3, 104, 106, 112, 130
hardware 17
Haresfeld 11
Hartoq & Denker 37
Hathaway & Co 38
Hathaway, F.S. 106
hats 107
Haurie & Nephews 21, 66
Havana 11, 16, 20, 23, 64, 67, 70, 72, 104, 128, 130
hegemony 4
Hellman, C. 22, 31
Hermanos, A. 16
herring 107
hides 11, 16–17, 22, 35, 67, 104, 106–7, 110, 128
Hill & Sons 16, 22, 80
Hinck & Co 73
Hoffman & Fils 104
Hoffmann & Dorrepaal 104
horses/horse hair 40, 107
House of Commons Parliamentary Papers 7
Howland Brothers 31–2
Howland, G.G. 31–2
Howland, S.S. 31–2
Huancavelica 42, 44–5
Huasco 36

Huffel, L.A. 18, 64, 73
Humphreys & Biddle 92
Huth & Co 1–8; agents 79–95; beyond bilateral trades 64–6; credit strategies 117–32; early years 18–23; expansion of firm (1820s-1830s) 29–46; financial services 66–71; founding 11, 13; German connections 55, 72–3; global enterprise 101–13; opportunities 136–44; quicksilver trade 41–6; risk management 117–32; role 136–44; South American branches 29–46; Spanish connections 55–73; trading operations (1820s-1840s) 34–41; US connections 89–94
Huth, C.F. 22, 43
Huth, Coit & Co 31, 33–4, 36, 82
Huth, F. 4–5, 7; agents 79–95; credit strategies 117–32; early life 11–23; establishing operations 30–4; first partnership 18–23; German connections 55, 72–3; global enterprise 101–13; opportunities 136–44; quicksilver trade 41–6; risk management 117–32; role 136–44; Spanish connections 55–73; standalone London merchant 15–18; trading operations (1820s-1840s) 34–41; training 11–14; US connections 89–94
Huth, Gruning & Co 29–30, 34–5, 37–41, 43–5, 79, 82, 108
Huth, H. 37
Huth, M. 59

Iberian peninsula 21, 66, 69, 72
Idria 42
imperialism 30
Indemnity Assurance Co 72
Indemnity Mutual 71
India 16, 29, 37, 105–7, 136
indigo 11, 86, 103, 106–7, 110–11
Industrial Revolution 4, 55, 136

industrialization 2, 5, 73, 117, 119, 136
information asymmetry 3, 22, 58, 61, 65–6, 71, 118, 137, 141–3
ING 7
ink 107
insects 107
insurance 1, 16, 35–7, 39, 41, 71–2, 113, 122, 128–9, 140–1, 143
intelligence gathering 4, 22, 80, 85–6, 143
interest rates 60–1, 120
intermediaries 1, 17, 42–3, 58, 61–2; credit strategies 117, 120, 123, 129, 131; insurance brokers 72; opportunities 141–2; Spanish connections 65, 68, 71
internationalization 29, 136
Ireland 82–3
iron 11, 21, 59, 80, 85, 90–1, 94, 104, 107–8, 131
Italian language 66
Italy 37, 105

Jacobs & Co 68
Jamaica 20, 103
Jancke, A. 37
Jaudon, S. 91
Jerez wine 21
jerked beef 20, 40, 67, 107, 128, 130
Johns, C.J. 73
Jones, C. 6
Jones, G. 3, 56, 102, 140
Jugo & Norzagaray 65

Karthaus, C. 90
Kennedy McGregor & Co 38, 125
Kindermann, A.H. 34, 82, 85–6
Kleinworts 4
knife handles 107
Knight & Co 67
Knight, M. 67
Konigsberg 73

La Guayra 70, 103

Lackersteen & Brothers 106
Lamb & Parbury 40
Lamikiz, X. 71
Lampson & Co 3
Lancashire 82–3, 88–9
Lancashire Record Office 7
Lasa, S. de 70
Latin America 7, 31, 41–2, 44, 65, 80–2, 84, 103–4, 106, 108–9, 140
Latvia 64
Launburg, J.D. 22
Laurie & Hamilton 82
Layseca & Co 20, 23, 64
Le Havre 12, 36, 125
lead 107
Leeds 7, 81–3, 88
Leipzig 72–3
Leland, Zimmerman & Davidson 41
lending 101–13, 118–19, 121–2, 125–6, 140, 143–4
letters of credit 41, 109, 118, 124–5, 128
Lillo, L. 63
Lima 31–2, 39, 41, 43
limited liability companies 2
Limpricht Brothers 41
linens 11–12, 65, 70, 82
liquidation 62, 85
Lisle-Williams, M. 2, 5
Liverpool 7, 21–2, 34, 36, 39; agents 79–94; branch opening 84–6, 91; credit strategies 119, 121, 125, 127–8, 130; global enterprise 104, 106, 108, 112; opportunities 137; Spanish connections 64, 69, 73; US connections 93
Lizardi & Co 91
Llano Brothers 17–18
Llano, J. 17
Llano, P. 16–17
Lloyds of London 35, 71–2
logwood 107–8
London 1–7, 11–23, 29–44, 64–6, 71–3; agents 79, 81, 83–7, 89, 91; credit strategies 118–20, 122–5, 127, 129–32; financial services 66–70; global enterprise 101–6, 108–13; opportunities 136–7, 139–42; quicksilver trade 42, 46; Spanish connections 55–63; US connections 89, 93–4
London Assurance Corporation 71
Longworthy Brothers 81
Loning, G. 19, 73
Lopez de Arce, Y. 64
Low Countries 63–4
Lucchesi & Co 89

McCrea & Co 40
McCurdy Aldrich & Co 92
McGrane, R.C. 6
McGregor, K. 106
MacWilliam, R. 84–5
Madrid 55, 62, 67, 69, 112
Magdeburg 73
Magniac Smith & Co 92
mahogany 107
Mainer & Co 130
Malaga 11
Malagamba, J. de 64
Malta 64
Manchester 66–7, 80–4, 87–8, 106, 112, 119, 123
Maneglier & Co 125
Manice Gould & Co 92
Manila 67, 70, 104, 106, 125
Manuela 18
manufactured goods 11, 16, 18, 21–2, 30; credit strategies 117, 120–4, 126, 130; expansion 34–5, 38; global enterprise 101, 104, 108–9; opportunities 136; Spanish connections 64, 66–7, 73; US connections 80–1, 85, 88, 91–2, 94
Maria Antonia, Princess of Asturias 59–60
Maria Christina, Queen of Spain 60–1, 63, 69
Marine Insurance Co 72
Marzagalli, S. 1

Marzal e Hijos 65
Marzal, P.C. 16
Matanzas 67
Mathiesen & Co 57
Matthaei & Co 73
Mayer & Fils 37
Mayfren, M.F. 13
Mayo, J. 42
Mazarredo, J. 64
Meier, H.H. 73, 104
Meinertzhagen & Co 40
Meinertzhagen, D. 84, 93
Menendez Mendive 130
merchant bankers 1–8, 14, 19, 21–3, 29–30; agents 79, 86–7; beyond bilateral trades 65; correspondents 110–12; credit strategies 117–20, 122, 125, 130; expansion 36, 39–40; financial services 66–9; global enterprise 101–4, 106–10; opportunities 136, 141–3; other activities 111–13; quicksilver trade 43; Spanish connections 55–8, 61–3
Mercier, P. 32–3
Merck & Co 81–2, 104, 106
Merck, H.J. 73
mercury *see* quicksilver
Merle & Co 91, 122
Mersey, River 84–6, 89, 106, 137
Mexican and South American Company 36
Mexico 20, 22, 29, 42, 44–5; credit strategies 119, 123; global enterprise 103–5, 108–9, 112–13; opportunities 141; US connections 82, 85
Mexico City 20, 37
Meyer Hupeden 91–2
military 4
mining 30
Mitchell & Co 65
Mitchell Cayley & Co 131
Molero Brothers 103
monarchy 59–64

monopoly 5, 43–4, 57, 64
Montevideo 41, 103, 130
moral hazard 123, 126, 128
Morales, J.M. 68
Moreno, J. 64
Morgan & Co 4
Morgan, J.S. 4
Morley 81
Morris Canal & Banking 61–3, 112
Morrison & Co 4, 102
Morrison Cryder & Co 91
Muir & Laurie 106
mules 40
Mulholland, A. 82
multinational trading companies 2, 5, 21, 65, 71, 101, 107, 139, 141
munitions 31
Muñoz & Funes 70
Muñoz, A.F. 60–1
Muñoz, J.A. 60
mustard 17, 85
Mutzenbecher & Co 37, 104

Nantes 84
Naples 60
Napoleon, Emperor 5, 13
Napoleonic Wars 4–5, 14–15, 17–18, 55, 60, 72, 103, 111, 136
neoclassical economics 65
Neptune Assurance Co 72
Netherlands 11, 17, 19–20, 29, 37; credit strategies 132; global enterprise 103, 105, 112; Spanish connections 58, 68, 73
network analysis 1, 3, 5–6, 12, 14, 18, 20, 22, 83–4, 118, 136–7, 139–41
Nevins Townsend 91–2
New Bedford 91
New Jersey 61
New Orleans 64, 91–2, 112, 121–2, 127, 130
New South Wales State Library 7
New York 31–2, 38–41, 89–92, 103, 113, 124, 131
New York Life Insurance & Trust 112

New York State 112
Newport 104
Nicaragua 107
nitrate 36
Nixon, Ariztia & Co 36
non-ferrous metals 44
North America 35, 39, 106, 109–10, 139
Norway 19, 22, 35, 103
Norwich, Connecticut 31
Nottingham University Library 7
nutmeg 107
Nye Gideon & Co 40, 106
Nye Parkin & Co 106, 122, 125, 127

Odessa 63, 86
O'Kelly & Co 68
Olver, J. 7, 80
Order of Charles III 63
Orense 65
Ostend 11
oxalic acid 107

Pacific 29–30, 32, 34–44, 85, 87, 91
paints 85
Palermo 113
Palmer McKillop & Co 92
panics 70, 130, 132, 142, 144
paper 107
Paris 19, 32–3, 36, 70, 104
Parkin & Co 38
partnerships 2, 7, 14, 30–1, 33–4; agents 62, 79–80, 84–5; credit strategies 121; expansion 37–8; Spanish connections 63, 72; US connections 86, 93
Passavant-Lemonitz 82
Pastor, J. 67
Paymasters Abroad 63
Peabody, G. 60, 102, 112
Pearson, R. 137
Pedrorena, M. de 69
Pennsylvania 92
pepper 16, 107–8
Perit & Cabot 89, 112

Perit, J.W. 38–41, 60–2, 91–3, 103, 106, 131–2
Perit, P. 91
Peru 6–7, 13, 20, 22, 29–30; agents 81–2, 85–7; beyond bilateral trades 65; credit strategies 119, 124; establishing operations 30–4; expansion 32–4; financial services 67; global enterprise 103–4, 106, 109, 113; operations (1820s-1840s) 34–41; opportunities 140–1; quicksilver trade 41–6
Petersen, Huth & Co 35, 37, 44
Petersen, L. 37
Philadelphia 38–41, 60–1, 89, 91–2, 103, 131
Philadelphia Loan Co 62
Philippines 38, 82, 106
philosophy 108, 111, 143
pianos 107–8
pimento 16, 107
plantations 20
Plate, River 12, 14, 17–18, 20, 22; agents 80; credit strategies 119; expansion 29, 32, 41; global enterprise 110, 113; opportunities 141; Spanish connections 67
Plymouth 80
Plymouth and West Devon Record Office 7
Poland 19, 103
pongees 107
ponies 107
Pons & Ziegler 70
Pope & Aspinwall 39–40
Porrua e Hijos 70
Portsmouth 80
Portugal 17
Portuguese language 66
Poschaan, B.J. 73
postal services 70, 137
Potosi 43
pottery 16, 107
Prado, A. 18, 64

Preusser & Co 73
Prevost & Co 103, 110
product trading coverage 107–8, 140
profit 31, 33–6, 42–4, 61, 64, 72, 79, 86, 111, 121, 140, 143
Protestants 12
Prussia 112
public opinion 62
Puerto Rico 20, 68, 70, 72, 103, 129
Putnam, H. 7
Putnam Papers 7

Queheille & Sons 129
quicksilver 7, 39, 41–6, 64, 107–8

rails/railways 68, 80, 84, 90–1, 94, 107, 117, 120, 131, 136, 140
Ralli Brothers 21, 103, 106–8, 142
Rathbone Brothers & Co 21, 103, 109, 111
Rawson & Saltmarshe 81, 120
Rawson, E. 81, 121–2
Real Consulado de Comercio 14
Reber, V.B. 6
refugees 5, 14
Reid Irving & Co 92, 131
reputation 4, 13–14, 29, 33, 39; credit strategies 120, 122, 124–5, 129; expansion 42; global enterprise 110; opportunities 137, 143; Spanish connections 59, 61–3, 69, 71
Respinger, C. 68
Rhodes, W. 126, 128
rice 107
Richardson, D. 137
Riga 64–5, 68, 70, 72
Rio de Janeiro 12, 23, 41, 103
The Rise of Merchant Banking 101
risk management 8, 117–32, 143–4
Rivadeo 16, 18, 64–5, 68
Roberts, R. 109
Robertson, W.H. 131–2
Rochelt Brothers 18, 64
Ross Vidal & Co 73, 104

Rothschild & Sons 4, 41, 43–6, 61, 91, 102–3, 106–7, 110–12, 142
Rothschild Archive 7
Rothschild, N. 71, 142
Rotterdam 104
Roux, A. 36–7
Royal Exchange Assurance Corporation 71
Royal Prussian Maritime Co 38, 125
Rubinstein, W.D. 4
rum 16, 20, 107
Rupe & Son 104, 110
Ruperti, J. 18–19, 73
Russell Sturgis 38, 106, 108, 125
Russell, T. 38–41, 124
Russia 13, 17, 22, 64, 68, 86, 131

Sadler Whitmore 57
Safont, J. 64
St Gall 37
St Petersburg 67, 104, 128, 131
St Thomas 20, 103
salt armoniac 107
salt volatile 107
Saltmarshe, A. 121
saltpetre 107
San Francisco 44
San Jacobo 72
San Juan 129
San Martin, J. de 32
San Sebastian 16, 66, 129
Sanchez, A. 35
Sandoval, J.J. 63
Santander 16, 55, 66–7, 70, 129
Santiago de Compostela 16, 55, 65, 68, 70
Santos & Co 65
sarsaparilla 107
sateens 38
Savoy 37
Schaezler, A.F. 85
Scheibler & Co 104
Scheibler, B. 104
Scheibler, E. 104
Scheibler, R. 104

Scheinert & Co 18
Scheinert, J.F. 18, 73
Scholtz, S.F. 31, 34
Schroder & Co 4–5, 86, 106–7, 109, 111, 142
Schroder, J.H. 5
Schutte & Co 18
Schutte, J.G. 18, 73
Scotland 7, 15, 21, 30, 80, 82
securities 1, 3, 57–8, 60–2, 70, 89–94, 111–12, 118, 137, 140–1
Seehandlung Societat 73
Serra Hermanos 69
Serra, M. 17
Seville 55
Sewell & Patrickson 36
shawls 38
Sheffield 21
sherry 21
shipping 1, 16, 18, 22, 32; credit strategies 120, 122, 126, 128; opportunities 140; Spanish connections 57, 68; US connections 85, 88
shipwrecks 72
Sicily 60, 113
Sierra & Hermanos 65
Silesia 12
silks 16, 36–8, 40, 104, 106–8, 122, 127
silver 17, 20, 22, 34–6, 38, 41–4, 104, 107–8
Simons Achenbach 73
skins 91, 107
slaves 20
Slovenia 42
Smith College, Northampton (US) 7
soap 41
social capital 2, 59, 137, 139–40, 142
Sociétés des Commerce 125
Sojo-Larralde 103
South America 13–14, 17, 22, 71, 82; agents 85–6, 89; credit strategies 119–20, 123–4, 126–7, 130; expansion 29–46; global enterprise 103–4, 106, 108, 110; opportunities 139–41; quicksilver trade 43–4, 46
Spain 3, 5–7, 11–22, 29–32, 35; agents 79–80, 83, 86; beyond bilateral trades 64–6; credit strategies 119, 132; expansion 37; financial services 66–71; global enterprise 103–7, 109–10, 113; insurance brokers 71–2; opportunities 139–41; panic 70; quicksilver trade 42–6; trade connections (1820s-1840s) 55–73
Spanish American Empire 5, 11–12, 16, 29, 31, 55, 57, 64, 67, 136
Spanish language 6, 14, 19, 32–3, 66
specie 42, 62, 124
Stansfeld, G. 83
Stansfeld, H.H. 82–4, 86–9
steam-packet companies 120, 137
sterling 67–9, 94
Stewart & Wilson 81–2, 106
Stewart and McAulay & Co 106
Stock & Sons 106, 121
Stockholm 64
Stockmeyer & Co 103
Stresow & Sons 68
sugar 11, 16, 20, 22–3, 37; credit strategies 124, 126, 128–30; expansion 41; global enterprise 103–4, 106–7, 110–11; Spanish connections 64, 67, 72; US connections 86
Supreme Court 63
Sweden 105
Swire & Co 21, 103, 106
Switzerland 37
Sydney 40

Tacna 33, 39
tallow 16–17, 22, 107
tar 85
Tastet & Co 14
Tastet, F. de 14, 19
Tastet, J.A. de 14
Tate, J. 22

tea 38, 40, 104, 106–8, 110, 113, 121–2, 125, 127
telescopes 108
textiles 4, 7, 15, 18, 21; agents 80–4; credit strategies 120–1, 123, 126–8, 130; expansion 30, 33–5; global enterprise 104, 106–9; Spanish connections 59, 66, 72; US connections 84, 87–8, 90, 94
Thayer & Brothers 93, 119
timber 22, 94, 107
The Times 7, 62
tin 107
tobacco 16, 20, 22, 41, 64, 67, 72, 91, 103, 107, 127
Torres & Co 65
tortoise shell 107
toys 107
trade 1–5, 8, 12–13, 15, 17–23; agents 79–94; credit strategies 117–32; expansion 30, 32, 34–41; global enterprise 101–13; opportunities 136–44; quicksilver 41–6; Spanish connections 55, 57–9; US connections 89–94
transaction costs 1, 17, 55, 57–8, 61, 66, 111, 117, 137, 141
Trieste 112
Trinius & Co 73
trust 13, 17, 19–20, 22, 33; correspondents 110; credit strategies 120, 122, 124–5, 129; expansion 42; opportunities 141; Spanish connections 57–8, 61–2, 65–6
turmeric 106
Tutein & Co 104

Uhthoff, C.F.A. 21
Ukraine 86
uncovered credits 129–30
underwriters 1, 35, 71, 128
Union Bank of Mississippi 61–3
United Kingdom (UK) 7, 21, 32–3, 56, 80, 92, 121

United States (US) 5–7, 14, 20–1, 29, 31–5; agents 85–6; credit strategies 117, 119, 121–2, 124, 128, 130–2; expansion 38–41, 44; global enterprise 103–6, 109, 111–12; opportunities 136, 142; Spanish connections 56, 60–4, 70; trading connections 79–94
University College London (UCL) Special Collections 6, 40, 140
University of Leeds 7
Urbieta, C. 13
Urbieta, J.A. 12–13
Urtetegui, H. 69

Valparaiso 12, 30–1, 33, 35–6, 38–45, 65, 82, 86–7, 137
Van Veen & Son 64
Varela & Co 65
Varela, F.A. 70
Venezuela 11, 67, 82, 103, 110, 129
Veracruz 16, 20, 37
Vidal & Sirven 20
Vidal, C.L. 22, 69
Vienna 112
Vilardaga & Reynals 65
Villanueva, G.M. 17
Virginia 91
Vivero 65
Vogeler & Co 41, 103
Vogelsang & Co 91

Wales 21, 35
walnuts 107
Ward, H.V. 34, 82
Ward, T.W. 91
Waterhouse, J. 81
Waterhouse, S. 81
wax 41
Weber, A. 68
Weber, E. 68
Webster & Sons 81
West Coast 34–9, 41–4, 46, 65, 82, 86, 88, 108
West Indies 119

wheat 16, 40–1, 65, 86, 94, 104, 107
Wiggins & Co 91, 102, 131
Wiggins, T. 91, 131
Wildes & Co 91, 131
Wildes, G. 91, 131
Wilson & Co 91, 131
Wilson, T. 91, 131
wine 16–17, 21, 65–6, 72, 107
wood 107–8
wool/woollens 7, 16–17, 21–2, 35, 38; agents 82–3; credit strategies 122, 126–7; global enterprise 106–8; Spanish connections 58, 66, 69, 72; US connections 86
worsteds 21, 38

Wuppertal 73, 104

Xerez 21

Ybarra & Co 57, 59
yerba mate 41
Yorkshire 82–3, 88–9
Yribarren & Sobrinos 70

Zaldarriaga-Sojo 103
Zellweger, U. 68
Zimmerman, Frazier & Co 20, 41, 103, 110, 113
Zimmerman, J.C. 41